Feb 2013

To June,

Happy Birthday! Larry & I were very inspired by this book. It's a wonderful book. So have fun celebrating your birthday with you en Leavenworth.

Love, Becky
and Larry

Remember, if you think you can or you think you can't — you're right? (Henry Ford) — Happy Valentine's Day — 2013. — L2

GREAT SOULS 10

I Want to Meet in HEAVEN

Also by S. Michael Wilcox

GREAT 10 SOULS

I Want to Meet in HEAVEN

S. MICHAEL WILCOX

DESERET
BOOK

Library of Congress Cataloging-in-Publication Data

Wilcox, S. Michael, author.
  10 great souls I want to meet in heaven / S. Michael Wilcox.
    pages cm
  Includes bibliographical references and index.
  ISBN 978-1-60907-137-0 (hardbound : alk. paper)
  1. Dead. 2. Biography. I. Title.
  CT121.W55 2012
  920.02—dc23
  [B]   2012027571

Printed in the United States of America
Malloy Lithographing Incorporated, Ann Arbor, MI

10   9   8   7   6   5   4   3   2   1

For Laurie—

Who I believe is now meeting these beautiful people

we both so love and admire.

*Study and learn, and become
acquainted with all good books, and with
languages, tongues, and people.*

—D&C 90:15

·······

*It is my will that you should hasten . . .
to obtain a knowledge of history, and of countries, and of
kingdoms, . . . and all this for the salvation of Zion.*

—D&C 93:53

CONTENTS

To Love—the Sharers

"The Beauty of the World"

Earth
Creation's Dawning

———◆———

Let us make man in our image,
after our likeness;
and it was so.
—Moses 2:26

Meditating on *The Meditations*

Every time I visit Rome I pay my respects to Marcus. There is a bronze equestrian statue of him that graces the center of Michelangelo's square on the top of the Capitoline Hill. There he sits in majestic benevolence overseeing the city as he oversaw the Roman Empire almost two thousand years ago. Marcus Aurelius was the last of the "five good emperors," a gracious, thinking, stoic king who ruled during the second century after Christ at the height of the Empire. After Marcus it was essentially all downhill for Rome. He was a humane, philosophical man who wrote a classic of world literature titled *The Meditations*. He begins this work by allowing his mind to remember all the people who had influenced his life for good and lists the qualities and life-changing values they instilled within him. They are beautiful tributes offered in praise and gratitude to others—a memorial of the mind.

I was impressed by Marcus's thoughts when I first came upon them and was at an age when impressions can chart life courses. I sat down those many years ago and began to reflect on people in my own life who had blessed me in a similar manner. It was an instructive, grace-filling, and humbling experience and I recommend it to the highest degree. My thoughts instinctively went, as did his, to family members: my mother, sisters, grandfather, my uncle at the ranch, special teachers. Just recognizing and writing down their contributions drew them deeper into my soul and made me even more desirous to graft their qualities into the tree trunk of my own growing life.

Having finished, however, the list seemed incomplete. So I added those I consider heroes and heroines from the scriptures. These were souls I had never met who were yet so much a part of my being. They were friends whom God himself wanted me to know; he was the mediator of our acquaintance. Having allowed my mind to peruse the scriptural past, however, other personalities began to surface, the non-scriptural breed of men and women. I realized how very many lives had touched mine. Perhaps more important, I understood how magnificent humanity was and how widespread God's involvement has been in the affairs of his children. He has many voices with which he speaks to bring truth and goodness and beauty into the world. These he has used at all times and in multiple places around the earth. This discovery had profound implications in my life, and I thank God for Marcus Aurelius meditating in Rome.

Over the years since that first moment of enlightenment, I have added dozens of men and women to the population of my mental city. I am at ease with them and enjoy our conversations across the ages. I feel that I am rich and prosperous in lives! We can all enjoy the vast wealth of wondrously lived lives and make such lovely friends. We are openly invited to explore and draw upon those personal, yet universally overflowing accounts of human experience as need arises. These singular people of the past move within my mind offering counsel, encouragement, comfort, and insight. I must admit that over the years I have also allowed numerous citizens into my mental city who never lived, drawn from the pens and souls of the world's finest authors, great characters in literature such as Jean Valjean, Atticus Finch, Benedick and Beatrice, Alyosha Karamazov, Don Quixote, Elizabeth Bennet. But that is a topic for another time. Here we will delve into the offerings of real people from history.

Ten Great Souls from the City

Shakespeare wrote a stirring description of man in *Hamlet*. His portrayal rivals David's own magnificent question in the Psalms with its wonderful concluding affirmation: "What is man, that thou art mindful of him? . . . Thou hast made him a little lower than the angels, and hast crowned him with glory and honour" (Psalm 8:4–5). In that same spirit we can read Hamlet saying, "What a piece of work is a man! How noble in reason, how infinite in faculty, in form and moving how express and admirable, in action how like an angel, in apprehension how like a god—the beauty of the world!"[1]

Sometimes it is difficult to believe such lofty thoughts are describing us and our fellow human travelers. It is certainly true we have, as a race, often not lived up to these divine potentialities. Yet man was created in the image of God, not only outwardly, but also inwardly, in the qualities of the soul. Humanity was the last act of creation, its crown! We shouldn't be surprised to see evidences of glory and honor in our fellowmen. Therefore, our journeys through the centuries of the past should uncover examples of "the beauty of the world!"

I've been carrying on my conversations with men and women of the past for as long as I can remember, even before Marcus Aurelius swung me into more formal recognitions. My imagination is perhaps too finely honed, but when I read or learn of someone admirable, I picture myself meeting them and temporarily being a part of their world. In this life, I can't go back in the past except in my mind, but I assume we will have the opportunity when we arrive at a more eternal destination to meet those who have gone before us and contributed so much to our lives. The Doctrine and Covenants promises we will see Jesus himself, then attests, "that same sociality which exists among us here will exist among us there, only it will be coupled with eternal glory" (D&C 130:2). Brigham Young once hinted at such associations when he said, speaking of the spirit world: "If we want to visit Jerusalem, or this, that, or the other place—and I presume we will be permitted if we desire—there we are, looking at its streets. If we want to behold Jerusalem as it was in the days of the Savior; or if we want to see the Garden of Eden as it was when created, there we are. . . . And when there we may behold the earth as at the dawn of creation, or we may visit any city we please. . . . When we pass into the spirit world we shall possess a measure of this power. . . . We shall enjoy the society of the just and the pure who are in the spirit world until the resurrection."[2] With those anticipated future introductions in mind, this book recounts the stories of ten such people that I intensely wish to meet, if for no other reason than to thank them for enriching my life to such a high degree. I am a better person because of the challenges, sacrifices, loves, and thoughts they faced and the records they left for the world. I assume that you will want to meet them too, though some of my choices may be at first a bit surprising.

Generalization of a culture, an age, or a religion is prone to misjudgment, dismissal, or ignorance, but when we contemplate humanity one life at a time, it is difficult not to find much to love and admire. Ultimately our compassion is expanded and our empathy enlarged. We gain in charity. We become more inclusive. We open ourselves up and invite wholeness. We may learn to see ourselves better in the light of another's example. This may invite reflection and change. The vast range of human possibilities and human experience broadens us and we are enlivened by it. Part of God being God consists in this universal but intimate view. We will not be able to develop his heart within us with only a surface understanding of our fellow-men—or with alienation because of difference, whatever the source of that dissimilarity. In this wonderful world of knowledge it is easy to learn. Is not this part of "the gathering"? We rightly call this age the "dispensation of the fulness of times." Notice that the phrase is plural—"times," not "time." We want all the best from every age and corner of the globe. The following pages contain the lives of ten souls from my own personal gatherings. They have tutored my soul as well as my mind, each with distinct and immeasurably valuable insight on what it means to be human. How I desire to meet them!

CHOICES

Taking a census of my mental city and selecting only ten inhabitants was probably the most difficult aspect of writing this book, the decisions becoming more difficult as I narrowed the list. I could hear many of my past friends' voices offering their compelling arguments and gracious gifts. I debated with myself for months about the tenth spot, and I will not reveal in what order I chose them. They are not presented in any kind of ranking from highest to lowest; one is not more valuable to me than another. So many other personalities circled through my brain who seemed to demand that their story also be told to the largely Latter-day Saint audience I am addressing that I felt often I had to apologize to them or perhaps stretch the number to twelve and quiet my conscience—but then it would never end. Finally, decisions had to be made. Fortunately, I could eliminate William Tyndale and C. S. Lewis, as I had already written about them. They could hardly complain, yet they have surely impacted my life profoundly. I have tried for balance in my leading coterie of ten. I chose them primarily because of their personal value to me—because of what their lives meant and what those lives taught, although there were other contributing factors. The inspiration they offer is open to all. I am convinced they will speak to you as they have done to me and they will soon be part of your own mind's citizenry.

I should make one disclaimer lest I be misjudged. My focus here is not on personalities from scripture or those from my own family, which obviously would top the list of persons we would wish to see in the hereafter. My scriptural (or "LDS") ten would quickly fill with Alma, Abraham, Rebekah, Rachel, Joseph Smith, and many others. And, of course, there is Jesus! The very first face I will look for when the curtain of death opens for me will be that of my Laurie. There are others among my family and friends with whom reunion will also be sweet and immediately sought after. That goes without saying. Having found Laurie, I might, however, while waiting for the line to meet Moses and Mary Magdalene to thin, seek out Patrick of Ireland, or Francis of Assisi, or Sir Ernest Shackleton, or Elizabeth Barrett Browning, or Khadija, Mohammad's first wife. My list of subjects here does not include Shakespeare, or Elizabeth I, or Abraham Lincoln, or Erasmus of Rotterdam, or Lady Jane Grey, or another ten who easily could have taken the top positions, largely because others have and their life lessons are more widely known, but it was painful to drop one or two to the eleventh or twelfth position. I also balanced my choices by covering a wide cross-section of the past, drawing from many ages and areas of the world and especially from different religious backgrounds. There are men and women, Christian and non-Christian, explorers and romantics, poets and warriors, saints, scientists, and sages.

We need to learn from one another. Of one thing I am certain: No single people, tradition, religion, governmental form, ethical program, moral code, or civilization has had sufficient wisdom and goodness to set the pattern and govern the world in the ways of peace, decency, and mutual respect. I do not believe God ever intended it to be that way. He wants us to reach out and learn from the wisdom he has given to humanity over broad sweeps of time and place and personality. How, for instance, can we of the Western tradition believe we can ignore—to the extent we have—a full half of humanity who have lived and thrived in Asia, especially China and India? Their civilizations were high, their ethics commanding, and in China they never endured the darkness that Europe went through for centuries after the fall of Rome. We should be as Erasmus of Rotterdam was: a citizen of the world, whose homeland is everywhere.[3]

"Friends"

Among the first ten people is a Chinese sage named Mencius. He taught that the wisest men of a village seek out others equally wise and good and commune with them. Not content with just the village, however, they seek out the wise and the good from their province, thus broadening their contacts and increasing the likelihood of deeper edification. Still not satisfied, they then reach out farther to embrace those of the empire. Even this will not quench their thirst for communion with the noble and humane and wise. They then turn to the past and search through the ages. Mencius called this "looking for friends in history."[4] The men and women in this book are some of my best friends in history. Most you know—or are familiar with— though perhaps only in brief glimpses. Some may be entirely new to you. I present them in the hope that you will come to know them better and be lifted by their goodness and all they have to offer in the great conversation of the ages and the nations.

REACH OUT WITH THE SEARCHING FOOT

India
Fifteenth Century B.C.E.

Truth is one,
The wise call it by different names.
—Rig Veda, 1.164.46

THE FIXED FOOT

AS A CHILD IN ELEMENTARY SCHOOL I had very illegible hand-writing—and I still do. Dextral coordination has never been my strong suit. I could not draw a straight line to save my soul, and the idea of drawing a perfect circle was beyond my wildest dreams. One day my teacher gave me a compass. It was a simple instrument with a sharp point on one leg and a pencil secured at the tip of the other. She showed me that by planting the pointed leg firmly and stretching out with the other leg, I could draw a perfect circle. I was spellbound by my newly acquired talent and merrily went around drawing circles on everything I could find. There was something magical in extending that movable foot out as far as it could reach and drawing the largest circle I could. I did not realize at that time what an important lesson about life I was being taught—a lesson that would in many ways define who I would become and how I would think. As I grew

1

I was taught how to draw another circle by a divine teacher, one that encompassed truth, beauty, and goodness. This spiritual compass also has two feet—one I call "the fixed foot," and the other, "the searching foot." We all have this spiritual compass.

As an LDS boy, I had heard numerous testimonies proclaiming, "I know this Church is true." I never doubted this; I maintain my boyhood faith to this day, but I think I assumed when I heard or said these words that truth was one, and it was *ours*. It took a good measure of spiritual maturity for me to realize that the great question of mortality was not really to find the one true church among all the false ones; rather it was to discover where truth and goodness and beauty had reached their most mature form and plant my fixed foot there. That is the critical starting point: Where will we place the fixed foot of our life's compass? There can be no true or complete circle without a center.

Having studied most religions, philosophies, and approaches to life, I believe and I affirm that truth and goodness and beauty in their most mature form are found in the teachings of Jesus of Nazareth. I do not believe you can find higher peaks in the mountain range of religion than the Prodigal Son, the Good Samaritan, or the Sermon on the Mount. This is velvet truth! There is a deep intuitive knowledge of God contained therein. Furthermore, I believe that the Restoration of the gospel through the Prophet Joseph Smith is the best lens with which to understand, apply, and internalize our Savior's life, teachings, and mercy—and the most secure pathway to happiness. Here I will place the fixed foot of my compass. One of the last gifts my wife gave me before she passed away was a golden navigator's compass, because she knew how much it represented my approach to life and learning. On one foot she had the words "Firmly Planted!" engraved. Then, in a gesture of love, graciousness, and touching compliment, she had my own name engraved on the searching foot.

THE SEARCHING FOOT

Placing the fixed foot is only half the task, not the whole of life's journey: We would draw the circle. We have another foot to consider—what will we do with the searching foot? Unfortunately, too many religions and cultures do little with it, believing that their own particular fixed position contains the essential and only believable truth, goodness, and beauty. They draw a tiny circle surrounding their own position and feel comfortable with life. Truth is too grand to be found in such small dimensions. It is scattered around the world, God distributing his wonders as widely as the sower throwing grain. God would have the harvest cover the whole field. Light is given not only in the scriptures or through prophetic inspiration, but in multiple ways. Our Father in Heaven is a light-giving God and dispenses it as widely as the stars. I believe God anticipates that as Latter-day Saints we will circumscribe the largest circle we can. May we become an inclusive as well as a discerning people.

I have learned that there is a tremendous amount of truth we can circumscribe if we reach out with the searching foot. Is this not as important as planting the fixed foot? We need to get them in the right order, of course. We do not wish to go dancing on both feet through the offerings of the world, picking up bits and pieces of truth here and there without ever taking the time, energy of thought, and introspection to find our fixed point. There is a certain intellectual and spiritual laziness in that approach. Discovering the right midpoint will give us the best perspective of the whole, the broad view from the peak, the best chance of encompassing all truth and avoiding error. Remember you cannot draw a perfect circle without an immovable center point. Having planted our fixed foot, we will learn that our Father in Heaven's engagement with his children is broad, constant, continual, and far-reaching.

I assumed while growing up that God spoke to the Hebrew

prophets of the Old Testament; sent his Son in the meridian of time who, with the help of the apostles, established his Church; revealed truths also on the American continent to Nephite prophets; and finally restored everything through the revelations and labors of Joseph Smith. I believed that my Father in Heaven is a loving God toward all his children. My idea of him was often difficult to align with this rather limited understanding of his interaction with humankind. What of the Chinese? What of those in India? He speaks often of his voice penetrating even the isles of the sea. What about those during the centuries of darkness we call the Great Apostasy? Surely God would speak to humanity through every voice he could find. I firmly believe this. God has many voices. If we cannot hear his voice in that of a prophet or apostle, perhaps we can hear it in that of a sage, or a poet, or a philosopher, or a playwright, or an artist. Their voices also find their roots in God. In time, I came to desire—to hunger for, really—these other voices. I sensed I would have to reach my searching foot far afield to bring them into my circle of understanding.

That reaching has made all the difference in my life and in my love of God. It has opened my heart to my fellow creatures and established my belief in the universal value of all God's children. There is only room for a fleeting encounter with ten magnificent men and women whose lives were rich and full. I have tried to offer a broad blending of humanity. I hope I have chosen those who are most interesting and have the greatest edification to offer.

"IN THY LIGHT SHALL WE SEE LIGHT"

Mormon gave an important address to those he called "the peaceable followers of Christ." It was so critical that Moroni included it in his own additions to the golden records. Therein Mormon taught his people that "every thing which inviteth and enticeth to do good, and to love God, and to serve him, is inspired of God." He counseled them to "search diligently in the light of Christ . . . [and] lay hold upon every good thing," and "cleave unto every good thing" (Moroni 7:3, 13, 19, 28). In a manner of speaking, he is saying, "Plant your foot in the light of Christ, then reach out." Let us search! The focus of Mormon's address is charity. Beyond our usual definition, charity is also an invitation extended to us to harvest truth, goodness, and beauty from all cultures, all places, and all people, anticipating that our search will be richly rewarded.

The Psalmist wrote, "In thy light shall we see light" (Psalm 36:9). I love this brief affirmation that could also be paraphrased as, "Take my truth, my goodness, my beauty, and find more." In these areas, we can be like the servant to whom the Lord gave five talents. Almost always in the scriptures, *light* is interchangeable with *truth*. The light of Christ is his truth—that which he has given us. With the light of Christ as our foundation, our point of planting, we are free to explore and encouraged to augment. We can find beauty and goodness in an almost inexhaustible number of people and places.

At times, I fear that we receive the Lord's beautiful light only to continually gaze at it reverently. Is not the purpose of light to push back the darkness? Is it not to see with greater clarity? As the Psalms testify, light was given that we might see with it and discover new and enhancing truth. The Doctrine and Covenants teaches that "light cleaveth unto light" (D&C 88:40). Solely and perpetually staring at it may ultimately result in a type of blindness that has afflicted too many men and women of every religion and every culture for too long. We may become exclusive, restricting, isolating, divisive, and intolerant. "We *seek after* these things" is undoubtedly the most appropriate ending for our Articles of Faith (Articles of Faith 1:13; emphasis added). Paul originally used the phrase *think on* (see Philippians 4:8). I believe Joseph Smith enlarged Paul's idea. *Seek after* is an active phrase. It defines who we are, what we are about, and what we want.

"He Greatly Marveled"

In the Pearl of Great Price, we have a vision recorded that Moses was shown. It was a mind- and soul-expanding moment for Moses. He "beheld the world and the ends thereof, and all the children of men which are, and which were created; of the same he greatly marveled" (Moses 1:8). The Lord withdrew from Moses for a time to let him contemplate the creative majesty of just this one world and its inhabitants. Later, Moses received the same vision a second time. "Moses cast his eyes and beheld the earth, yea, even all of it. . . . And he beheld also the inhabitants thereof, and there was not a soul which he beheld not; and he discerned them by the Spirit of God; and their numbers were great" (Moses 1:27–28).

Why did the Lord show this to Moses? I think he was saying, "The world is more than you know, Moses. Look! See all the nations. Here are the Chinese. They too are the workmanship of my hands. And here is India, with its teeming masses, and Africa. There are continents across the sea and islands in its midst. The world is not just the Israelites, not just Egypt and Canaan, but much, much more. If I am concerned about slaves laboring in the mud pits of the Nile, I will surely be concerned with these others." The Lord then expanded Moses' understanding to include "worlds without number" (Moses 1:33)—the ongoing grace of continual creation: past, present, and future.

The Lord taught Peter a similar lesson in a thrice-repeated vision on a rooftop in Joppa. He was shown a vessel filled with all kinds of unclean animals, which he was commanded to eat. Peter turned away from this command, which went against everything he believed in, but the Lord was insistent, teaching Peter, "What God hath cleansed, that call not thou common." Peter testified later, after he had met the Roman centurion Cornelius, "Of a truth I perceive that God is no respecter of persons: But in every nation he that feareth him, and worketh righteousness, is accepted with him" (Acts 10:15, 34–35). A Jewish fisherman learned that a Roman centurion was well within the circle of God's deepest concerns.

Mindset of the Believer

I have included in the ten souls herein those from other religious traditions, from Catholicism to Islam—and even one whom we view as hostile to religious belief: Charles Darwin. When we study other faiths, eras, or cultures, if we are to understand them and appreciate what they have to offer, we must suspend our tendency to disbelieve. We must avoid slipping too quickly into judgment. We must try, inasmuch as we can, to create the mindset of the believer. If I were Buddhist, why would I find this teaching or that story compelling? If I believe in a stone box containing golden plates with lenses to help in translation, if I believe a man walked on water, it would not strain my faith gene to believe that a bowl can float upstream to assure Siddhartha he could reach enlightenment or that a Meccan merchant would be asked to recite from the top of Mount Hira.

We must also curb the natural propensity to look for motes and beams, or to compare all that is best in our own faith or culture with all that is worst in others'. This would neither be fair nor wise. The Buddha taught that such an approach was akin to fettering the mind. All these men and women were human, complete with all the faults and frailties to which we are subject. Their teachings and actions were not perfect. What I marvel at is how much God has accomplished with ordinary people who are also part of flawed humanity. We can't have pure saints—or prophets, apostles, or holy men for that matter. We need to quit perpetuating the myth that they exist. We risk faith-damaging disappointment when we believe this. Other than Jesus Christ, imperfection has been true for Joseph Smith, Moses, Peter, President Thomas S. Monson, or any other scriptural personality or living leader. To believe otherwise is to deny humanity. The souls I have chosen to write about obviously lack perfection in some manner and display failings that we can condemn—if that is what we are looking to do. Shallow assessments are easy to make; turning away is the frequent result.

Nor must we dismiss an entire approach to life or belief system because it has something within it with which we disagree, something that keeps our searching foot from reaching quite that far. This is to be expected. The greatest personalities are still part and parcel of their surrounding culture. For Siddhartha, that meant reincarnation, and for Saint Francis, it meant living a celibate life. We simply cannot judge their challenges and achievements outside the context of their own times and belief systems. I do not dismiss the Gospel of John because he describes with perfect acceptance the belief, bordering on superstition, that an angel troubled the water at the pool of Bethesda and the first one in was healed. We also give Moses the benefit of the doubt for killing an Egyptian and Joshua for the slaughter at Jericho.

It is also wise to remember when "making friends in history" that, in many cases, layer upon layer of legends and folklore have accrued that were never part of a person's original life or teachings. Humankind seems to have an almost unending ability to complicate the simple and ritualize the innovative into rigidity. With the help of the Holy Spirit we'll have to do a bit of winnowing, but I have found very little chaff I need to blow away in the lives I present here. The Lord gave instructions in the Doctrine and Covenants about the Apocrypha that we can readily apply to our friends in history: "There are many things contained therein that are true. . . . Therefore, whoso readeth it, let him understand, for the Spirit manifesteth truth; and whoso is enlightened by the Spirit shall obtain benefit therefrom" (D&C 91:1, 4–5). The Lord leaves it up to us to search and reach with the discernment of the Holy Spirit. Then we will "obtain benefit." We will also discover that though we may not accept all the conclusions our friends in history reached, their lives are triumphs of the human spirit. I do not accept all of Darwin's conclusions, but I am convinced that every one of us would have liked him as a person and thus he has much to offer us.

A Thousand Different Voices

As we reach out with the searching foot, we will be surprised to discover there are areas (of thought, behavior, practices, or beliefs) in which other traditions have reached a more mature level than our own. This requires a good deal of healthy humility and a fair assessment of the achievements of others.

An example may serve to illustrate. In our own religious faith we are told to control our thoughts. Benjamin acknowledged that it is critical to "watch yourselves, and your thoughts" (Mosiah 4:30). Jesus warned that to lust after a woman was to commit adultery already in our thoughts. Isaiah has the Lord teaching, "My thoughts are not your thoughts" (Isaiah 55:8), with the understanding that one must change his or her thoughts and bring them in line with the Lord's. The Doctrine and Covenants tells us we must "cast away [our] idle thoughts" (D&C 88:69) and "study it out in your mind" (D&C 9:8). There are other scriptures to which we might refer. The point is that controlling our thoughts is an important part of our mortal stewardship, but once we've been impressed with the importance and the magnitude of the mind and the necessity of controlling it, we leave each individual to his own strategy. We speak of pondering, but there are no essential religious practices in our faith that specifically deal with focusing and controlling our minds. Usually when we speak of our thoughts needing restraint we focus on specific negative thoughts, including avoiding excessive anger, covetousness, or dwelling on improper sexual images. These negative thoughts, we are sometimes told, can be cleansed from the mind by singing hymns, or otherwise replacing the bad thought with a good one. This is good counsel, but we are not masters of dealing with the mind. Our faith's focus lies more in behavior, in service, and in active participation in goodness.

However, Eastern religions—Buddhism in particular—teach one how to deeply control mental processes, not only to remove unwanted thoughts, but also to instill positive, compassionate, empathetic ones. One learns to quiet the mental busyness, the darting, egocentric, racing mind, and open up the calmer, more serene, and joyful one. This is a state that invites insight and, in our terminology, revelation. The mind is a wonderful instrument. In this particular area Eastern religious practice has achieved a higher maturity than we have. Now, I don't have to bear my testimony in the next fast meeting about the Buddha's meditative epiphany under the Bodhi tree, or the washing of Mohammad's heart, or Saint Patrick's vision of the Irish letters, or Joan of Arc's voices, or the comfort of Shackleton's fourth man, but I can recognize God moving in their lives to the benefit of myriads of people. These too resonate with the compelling voice of the divine.

Nephi expressed regret over the future Gentiles' unwillingness to accept the Nephite writings, indicating they would cry, "A Bible! A Bible! We have got a Bible. . . . And we need no more Bible" (2 Nephi 29:3, 6). These he called fools. I sense the tone of his words is not derisive or condemnatory, but lamentable—sadness mingled with compassion. He later wrote that the Jews, the Nephites, and the lost ten tribes would receive knowledge and write it. He then added the Lord's own words, which we might miss without careful reading, "I shall also speak unto *all nations of the earth* and *they shall write it*" (2 Nephi 29:12; emphasis added). Perhaps all these writings are yet to come forth, but I suspect many of them are already available.

I repeat: God has many voices. I believe he desires to get as much goodness, beauty, and truth as he can into the lives and hearts and minds of the people of this world. If we asked him, "Where are your words to the Chinese?" he might reply, "Have you not read Mencius, or Confucius, or Chuang Tzu?" "Know ye not that there are more nations than one?" the Lord asked (2 Nephi 29:7). Let us answer, "Yea, Lord, we know. We have reached! We have searched! We have found thy divine footprint among the nations and in the lives of humanity! All of the world's beautiful truths reverberate in our souls. We have heard the divine song in a thousand different voices in a hundred different tongues!"

To Hear—the Saints

Also I heard the voice of the Lord, saying,
Whom shall I send, and who will go for us?
Then said I, Here am I; send me.
—Isaiah 6:8

CHAPTER ONE

"The Voice of the Irish": Saint Patrick

Ireland
Fifth Century C.E.

Though a rustic, a fugitive, . . . unlearned . . .
I was like a stone that lay in the deep mire, and He, who
alone is powerful, came, and in his own mercy, raised me,
and lifted me up, and placed me on the top of the wall.[1]
—The Confession of Saint Patrick

The Landing

A SMALL BOAT GLIDED THROUGH the waters of the Irish Sea, the bright green of the land lying to the west just coming into view. Its emerald skyline, though inviting, promised hostility. Yet the man who sat in resolute silence with his small band of fellow missionaries, staring at the pagan shoreline that contained so many painful memories of the past, directed the boat forward until it landed in a small bay by the mouth of a stream. The men hid their boat, the old legends say, and walked inland, seen by a swineherd who ran quickly to tell his master, Dichu, of the tiny troop of invaders. Surely they were thieves, pirates from the hostile shores of Britain come to steal or raid. The Irish master approached, prepared to slay the strangers, yet there was something in the quiet stare of their leader, a look of unfearing compassion, a spark of holiness that stopped him, and he extended instead the hospitality of his home. Therein, sitting throughout the daylight hours and into the night beside his host's bone-warming fires, the apostle to the Irish offered the warmth of another fire, the fire of Christ, and Dichu believed—his first convert, the Cornelius of Hibernia. And who was the man whose face of firm conviction and unyielding compassion lowered the sword of fear and distrust? His name was Patrick, the year was 432 c.e., and this was not the first time his feet had touched the shores of Ireland.

The Slave Who Was Not Irish

People are always surprised when I tell them that the single most revered man in Irish history, the man whose very name sings of the beauties of Ireland, was not Irish at all—at least not by birth or heritage. That he became the incarnation of the Irish soul is the wonder of his story and the seed of the truths that his life has to offer us. Patrick, or Patricius, was born sometime near the fourth century's end into the world of a fading Roman civilization on Britain's west coast. As Rome declined and the legions of the empire were pulled off the island, life became precarious and uncertain, with increasing raids from the Scots to the north, Germanic tribes from the Continent, and Irish pirates just a short sail to the west. Patrick's father, Calpurnius, was a deacon of the Christian church and owned a small villa in the countryside along the western coast of England, which Patrick describes as near the settlement of Bannaven Taburniae, a location still debated to this day.

During his sixteenth year he was surprised by a band of slavers who took him, along with many of his father's servants, captive and transported them across the Irish Sea. There they sold Patrick as a slave to a petty chief named Miliucc, who put him to watching his herds in the hills of Antrim. In his own words, he was now among a people "at the ends of the earth,"[2] and his tutorial of misery began. "A beardless boy, I was taken captive before I knew what I should desire, and what I should shun."[3] In the cold and persistent rains of Ireland's northern quarter, Patrick thought on his youth. "I did not, indeed, know the true God . . . for quite drawn away from God, we did not keep his precepts nor were we obedient."[4] But he was molded in the freezing rains and hungers of his servitude by his God, who had plans for this boy, seemingly alone and forgotten among an alien people.

Profound moral and spiritual changes slowly transformed him. Turning to the largely ignored God of his youth, his misery brought him to his knees and he began to pray. "The Lord opened my mind to an awareness of my unbelief, in order that, even so late, I might . . . turn with all my heart to the Lord my God, who had regard for my insignificance and pitied my youth and ignorance. And he watched over me before I knew him . . . and he protected me, and consoled me as a father would his son."[5] Moved by the unseen hand of his Father in Heaven, Patrick often said "as many as a hundred prayers" in a day and "in the night nearly the same."[6] In these moments of intense turning, "the love of God, and His faith and fear, increased in me more and more."[7] Devoid of scripture, consumed with homesickness, without friends or any other form of moral guidance, prayer became his only comfort in the tenuous circumstances of his life. "Even before the dawn, I was roused to prayer, in snow, and ice, and rain."[8] But in time, the metal of God's newest instrument was forged and ready for the final imprint that would change a nation, breathe life into Christianity, and in so doing transform the world. Though the Great Apostasy was looming in the Christian world with its ceaseless debates and increasing obscurity, a light burned in Ireland. God had chosen a new torch.

Through it all, though, hope of returning to the civilized world of Patrick's British patrimony never left him. In time, his ear, now more keenly tuned to the voice of God through suffering, listened in the stillness to offered comfort. "One night I heard a voice, while I slept, saying to me: 'Thou dost fast well; fasting thou shalt soon go to thy country.'" Not comprehending the meaning of the message, he waited, and the voice came again, "'Behold, thy ship is ready.'"[9]

Bound for Gaul

Patrick had been a slave for six long years, but with faith in the promise of his inner voice, he fled from his master, heading southward for two hundred miles to a place he "had never been . . . nor did I know any one who lived there. . . . And I came in the strength of the Lord, who directed my way for good; and I feared nothing until I arrived at that ship."[10] Somewhere along the southern coast of Ireland, probably near the present-day towns of either Wexford or Wicklow, Patrick found a ship on the verge of departing for the Continent with a load of Irish wolfhounds. A runaway slave had few options, but Patrick was being guided and, approaching the captain, asked for passage. He was curtly refused. "'Do not seek to go with us,'"[11] he was answered. As he walked away, no good alternatives ahead, a fervent prayer filling his thoughts, he heard a voice behind him calling him back. "'Come quickly, for these men are calling you.'"[12] In an unexpected change of mind, the sailors, whom Patrick informs us were barbarians, admitted him to their rough fellowship "in good faith."[13] A short time later his days of fear and bondage in Ireland were over as they put out to sea.

A three-day voyage landed them somewhere on the coast of France. But Patrick's trials were far from over. Everywhere they traveled, all they found was desolation. Perhaps it was due to the Germanic invasions sweeping across the fading Roman Empire of the time, but whatever the cause, for twenty-eight days they found neither person nor any food and were on the verge of starvation. In their desperate state, the steersman turned to Patrick with a challenge for his Christian God. "'What sayest thou, O Christian? Your God is great and all-powerful; why canst thou not, then, pray for us, since we are perishing with hunger?"[14] Evidently Patrick had not hid his Christian faith from his new companions and answered by promising them if they would turn to his God with all their hearts, nothing was impossible and he would send them food that very day to the full satisfying of their hungers, for God was everywhere. By this time many of the dog traders had laid down to die, the weakness of hunger taking its toll, but true to Patrick's assurance, "a flock of swine appeared in the way before our eyes, and they killed many of them . . . and [were] much refreshed and filled."[15] They discovered wild honey as well. This sustained them until the day they ran out of food, when they came upon a town.

On the night the swine herd appeared, Patrick survived an attack by the adversary (similar to that of Joseph Smith just moments before the First Vision), which he testified "I shall be mindful as long as I shall be in this body."[16] A tremendous weight, "as it were, a great stone," fell upon him with such force that he had no strength to resist and all the members of his body were powerless to remove it.[17] But gathering the strength of his voice and mind, he called upon the prophet Elias to help him, but was ignorant of why he found himself calling upon that particular Old Testament prophet. Help came! "While I cried out Elias with all my might, behold! the splendor of the sun was shed upon me, and immediately shook from me all heaviness."[18] I have been struck more than once while reading Patrick's *Confession* how closely in many ways it parallels the life of Joseph Smith—the quotation at the head of this chapter being an example, for Joseph also compared himself to a rough stone shaped by God for the salvation of man. I cannot help but remember as I read the above account of the Irish saint the words from the First Vision, "I saw a pillar of light exactly over my head, above the brightness of the sun, which descended gradually until it fell upon me. It no sooner appeared than I found myself delivered from the enemy which held me bound" (Joseph Smith–History 1:16–17). It should not surprise us that we see such parallels in these experiences, for Joseph's God was also Patrick's God.

There is uncertainty about Patrick's activities after he left his fellow travelers, but he did not return home to Britain until a "few years" had passed.[19] There is some evidence he remained in Gaul (France) studying with the monks at Lerins. His family rejoiced to see the boy they had thought was forever lost to them and asked him "that then, at least, after I had gone through so many tribulations, I would go nowhere from them."[20] Perhaps the reunited family sensed the deep changes in Patrick, his intensity of fervor, and that spiritual power which God would soon call upon in the most unexpected way.

The Voices of the Children

Home now for only a short time, the voice that had so mercifully guided him out of slavery spoke again in the visions of the night. Patrick saw a man named Victoricus, perhaps someone he had known during his exiled years in the hills of Antrim, coming from Ireland with innumerable letters in his hands. Patrick was given one of the letters and began to read. He read no further than the words, "'The Voice of the Irish,'" and something deep within him opened and filled him with an abiding love. "As I read aloud the beginning of the letter, I thought I heard in my mind the voice of those who were near the wood of Focluti, which is near the western [Irish] sea; and they cried out: 'We entreat thee, holy youth, to come and walk still amongst us.' And my heart was greatly touched, so that I could not read any more, and so I awoke."[21]

The story of Patrick's call to bring Christ's teachings to the land of his former bondage, as it has been told and retold through centuries, tells us that the voices Patrick heard were the voices of young children, not only those living, but also the countless thousands yet unborn who would live and die without the knowledge, the beauty of all that Jesus taught. What pierced the heart of Patrick and pressed the Irish people unrelentingly into his soul was the dawning understanding that generations of future Irish children must know the sweetness of the Prodigal Son, the humanity of the Good Samaritan, the majesty of the Sermon on the Mount, the yearning inclusiveness of Paul's description of charity, and innumerable other truths. Yet, as we all might, Patrick hesitated. The land he was called to was the land and people of his years of misery, those who had enslaved him with memories of terror, freezing nights, hunger, and the perils of his eventual escape. Besides all this, he was unlearned, something that would haunt him to his death. The years he would have spent in study were wasted with the flocks and herds of his captivity. "I was hindered from learning in my youth," he once wrote. "Therefore I blush to-day and greatly dread to expose my ignorance, because I am not able to express myself briefly, with clear and well-arranged words, as the spirit desires and the mind and intellect point out."[22] Did not Enoch, and Moses also, counter God's calls with the poignant words, "I am slow of speech; wherefore am I thy servant?" (Moses 6:31; see also Exodus 4:10). Joseph Smith once, while thinking "upon eternal wisdom engraven upon the heavens," prayed, "O Lord, deliver us in due time from the little, narrow prison, almost as it were, total darkness of paper, pen and;—and a crooked, broken, scattered and imperfect language."[23] "I did not promptly follow what was shown me," Patrick wrote, "and what the Spirit suggested; and the Lord had compassion on me among thousands and thousands, because he saw my good-will."[24]

God's way is a path of mercy. He knew that Patrick, like Gideon in the book of Judges, needed the confirming comfort of "fleeces." Once again in the silences of the night, the voice of God spoke: "'He who gave His life for thee is He who speaks in thee': and so I awoke full of joy."[25] In Patrick's deepening humility and sense of inadequacy, the Lord responded and a second fleece was granted. In this vision Patrick sensed God praying within him, giving voice to the hidden recesses of his soul: "I was, as it were, within my body, and I heard, that is, above the inner man, and there he prayed earnestly with groans."[26] As Paul had taught, there are times when the Spirit intercedes for us in prayer, expressing the things too deep for our own understanding and wisdom (see Romans 8:26). The compassion of Christ, which caused him to groan within himself at Mary and Martha weeping over the death of Lazarus, descended upon Patrick. That level of love was enough. He would return to Ireland.

Betrayed Confession and Disgrace

Patrick, ever mindful of his woefully inadequate education, returned to Gaul—probably to Lerins or Auxerre—to learn to read, understand, and teach the scriptures and church doctrines. Patrick faced stern opposition from the time the Lord called him to teach Christianity to the pagan Irish until that climactic moment when he stepped from a small boat onto Ireland's rocky shores. The whole enterprise was filled with risk. Ireland had never been part of Rome's civilizing influence. No encouragement came for one so rustic and unlearned. From Patrick's own confession, we see he gained a commanding grasp of scripture, yet in spite of all his efforts, he did not gain the church's official sanction. And there was another matter which brought Patrick abiding pain.

In the early Christian church, one could confess one's sins before a close friend—not necessarily a cleric. Patrick had something deeply troubling on his mind. To ease his guilt he confessed to "my dearest friend, to whom I would have trusted even my life."[27] Relieved that he had lifted the burden from his shoulders, he continued his preparations. In time, his love for the Irish people pressed so fully he sought church sanction and ordination as bishop for Ireland. At this critical moment, the unveiling of his soul was publicly revealed by his friend. Patrick despaired. They "brought against me words that I had confessed before I was a deacon; from anxiety, with sorrow of mind, I told my dearest friend what I had done in my youth, in one day, nay, rather in one hour, because I was not then able to overcome. I know not, God knows, if I was then fifteen years of age."[28] "How, then, did it happen to him that afterwards, before all persons, good and bad, he should disgrace me publicly, when he had before this freely and gladly praised me?"[29] We do not know the nature of Patrick's teenage sin, but the disgrace and public disclosure was enough that he nearly gave up. He wrote, "Many were hindering my mission, and were talking behind my back."[30] On the night of his formal humiliation, his God did not forsake nor condemn him, but revealed a vision in which a document was laid before his eyes on which was written the Lord's message: "'He that touches you is as he who toucheth the apple of my eye.'"[31] Assured of God's full forgiveness and acceptance, he confidently wrote, "Therefore I dare to say that my conscience does not reproach me now or for the future."[32] Forgiving ourselves through fully believing in God's cleansing pardon and letting go of our sins—even if others cannot—is a wonderful thing.

Patrick was not to be denied. In time, an official ordination and call came. His burning love for the Irish, which had blossomed in his heart through the intervening years, had its fulfillment on the day when he sat by the pagan Dichu's warming fire and began a lifelong conversation that resulted in the conversion of thousands.

The "Twelve Trials" of Persecution

Patrick does not tell us all the labors, persecutions, and sacrifices he endured. We receive only hints in his *Confession,* including these few:

- "God often delivered me from slavery and from twelve dangers by which my soul was threatened, besides many snares, and in what words I cannot express."[33]

- "I came to the Irish people to preach the Gospel, and bear with the injuries of the unbelieving, and listen to the reproach of being a stranger, and endure many persecutions, even to chains."[34]
- "Among you and everywhere for you I endured many perils in distant places, where none had been further."[35]
- While in these outermost regions he was seized with his missionary companions: "One day they wished to kill me. . . . They put me in irons, and carried off all we possessed. But on the fourteenth day the Lord released me from their power, and what was ours was restored to us through God."[36]
- Though he was successful beyond his highest dreams, still, "I daily expect either death, or treachery, or slavery."[37]

And what of his former master? Tradition tells us that Patrick returned to the hills of his bondage intending to repay Miliucc the price of a slave as redemption for his escape. But the old chieftain—out of fear, shame, or defiance—gathered his possessions into his house, set all on fire, and died in the flames.

Patrick was not the vision of a saint who grew from holiness to holiness. He wrestled with his mortal state until the day he died. His humanity draws us to him for the honesty of his words and humility of his mind. "I hope that which I am bound to do, but I trust not myself as long as I am in this body of death, for he is strong who daily tries to turn me from the faith, and from the sincere religious chastity to Christ my Lord, to which I have dedicated myself to the end of my life; but the flesh, which is in enmity, always draws me to death—that is, to unlawful desires, that may be unlawfully gratified—and I know in part that I have not led a perfect life like other believers."[38] Though it often offended the chieftains who presented gifts to Patrick "with sorrow and tears,"[39] he consistently turned them down, as had the

Apostle Paul, for the greater good of his ministry. And always he felt the inadequacy of his education and his poor ability to express in words the grand nobility of the message he preached. His courage, however, can never be questioned; he knew the power of the dramatic symbolic act. On the night of a Druidic rite when no one was allowed to light a fire until the Druids had lit their ritual fire in the home of the high king, Patrick climbed to the top of an opposing hill and lit a fire first in honor of Christ.

Patrick was not alone in facing persecution and adversity. His heart was greatly distressed at the suffering of those who believed him. "Those who are in slavery are most severely persecuted," he lamented. "Yet they persevere in spite of terrors and threats. But the Lord has given grace to many of my handmaids, for they zealously imitate him as far as they are able."[40] Of course, the former captive of the Antrim hills would feel the yearning pull of compassion for the suffering of slaves. He was one of them, understood their hopes and their fears, and could openly pray, "may my Lord never permit me to lose His people whom He has gained in the ends of the earth."[41]

SPREADING FORTH THE NETS

Through it all, year by year, the message spread and Patrick triumphed. He saw his mission as the fulfillment of prophecies, many of which were the same utterances that would become foundational truths of the Restoration. "I am truly a debtor to God, who has given me so much grace that many people should be born again to God through me, and that for them everywhere should be ordained priests for this people, newly come to the faith, which the Lord took from the ends of the earth, as He promised formerly by His prophets: . . . 'I have set thee to be the light of the Gentiles, that thou mayest be for salvation unto the utmost parts of the earth.' . . . Therefore we ought to fish well and diligently; as the Lord taught and said: 'Come ye after me, and I will make you fishers of men.' And again: 'Behold, saith the Lord, I send many fishers and hunters,' etc. Therefore we should, by all means, set our nets in such a manner that a great multitude and a crowd may be caught therein for God."[42] Patrick's labors fulfilled the words of Joel, the same prophecy that Moroni quoted to Joseph Smith, which Patrick also quoted to explain his own tremendous success: "I will pour out my spirit upon all flesh; and your sons and your daughters shall prophesy, your old men shall dream dreams, your young men shall see visions: And also upon the servants and upon the handmaids in those days will I pour out my spirit" (Joel 2:28–29).

"We"

As the years passed, the Roman Christian slave from Britain became more Irish than the Irish; the love first placed in him when he reached for the letters and heard children calling to him from the turning pages of future history grew until he became so. That love rises from the pages of his *Confession* as he writes, for example, of "one blessed Irish maiden, of adult age, noble and very beautiful, whom I baptized."[43] Or from the only letter we have of his, written to the people of Britain when a party of Christian soldiers under the command of a man named Coroticus slaughtered and enslaved some of the newly baptized Irish. Over fifteen hundred years later, his pain can still be felt today: "On the day following that in which they were clothed in white and received the chrism of neophytes, they were cruelly cut up and slain with the sword of the above mentioned. . . . I know not whether I should grieve most for those who were slain, or for those whom the devil insnared into the eternal pains of hell."[44] "What shall I do, O Lord? I am greatly despised. Lo! thy sheep are torn around me, and plundered."[45] Yet when he sent fellow laborers to plead for the release of the living who were now enslaved, "they laughed at them."[46] Patrick is left to lament and comfort as best he can with words that echo the pain that his contemporary, Mormon, felt at the loss of his people after the last great battle in the Book of Mormon: "O you fair and beloved brethren and sons whom I have begotten in Christ, countless of number, what can I do for you? . . . The wickedness of the wicked hath prevailed over us. . . . Perhaps they do not believe we have received one and the same baptism, or have one and the same God as Father. For them it is a disgrace that *we are Irish.*"[47] There is something wonderful in Patrick's use of the phrase "*we* are Irish." The transformation is complete; he is Ireland's, body and soul. His pain echoes from the cavernous depths of his compassion as he speaks to the slain through the veil of death: "I grieve for you, I grieve, my dearly beloved. . . . If this horrible, unspeakable crime did happen—thanks be to God, you have left the world and have gone to Paradise as baptized faithful."[48] He is then granted the comforting solace of vision: "I see you: you have begun to journey where night shall be no more, nor mourning, nor death; but you shall leap like calves loosened from their bonds. . . . You then, will reign with the apostles, and prophets, and martyrs. You will take possession of an eternal kingdom."[49] He is now not only Irish, but has become the very soul of the Emerald Isle.

Perhaps this in part explains why he felt he could never go home or leave—even for a short time—those the Lord gave him as brothers and sisters to love and to become one with. He writes of a time when he desired to return home or to visit the friends he left behind in Gaul, but the Lord forbade it: "Therefore, though I could have wished to leave them, and had been ready and very desirous to go to Britannia, as if to my country and parents, and not that alone, but to go even to Gallia [Gaul]. . . . But I am bound in the spirit . . . and not I, but the Lord Christ, who commanded me to come and be with them for the rest of my life."[50]

"Turning Darkness into Light"

Patrick died in 461, in an age I grew up believing was dark with the silences of heaven. But light was shining in Ireland; Patrick's example fired the imagination and desires of the succeeding generations. In one of the great ironies of history, the unlearned missionary from Britain infused a love of learning into the Irish soul. He brought the gift of Latin literacy to the island, and the Irish took to words and scholarship like a bird rises in flight. Soon monastic communities sprang up in the valleys, along the rivers and lakes, and on rocky isolated islands. Here the monks labored, dedicated to copying and enhancing with beautiful illumination the scriptures—and vast quantities of classical literature which would have been lost forever were it not for their efforts. Then, like the unlearned former slave who inspired them, their coveted Biblical manuscripts packed into leather pouches, they spread the gospel message back across Britain and the Continent, establishing scores of monasteries and centers of learning. The sixth, seventh, and eighth centuries were dominated by learned holy men from Ireland—until the Viking raids of the ninth century devastated Patrick's beloved island, leaving only an echo of its former voices.

The spirit of their values and the power of Patrick's legacy are marvelously captured in a poem, "Pangur Bán," written by an Irish monk in Saint Gallen, Switzerland, during the ninth century. A copy of this poem is given to every visitor to Trinity College, Dublin, who line up by the thousands to see the illuminated Biblical beauty and wonder of the Book of Kells. The combination of humor, love of rhythmic wordplay, and delight in truth is so indicative of the Irish spirit and of the great Saint, himself.

Pangur Bán

I and Pangur Bán, my cat,
'Tis a like task we are at;

Hunting mice is his delight,
Hunting words I sit all night.

Better far than praise of men
'Tis to sit with book and pen;
Pangur bears me no ill-will
He too plies his simple skill.

'Tis a merry thing to see
At our tasks how glad are we,
When at home we sit and find
Entertainment to our mind.

Oftentimes a mouse will stray
In the hero Pangur's way;
Oftentimes my keen thought set
Takes a meaning in its net.

'Gainst the wall he sets his eye
Full and fierce, and sharp and sly;
'Gainst the wall of knowledge I
All my little wisdom try.

When a mouse darts from its den,
O how glad is Pangur then!
O what gladness do I prove
When I solve the doubts I love!

So in peace our tasks we ply,
Pangur Bán, my cat, and I;
In our arts we find our bliss,
I have mine and he has his.

Practice every day has made
Pangur perfect in his trade;
I get wisdom day and night,
Turning darkness into light.[51]

That is what Patrick did—he turned darkness into light! I have been lifted by his story, by its assurance that God still spoke to men even through the darkness of Europe's night, and by the transforming power of the word, which has always been and always will be more powerful than the sword. Patrick's story reminds us that God can use any experience to school us to his purposes. When all appears to be against us, just the opposite may be true. Most of all we learn that good can be returned for evil as Jesus so beautifully taught.

How wonderful are God's ways of instructing his children! He took an outcast, a slave, who had endured misery for six long years, and placed in that man's heart an abiding love for the very people who created his distress and deprivations, who separated him from home and family. God led that man through countless oppositions to embody the heart and soul, the very birthright itself, of the people he had considered barbarians and enemies, a people from whom he longed to escape. As a good Irish friend once said to me when I told him of my love for Saint Patrick, "We are all called Patrick here!"

As long as the story of Patrick is told there will be hope that the hearts of men can be changed, that forgiveness and compassion truly are greater than hostility and vengeance, and that those of different languages, backgrounds, and nationalities may yet become one in the manner that Christ taught us to be one. In a world of divisiveness, of ethnic exclusiveness, of distrust and violent separation, where we are often bound together only in the cultural community of Coca-Cola, Levi's, and cellular electronics, may Patrick's light brighten our understandings and leave us inspired to look with new eyes on those who inhabit the next island, be that island just across the Irish Sea or far beyond the horizon. They may have hurt us, or frightened us; they may belong to an alien religion or distant culture, but, as Patrick would testify, with God's help they may rest one day lovingly in our hearts and we can say, "O you fair and beloved brethren and sons . . ."[52]

"They," in the providence of God, may yet become "We!"

I testify in truth and in joy of heart,
before God and His holy angels,
That I never had any occasion,
except the Gospel and its promises,
For returning to that people from whom
I had before with difficulty escaped.[53]

CHAPTER TWO

"ALL CREATURES OF OUR GOD AND KING": SAINT FRANCIS OF ASSISI

Italy
Thirteenth Century C.E.

God could not have chosen anyone less qualified, or more of
a sinner, than myself. And so, for this wonderful work He intends to
perform through us, He selected me—for God always chooses the
weak and the absurd, and those who count for nothing.[1]
—SAINT FRANCIS OF ASSISI

SONG OF FORGIVENESS

THE CROWDS HAD BEEN GATHERING all morning. The area before the bishop's palace was packed with tension and anticipation. Two great enemies, whose politics and power struggles were so endemic to the Italian city states—and the cause of so much violence—glared angrily at each other. One antagonist, Bishop Guido, was a supposed representative of Christ; the other, Oportulo de Bernardo, was a civic leader, the mayor of Assisi, commissioned to maintain order and justice. One threatened with the weapon of excommunication; the other with that of chains and confinement. The crowds stilled as a dying man, too weak to walk, was carried before the two powerful men on a stretcher. Clothed in a simple brown habit with a rope for a belt, he had requested the two enemies meet him outside the palace. There would be no sermons, no reading of scripture, no reminder of Christ's forgiving words from the cross. Instead he sang his "Canticle of the Sun," having added new verses to his joyful celebration of all creation. They were verses of forgiveness and peace. His voice flowed out over the crowd in the quiet calm his presence inspired:

> *Praise to You, my Lord, for those who forgive,*
> *For the sake of your love*
> *And bear weakness and tribulation.*
> *Blessed are those who endure in peace,*
> *For by You, Most High,*
> *They shall be crowned.*[2]

The voice ceased and as muffled whispers slowly rose from the gathered crowd, the two chastened men were reconciled—softened by the fading voice of a dying man. Lying down again, the tiny wasted figure in the brown robe was carried back to his room, where he would prepare for his death. His name was Francis, and we have all sung the earliest stanzas of his "Canticle of the Sun." We call it "All Creatures of Our God and King."[3]

CAREFREE MINSTREL OF ASSISI

He was born in 1182 to an Umbrian cloth merchant who was absent in France when his French mother, affectionately called "Pica," had him christened Giovanni. When Pietro di Bernardone returned and learned his son was named after the Baptist, his temper rose and he changed the sickly child's name to Francesco [Francis], meaning "the Frenchman," and Francis it would remain. These were days when the romance songs of the French troubadours and the heroic deeds of the Crusaders circled through the streets. Though in reality the Crusades were brutal, violent, intolerant affairs and displayed the most un-Christlike behavior, the magic of their mythology captured young men's imaginations, even as today their heroic spirit is still immortalized in such songs as "Onward, Christian Soldiers." Francis's mother sang the lilting melodies of the troubadours to her son, and he thrilled to hear stories of gallant knights. As he grew, his father took him to France and the boy's soul filled with the music of love and heroism. Always a dreamer, he endured a few years of education from Assisi's village priest and aspired to great deeds of knighthood.

His joyful, lighthearted spirit and lavish generosity made him the center around which the youth of Assisi gathered. He became a "master of revels." But there was a shallow emptiness in his joking, his irresponsible strutting, and his quest for constant entertainment. His father was increasingly distressed at Francis's apathetic attitude toward the family business. Even on trips to France he was more interested in the latest minstrel's verse than the quality and price of cloth. But he dressed to the nines in the latest fashion and enjoyed his idle life reveling with the youth of Assisi. He sang when he was happy, while the serious side of life could whistle its own tune for all Francis cared. Francis later gave a simple summation of this time in his life: "I lived in sin."

Events would change him, slowly at first. After turning away a beggar, he heard something inside ask, "If that poor man had asked something of you in the name of a great count or baron, certainly you would have given him what he asked for. How much more ought you to have done it for the King of kings and Lord of all!"[4] While riding horses with his friends, they came near the "lazaretto," where the lepers were confined. The stench pushed its way out into the clean air and the boys, smelling the foul odors, wheeled their horses around and sped away. Human misery could not always be ignored. Filled with a shame that he remembered all his life, Francis turned his own horse and raced after his companions. More of the realities of life awaited him.

THE PRISON YEAR

This was medieval Italy, a world of factions, the *vendetta*, fierce flashing anger, and blood feuds in which the enemy could be the family in the next street or in a city miles away. And so it was that on a December day in 1202, Francis, battlefield heroics claiming his heart and dressed in shining armor as befitted an aspiring knight, went to fight at Perugia. Just twelve miles away, Perugia was Assisi's traditional enemy and had joined with the discontented aristocrats of Assisi against their rising middle class.

As often happens in war, the initial celebration of courage and manly valor ended in tragedy and disenchantment. War can be a vile thing. Francis was captured and found himself rotting in the dark, unsanitary squalor of Perugia's jail. He nearly died of malaria, his already weak constitution broken even more. For a year he waited; the joyful mischievous boy changed as the hopelessness of his situation became apparent in the damp, polluted quarters of the dungeon. In time he was ransomed, but something was lost in Perugia's miseries. The carefree boy filled with the songs of the lark returned to Assisi subdued and reflective, seeing himself devoid of value.

Yet something was won also through the heat of malarial fevers and the despair of dank stone walls and military failure. There was now in his heart a holding place for a higher commission than that championed by the knights "marching as to war, / With the cross of Jesus / Going on before."[5] He had taken a critical step on the lifelong road of his full conversion. Saints are not made in a moment. He was now twenty-two.

He suffered from tuberculosis when he returned to Assisi and for a time walked with a cane. He tried one last time to win glory, joining himself to a nobleman, dressing once more in a knight's expensive costume, but his already weak body had suffered too much and he was forced to quit. His bold assertion that he would one day become a great prince faded in the labored coughing of his diminished lungs and the return of malaria. In his fevered condition he thought he heard a voice asking him, "Who can do better for you, the servant or the lord?"

"The Lord," he replied.

"Then why do you seek the servant rather than the lord?"[6]

When he asked what he should do, he was told to return to Assisi and it would be shown him. In the summer of 1205, purged of his vainglorious boyhood days, his life would be rechanneled by a plaintive voice speaking to him from the crumbling ruins of a tiny chapel called San Damiano. Here he would come to know his Savior and begin the first footsteps on the road that would make him, in many minds, the most Christlike man since the death of the apostles. Here his joyful, singing soul would burst again into flame, but a flame made pure by his love for God, for his fellowmen, and for all created things.

My Church Lies in Ruin

Francis's exuberant nature had been subdued. A much more reflective young man entered San Damiano, where dim light showed the broken stones and destructive wear of time. Yet in the midst of the decay and ruin an intact crucifix made of wood and painted linen was still affixed to the wall of the sanctuary. Jesus' face on that crucifix—which can still be seen today in Assisi—has a touch of softness; the eyes beckon with uncondemning invitation. Francis thought he heard a voice penetrating his thoughts, a voice filled with tenderness and pleading. The voice struck his heart with gentleness and shaped something inside he could never quite explain afterwards. "Francis," the voice of the Savior called, "go, repair my house, which as you see is entirely ruined."[7]

This experience was Francis's burning bush, his holy ground

consecrated for communion with heaven. He had turned aside to "see this great sight," would reply, "Here am I" (Exodus 3:3–4), and the grand commission, the conversation with heaven that would spill over in goodness, began. He had been saved from his selfishness—a condition more damaging than that of the prison at Perugia.

Yet as is often the case, Francis did not understand the measure of his call. With limited vision, he believed he was to repair the tumbled stones of the small chapel in which hung the image of Christ, whose voice he had heard. As yet he had no understanding that the church he was called to repair was the one whose beauty began in Bethlehem with the angelic announcement to shepherds and the call for "peace on earth, good will toward men" (see Luke 2:14). Francis would now devote his life to that peace.

He was always a bit dramatic, this young man who wanted to be a knight and loved singing the romantic ballads of the French minstrels. Removing his fashionable clothes, he donned rough peasant garb, and cinched it with a belt, which he later traded for a bit of rope, foreshadowing the traditional robes of the Franciscans he inspired. In time he took Jesus' words to the apostles literally: "Provide neither gold, nor silver, nor brass in your purses, nor scrip for your journey, neither two coats, neither shoes, nor yet staves: for the workman is worthy of his meat" (Matthew 10:9–10). "This is what I want," he said, then simplified his life, living at first in a hermit's cave. The words of Jesus were not to be argued over or allegorized, they were to be lived.

Still not comprehending the extent of his life's work, he restored the ruins of San Damiano stone by stone, often beseeching passersby to help him if only through providing another stone for the walls. Needing money for the reconstruction, he took several bolts of cloth from Bernardone's stock while he was away, sold them, and took the bag of coins to the old church. Furious not only for the loss of his merchandise, but scandalized by the bizarre behavior of the son upon whom he had lavished so much, the embarrassed father dragged Francis home, beat him, locked him in a room until he would come to his senses, then left on another trading journey. His mother's tender heart could not maintain the locked room and, pleading with Francis to please his father, she let him out. But Francis's destiny was sealed in his growing love for Christ and he returned to a life of poverty.

Frustrated to despair, Francis's father brought a formal complaint before Bishop Guido of Assisi. In one of the celebrated moments of his life, Francis met his father and the bishop in front of townspeople gathered in the piazza before the cathedral. His flair for drama and symbol dominated as he appeared dressed in his old elegant clothes as the proper son of Bernardone, the money bag from selling his father's cloth in hand. Here he divested himself of every bit of clothing and laid them at the feet of his father, the coins crowning the pile. Naked before the world, he said to the stunned crowd: "Henceforth I may freely say: 'Our Father who is in heaven,' not father Peter Bernardone, to whom, look, I not only give back the money but resign my entire clothing. Therefore I may proceed naked to the Lord."[8] The shocked bishop wrapped his own richly decorated cloak around the naked man and embraced him. We are not told of his stunned father's actions.

BEAUTY ALL AROUND

Since Jesus had exhorted his disciples to reach out into the world and preach the good news of forgiveness and love, Francis did the same. The leper no longer repulsed him. His natural cheerfulness and love of song returned and with joy he traveled into the poor villages and farmland of Umbria, gathering followers attracted by his soul's simplicity and gladness of heart and the earnestness of his teaching. The world was a beautiful place, filled with God's grace; all things were our brothers and sisters. Here was splendor above the latest scarlet cloth.

As those who followed Francis increased, Pope Innocent III granted them the blessing of an organized order of traveling friars, but Francis was not one for lists of rules, nor strict discipline. He had married what he considered the most beautiful woman of all—lady poverty—and love, kindness, compassion, gentleness, and joy needed no commanding laws nor channeled monastic vows. When later in his life he was compelled to put something to paper to guide his monastic order, he drew up a list of basic affirmations. Among those affirmations were: "We give thanks for the beauty of the world," and "We prefer the celebration and the living out of faith rather than disputing about it—hence we go among unbelievers and preach to others mostly by example."[9] His Franciscans, whose very name still sings with gentleness and has become synonymous with brotherly love, fanned out two by two, as the New Testament instructed, and preached the simple message of Jesus inherent in the parables of the Good Samaritan and the Prodigal Son—which Francis would probably have renamed "The Loving Father." He taught his followers that they were not to be angered or alienated by another's sins, for these emotions were a barrier to charity. We were to love, not judge. It was that simple!

In an age when the world was seen as fallen and sin-filled, a world of flies, fleas, and fevers, Francis saw color and music—the majesty of God displayed in every rock and tree. He loved all things, celebrated all things, and greeted all things as equally reflective of God's goodness and glory. Soon the mocking laughter that first greeted the rich, indifferent, spoiled boy—whose strange ways now compelled him to dress in peasant brown instead of nobility's scarlet—turned to awed admiration and devoted emulation.

One could not help but love Francis. His own love radiated out into the world and returned to him double. He humbled the proud of the church, whose eyes were too often centered on power and wealth, with the cheerful gladness of his own poverty. Sometimes the world needs the shock of radical contrasts to wake it from its accustomed lethargy. Neither honors nor comforts drew him. Owning nothing, judging no one, accepting everyone, reaching out to all—leper, beggar, bishop, or king; the brother of all, who never really enjoyed full health, walked the roads of Italy, his own life his greatest message. "Give, and it shall be given unto you; good measure, pressed down, and shaken together, and running over," was his mantra (Luke 6:38).

With no desire for possessions, the natural selfishness of man could be conquered, he taught. Where was the fear of loss when the heart was not centered on mere things? There was a radiant happiness in these ragged men in brown. Life was to be enjoyed! Sadness and melancholy were not of God. God wanted his children to be happy, and possession of things was not happiness. Neither was life a constant preparation for the glory to come, something to be endured. It was not a struggle to accumulate, rather it was a time for hope and rejoicing even in a world that was filled with hardship. We must do what we can to lift suffering. This he strived to do. Ever courteous, filled with compassion, he was Christ's knight, a patron of God's true chivalry.

He labored with his hands, for idleness was to be avoided, and always believed his own example was his most powerful tool. His teaching style was visual. He taught a wordless sermon to the Poor Clares (the female equivalent of the Franciscans), who were tempted to obtain property, by sprinkling ashes on his head and drawing a circle around him with them, then leaving the women to reflection. Remember you are mortal, his actions said. Dust to dust, ashes to ashes we all return.

In Greccio one Christmas, he thought the illiterate poor of the town would come to understand and love the birth of their dear Savior more if they could see the circumstances in which he came to earth. Was not Jesus first and always poor and simple as were they? He created a manger, placed next to it a mother, father, and infant from the local village, and brought in animals, the ox and donkey, and the straw to soften the bed for the baby Jesus. In the surroundings of this unadorned crèche he told the story of the shepherds and the child in swaddling clothes. The nativity scenes of our own time reach back in history to Francis's first attempt to draw the heart closer to the baby of Bethlehem. His love for the visual is duplicated across the world each Christmas and plays out in our own family home evenings and Primary programs.

IMPERFECT SAINT

He did not consider himself a saint. He did not consider himself at all. Yet he knew the temptations of the flesh and could understand the difficulties of living as Jesus asked us to live. He was always cautious around women, though he helped Clare of Assisi found an order of nuns called the Poor Clares, and he shared the Christian mentality that valued martyrdom too highly. On occasion, there was also in him a leaning toward excessive fanaticism in some areas, particularly in his ideas on poverty, yet in almost all things his cheerfulness and love kept him in balance, a rare thing for the times in which he lived. When people began to greet him as "The Saint," he gently rebuked them: "Don't canonize me too quickly," he warned, "I am perfectly capable of fathering a child."[10] Though said with that touch of merry humor which never left his heart, he was more than aware of the frailties of men. Yet his view of such weakness was neither condemnatory nor indulgent, but filled with understanding and empathy. His was not the voice of railing accusation, but of comforting invitation. He once mildly rebuked a brother for being too circumspect with his conscience, for constantly examining himself and finding fault. Those who believe in God should always present the face of hope and joy to the world, he assured him, or why would anyone want to follow the Savior or embrace his teachings?

He once sent a poignantly shy and stuttering brother named Rufino into the church to preach. Though he pleaded with Francis that he could not do such a thing, Francis was adamant. The poor man obeyed and soon became the object of laughter. Francis, realizing he had been wrong, rushed to the church to stand in the pulpit next to the terrified young man and preached the love of Christ so tenderly that all eyes turned to him. Had not Jesus also been mocked during the final hours of his Passion? Silence prevailed and the disrespectful ribaldry ceased. Rufino became one of Francis's dearest companions from that day forth.

Francis was not against learning, but preferred his brothers to stay focused on the Gospels alone—let the other orders amass libraries. He was somewhat perturbed when a young novice asked permission to have a Psalter. "This will lead to wanting other books," the novice was told. Still, over the next days the young friar persisted, until one morning in the road the normally gentle Francis impatiently lashed out at the young man, who turned away in humiliation. Francis watched him walk down the road until he was small in the distance, then ran after him, beseeching him to return with him. In silence, the two men retraced their steps until they arrived at the very spot Francis had lost his temper. There, kneeling in the dust, Francis asked forgiveness, admitting, "I have done wrong."[11] There are times in all of our lives when we must retrace our steps, return to the spot in the road where we committed an offense, and ask for pardon.

Francis could also receive chastening without the contentious defenses we so quickly erect when our own ideas or self-awareness are challenged. Notwithstanding his empathy with all the brothers and sisters of God's creating, he was harsh on his own body. In this he still reflected the excesses of his age with their perception that it was necessary to subjugate, not merely conquer, the flesh. He would need to learn that his own body also was a masterpiece of the Lord he loved. He was once asked by an attending friar if his body had not obediently served him. Yes, came the reply. "Then how hast thou treated it in return?" Francis, properly rebuked, then addressed that temporal side of himself he had so abused throughout his life as "Brother Body."[12]

CANTICLE OF CREATION

Francis's fellowship with nature was founded in gratitude to have been part of something so grand. The story is told of his stopping in the road to preach to the birds, who sensed they had nothing to fear from this man who looked up at them so admiringly. They rested in the trees as he told them to praise God for giving them the colored beauty of their feathers and freedom and independence in flight. And, for Francis who so loved song, he told them to praise God for the light-hearted joyfulness of music, each bird with its own uniquely created voice. Had not Jesus also loved the birds of the field whom his Father fed and did he not notice the fall of the sparrow?

The legend of the wolf of Gubbio is loved by children. Though it was in all probability created after his death, its spirit is pure Francis. The village of Gubbio was being terrorized by a wolf who preyed upon the flocks of the village and its inhabitants. Francis walked into the forest to talk with "Brother Wolf." Tamed by Francis's gentle nature and strong belief in the power of God, the wolf walked into the town at Francis's heels and from then on was fed by the townspeople. He told them that if they would feed the wolf, they need not live in fear.[13] The tradition is indicative of the need to believe in miracles, though Francis never claimed any of himself. Though the story is undoubtedly pure fancy, its message echoes the heart of the man who saw all life, even the wolf, as part of God's creation and felt a reverence for all that came from His hand. A dear friend once gave me a beautifully carved wooden statue of Francis. The face is gentle and soaked in mercy; Francis gazes at a sparrow in his left hand, his right tenderly stroking the head of the famous wolf of Gubbio. It holds an honored place in our home.

It was the minstrel in Francis, coupled with his awareness of that beauty, who composed his famous "Canticle of the Sun," parts of which we still sing to this day as "All Creatures of Our God and King." Francis was nearing the end of his life and, soaked in pain, called one of the brothers into his cell and had him write down the words as he recited them. He had experienced so much joy even in the midst of trials, and, of course, creation had to be celebrated. He was a lover of landscapes and the views from high hills. All under heaven—and in it—were cause for praise and gratitude. Here are some of the beauties Francis rejoiced in even as he descended into the darkness of an eye disease and tortured agony:

> *Praise to You, my Lord, for all your creatures,*
> *Especially for Brother Sun,*
> *Who is the day through whom You give us light.*
> *And he is beautiful, radiant with great splendor:*
> *Of You, Most High, he bears your likeness.*
> *Praise to You, my Lord, for Sister Moon and the*
> *   stars:*
> *In the heavens You formed them bright, precious,*
> *   and beautiful.*
> *Praise to You, my Lord, for Brother Wind,*
> *And for air and clouds*
> *Serene and every kind of weather*
> *By which you grant sustenance to every creature.*
> *Praise to You, my Lord, for Sister Water,*
> *She is very useful and humble*
> *And precious and pure.*

Praise to You, my Lord, for Brother Fire,
Through whom You illuminate the night:
He is beautiful and playful
And robust and strong.
Praise to You, my Lord, for our Sister,
  Mother Earth
Who sustains and governs us
And produces diverse fruits
With colored flowers, and herbs.[14]

To receive the full power of Francis's meaning, we must realize he deliberately alternated throughout the "Canticle to the Sun" the masculine and feminine, Brother and Sister equally loved in the splendid symphony of creation. If you want to connect to the pure beauty of Francis's soul, listen to Jenny Oaks Baker's arrangement on the violin (an Italian instrument) of "All Creatures of Our God and King."[15] She catches the majestic joyfulness, the complete adoration of the Giver of Life, the sheer love of all things that directed Francis's paths, greater than anything I have ever read or listened to before about the Italian saint. "We are minstrels of the Lord," he said of the Canticle. "What are the servants of God if not His minstrels, who must move people's hearts and lift them up to spiritual joy?"[16]

THE CRUSADE OF PEACE

Francis lived in a time of intense intolerance, mutual distrust, and hatred. With the Fifth Crusade raging against Islam in the East, Pope Innocent III launched another crusade against the heretical Cathars of southern France, which would within a few years be almost depopulated as a result. Dominic of Spain founded a new order of monks dedicated to rooting out heresy wherever it was found. This was the beginning of the Inquisition, which would, roughly three centuries later under Ferdinand and Isabella, light hundreds of fires in Spain and silence Galileo in Italy. In this world of hostility and hatred, Francis, the one-time aspiring knight, decided to go on a crusade of his own, for God was love, not "threatenings and slaughter" (Acts 9:1). He would try to negotiate a peace between the Muslims and Christians if not outright convert the followers of Mohammad. Distressed over the animosity of the Crusades, deeming even the Muslims his brothers, he boarded a ship and sailed to Egypt, where the latest Christian attempt to bring the infidels to heel was raging.

Many of his brothers accompanied him to the port of departure, wishing to travel to Egypt with him. In characteristic diplomacy, he turned to a nearby child and told his friends the child would choose. The child's little finger pointed to twelve friars. Though disappointed, the others accepted Francis's wisdom.

In Egypt, Francis was shocked by the brutality and violence of the Christian forces. Though warned by them that he would not return, he walked across the battle lines to meet with the Muslim sultan, an intelligent and noble man named Malik al-Kamil. One can almost picture the diminutive, brown-robed man alone against the splendors of Islamic Egypt and the temples of the Pharaohs. Curious about the little man with the rope belt, al-Kamil received Francis graciously and a religious conversation that lasted a number of days followed.

One is tempted to think of Paul's bold teaching of Christ before King Agrippa, which ended in Agrippa saying, "Almost thou persuadest me to be a Christian" (Acts 26:28). The two men, mutually respectful of each other's beliefs, present an image of such open possibilities and spiritual maturity. Francis was one of the earliest peace-seeking diplomats, and the tragedy of his failure was not grounded in the infidel Muslims, but in his own fellow Christians, who refused to see good or truth in any other faith. Francis learned that belief in God, faith, and truth could be discovered outside of Christian teachings. He was particularly impressed by the call to prayer five times a day and he personally prayed in the mosque. When criticized for so doing he replied, "God is everywhere."[17]

Francis returned from al-Kamil's palace convinced that the only way to win souls for God was through gentleness and loving example. Understanding and rapprochement based on respect and shared values were surely possible. He met with Cardinal Pelagio, head of the Christian forces, arguing that peace could be formed with the Muslim ruler, but was rebuffed by the insistence that Christians and Muslims could not find common ground and to attempt to do so was offensive in the sight of God. Francis, feeling a failure, returned to Italy and prepared for his death. His childhood dreams of crusading glory died in the graciousness of a Muslim ruler and in the brutality of his own fellow Christians.

SISTER DEATH

He returned from Egypt with an eye disease; the light of the sun he so loved now brought excruciating pain. In the darkness of his cell he endured the medical madness of his times as hot irons were pressed against his temples to cure his eyes. From the loss of his eyesight and the growing anguish that affliction stirred in him, he received a balancing blessing. The inner voice he had come to trust told him to rejoice, as if he already shared God's kingdom. Thus prepared, he submitted to the ordeal of the searing iron laid against his temples. The brothers offered him a sedative of some kind, perhaps an opiate made from powdered poppies. He refused. When the glowing iron came to cauterize ears to eyebrows, his fellow friars, unable to bear the sight, left the room. Only one remained, Brother Elias, who heard him offer a childlike prayer to his beloved Brother Fire: "'My Brother Fire, the Most High has given you a splendor that all creatures envy. Show yourself now to be kind and courteous to me. . . . I pray the Magnificent Lord to temper his fiery heat so that I may have the strength to bear his burning caress.'"[18] The procedure was, of course, a failure, but it was during this period he was carried to the bishop's palace to sing forgiveness into the hearts of Assisi's two powerful antagonists.

He had one final addition to compose for his "Canticle to the Sun," the one preparing him for death. Death was part of the loving care of his God and he would not turn from it in fear or regret. Calling in three of the brothers, he asked them to sing for him his Canticle, then quietly told them he wished to add a verse:

> *Praise to You, my Lord, for our Sister, bodily*
> > *Death,*
> *From whom no living man can escape . . .*
> *Blessed are those whom Death will find in Thy holy*
> > *will.*
> *The second death will do them no harm.*
> *Praise and bless, my Lord,*
> *And give Him gratitude and serve Him with great*
> > *humility.*[19]

His health had never been robust. The last years of his life were one continual round of disappointment and enduring pain. During the final few days he was comforted each evening, he told his closest brothers, by the larks who sang noisily around the church. He had always loved them. Music had never left his soul, and the birds were God's singers. Spending most of his time in the darkness of his cell to keep light from adding to the burning in his eyes, sounds became more precious to him.

In these circumstances he gave his final teachings and instructions to the brothers of his monastic order. May they always love one another as Jesus taught, for then they were truly his. May they embrace Lady Poverty and stay true in faith. He requested a last taste of almond cake made by one of the Poor Clares who was a dear friend, then asked to be laid naked on the floor of his cell. Naked he came into the world, and naked he would leave it. To the end, his appreciation for the dramatic and symbolic act remained—that too was in his soul. He wished to die alone with his God. He told the brothers to walk away slowly for about a mile, then return. As they did so, they could see an *exaltation of larks* (that is the correct collective noun) singing joyfully in the evening dusk, wheeling and circling the place where Francis lay—a final tribute of the birds to whom he once preached, a last celebration of the natural world in which he found such pleasure and beauty. When I visited Assisi on my own pilgrimage to honor the diminutive Italian friar, I could still see the winging birds in my mind's eye hallowing the spot where the great saint lay and hear their joyful haunting song.

NOURISHER

Francis taught us to possess our soul in joy, not find joy in possessiveness. He allows us to believe that even the most holy souls may yet display human frailty. He encouraged us to see good in all things and to feel celebratory rejoicing in each act of creation. God's splendor was in Brother Fire and Sister Moon, in the wolf's hunger, and the simplicity of the birds' songs, in the sweeping landscapes of green rolling hills, in the silent wonder of the night sky, and in the quiet mystery of the crèche of Bethlehem. He helped us feel God in the breeze and recognize his love even in the pain we often must endure. Above all, he helped us to see God's nobility in each other and to love what we see, even in those whose beliefs are so different from our own, for the Muslim and the Cathar were also God's children. We are not measured in bolts of scarlet cloth, or the number of prayers we offer each day, or in great deeds of chivalry, but in our common humanity, in our kindness to each other, in the actions brought on by our "good Samaritan" hearts.

For a Christianity that seemed to value and teach orthodoxy and doctrinal conformity more than morality and open-hearted compassion, Francis was a breath of fresh air. Sadly, it would take the humanism of the sixteenth and seventeenth centuries, not the formal church itself, to show Christianity what it should have known and been practicing openly and comprehensively from its foundation. Herein is an invitation to discover the blessedness of the Enlightenment's great lives and the goodness they had to offer as seen, for example, in the humanists Voltaire of France and Erasmus of Rotterdam.

Francis condemned no one. He judged no one. He was intolerant of no one. He railed at no one. He avoided no one. In light of the sad history of religions and some religious people who, unfortunately, find it far too easy to search out the motes and beams in the other's eye, Francis is in some ways an anomaly. And though we remember him for his exuberant, joyful love of living things and for his assurance that God reveals himself in nature's beauty, perhaps the greatest testimony of God's reality is to be found in the goodness, kindness, and sacred selflessness of humanity. Holiness in the individual is the highest holiness of all, the greatest sanctification, above that of temple, cathedral, mosque, or synagogue, for it is in the human heart that God's spirit reigns so supremely. The brilliant luminosity of Francis's imperfect, but listening, life witnesses to the higher Light he worshipped and makes all of us shine with a nobler glow.

The Lord revealed to John in Revelation that his church would flee into the wilderness of apostasy, but not that everything would be darkness. He would feed and nourish his bride even in that extremity (see Revelation 12:6, 14). The same truth is told in Jacob's famous allegory of the trees in the vineyard. Though the grafted-in branches had gone wild and were producing all kinds of bad fruit, yet they had nourished the roots and kept them alive! (See Jacob 5:34.) Francis of Assisi was, as was Patrick of Ireland, a "Nourisher." He was once asked by a fellow brother, "Why you?" Francis replied, "God could not have chosen anyone less qualified, or more of a sinner, than myself. And so, for this wonderful work He intends to perform through us, He selected me—for God always chooses the weak and the absurd, and those who count for nothing."[20] Those words find their echo in the Doctrine and Covenants (see D&C 1; 133:57–59).

The Sound of Their Footsteps

As a child in California, I visited the Franciscan monasteries and heard the tales of the sandaled friars who first wandered along the coast from the Mexican border to the redwood forests, establishing missions to teach the Indians and settlers. The trip up the coast to San Francisco was a yearly pilgrimage. I remember to this day the feeling of gentle love those places invoked, and still invoke, in me. The crumbling adobe seemed consistent with the spirit of Francis, not one for ostentatious show or luxury.

He had an early vision of the wide extent his movement would engender, which surprised him. "I can still hear the sound of their footsteps," he said to the small group of followers who were the genesis of his brotherhood, speaking of the coming generations of Franciscans. He had no idea those footsteps would take his brothers to the shores of a yet-to-be-discovered continent. He had no idea they would echo in the soul of an LDS boy caught up in visions of brown-cloaked and rope-belted men walking the earliest paths of the California he so loved. I recall my son relating to me an experience of being graciously helped by a Catholic cleric in South America. He was impressed with the joyfulness of this cleric's spirit and the love he extended.

I asked, "Was he dressed in brown with a knotted rope belt?"

"Yes," came the answer.

I smiled, knowing the spirit of Francis was alive and burning in a world which still so fervently needs his example. "I have done what is mine," he told the brotherhood just before his death. "May Christ teach you what is yours to do."[21] With the joys and loves of Francis in our hearts may we so learn that the world may be a better place as we pass through it, as it is a better place because *he* passed through it. "May the Lord give you peace," was his perpetual greeting. May it be ours also!

Let us begin, brothers, to serve the Lord God—
For up until now, we have done little or nothing.[22]
—SAINT FRANCIS, JUST PRIOR TO HIS DEATH.

CHAPTER THREE

"We Have Burned a Saint": Joan of Arc

France
Fifteenth Century C.E.

Forward, gentle duke, to the assault!
Have no fear! It is the right time when it pleases God.
We must work when it is His will.
Act and God will act.[1]
—Joan of Arc

The Stake at Rouen

THE English soldiers were in a festive mood. They had waited for this moment many long months. The heretical witch that had demonized their efforts to fully subjugate France would be burned this morning. The scaffold awaited; the crowd who had gathered for the spectacle muttered their approval, eager to see the suffering of their fellow man—in this case a French peasant girl, not yet twenty, whom the court had condemned. Only the formalities remained.

When told early on the morning of her execution that she was to be burned, she cried out sorrowfully, pulling at her hair. "'Alas!' she cried, 'will they treat me so horribly and cruelly, and must my body, which has never been corrupted, be burned to ashes to-day! Ah! I would far rather be beheaded seven times than burned.'"[2]

She was simply a girl now, not the leader of armies nor the

53

crowner of a king, and filled with terror. Yet she calmed herself and walked toward the Old Market of Rouen, where platforms had been erected, grandstands for the nobility and prelates of the church, and one for her whose only feature was the stake, chains lying at its foot to secure her to it. Through the jeering crowd of soldiers she went, barefoot, silent, self-protecting in her downward stare, enfolded only in the peace that her voices had offered her: *Thus it must be.* She wore a long white robe, the color of purity. When she approached the stake, she collapsed and wept, the roar of the crowd engulfing her. Then, trying to quiet herself, she knelt, pardoned her persecutors in the spirit of Christ's own forgiving words from the cross, and asked everyone to pray for her.

In inquisitorial tradition, a paper hat was placed on her head labeled "heretic." The armed men grew restive. She was made to listen to a long sermon detailing her sins and apostasy when a voice cried out, "Priest, are you going to let us get done in time for dinner?"[3] Wresting her from the hands of her confessor, they chained her to the stake and lit the fires. She asked for a crucifix, and one sympathetic soldier, drawing two sticks from those piled around her, quickly made a cross and handed it to her. She kissed it, then placed it next to her breast under her clothes. A Dominican friar named Isambart rushed into the nearby church of Saint-Laurent to obtain a cross and held it high above the crowds directly before her face and kept it there while the flames began to rise. She never ceased to pray, calling on Jesus repeatedly with a strong clear voice through her agony. "While surrendering her spirit," a witness testified, "and letting her head fall, she uttered the name of Jesus as a sign that she was fervent in the faith of God."[4] Then she slumped against the chains and fell silent.

The raucous voices of the crowded men were subdued; quiet prevailed except for the cracking noises of the fire. Most now were moved to pity, and some wept. The king of England's secretary, Jean Tressart, returning from the execution in deep agitation, voiced what would become the verdict of history, "We are lost, for we have burned a good and holy person."[5] One of her judges concurred, confessing his guilt with the words, "I wish that my soul could now be where that woman's soul is."[6] The date was May 30, 1431. Her name was Jeanne, but she always referred to herself as "the Maid." We call her "Joan of Arc."

Alone and Unequaled

How does one assess Joan? There is really no one in history like her. She stands alone, unequaled, never imitated. Even Deborah in the Biblical book of Judges does not rise to the summit upon which Joan stands. She was cut out of the cloth of no previous pattern and no one since Joan has walked in her footsteps. The path she followed was hers and hers alone. There is no sufficient explanation for her. No theory encompasses the facts that became her story. Had her life been fiction, we would have accused the author of straining our suspension of disbelief. Was she born a natural inspirer of men, a genius? Do we define her in terms of miracle, of faith, of God moving in mysterious ways? Against any odds, she was successful in the three critical things she set out to accomplish, yet her influence over events amounted to less than a year. Let us never forget she was a young girl moving in a man's world, even that most masculine of pursuits, war. Within weeks, she was conferring with men as equals to whom she would not have dared to speak while in the pastures of her village, Domremy. She was almost always the youngest person on the battlefield and certainly the only woman. It was given to the French to produce one of the singularly most splendid women in history.

I have been fascinated by Joan since my mission to France. One cannot live in that country and not be captivated by the girl who, in countless ways, embodies so much of what is heroic and noble in the French soul, for therein Joan sits as perpetual inspiration. She is the spirit of commitment which knows no fear, confident in the outcome and in the righteousness of a cause. Yet she showed no religious zealotry, no fanatical streak that too often justifies the greatest horrors in the name of God. And she never lost her woman's heart, distressed perpetually at the brutality of war, weeping at a collapsing bridge which drowned her English foes, and cradling the head of a senselessly beaten English captive in her lap while listening to his dying confession of faith.

Thinking of her has healed me more than once of my preoccupation with the trivial and inconsequential. She triumphs for women and youth, for she teaches them—and all of us regardless of sex or age—that there is very little any of us cannot do if we hold nothing back. She inspires us to stretch ourselves to the farthest limits. We can do things we never dreamed we could do because she did things no one had ever seen a peasant girl do—or any girl, for that matter. That is the genius or miracle or message of her life. That is why I believe God sent her not only to the French but to us in general. That is all that matters in the multitudinous discussions of Joan of Arc.

The cautions of a more commonsense approach never deterred her. She could leave her family, speak to knights, to bishops, to a king, wear armor, wield a sword, go into battle, lead men, bear the pain of arrows that pierced her body and return to the fight, leap from towers, even crown a king. And when all this was over, she could bear up under the relentless questioning of the most educated men of the day who tried, hour after hour, week by week, to pinion her into confessing heresy, to abandon faith in her mission, and betray the message God had sent her to achieve. Yet she held her own, until broken at last, she was led weeping to her painful death. She knew she was right, that she had been called of God to save her beloved France. This she would do for she could do nothing less.

In addition, she was engaged in affirming the proposition still so necessary today that no people should be dominated and oppressed by another. Each nation has the right to control its own destiny independent of outside forces that would violate that sovereignty. Her decisions and actions were spurred by this passion and her faith.

Her weeping collapse at the foot of the scaffold in the Old Market in Rouen reminds us of the one most pertinent fact of her remarkable life we must never forget: She was over and above all a teenage girl. We wonder at her independence, her vision, her bold, guileless, doubting-nothing life. She feared nothing but the final fires, maintaining even her sense of humor to the last. There will never be another Joan. A world produces during its existence only one.

"I Always Saw a Bright Light"

She was born in the village of Domremy in eastern France during the last phases of the Hundred Years War with England—a senseless war fought between a few noble families for the right to rule France. As always, it was the commoners who suffered, especially the peasants of France, who were subjected over and over again to pillage, rape, and destruction by roving bands of soldiers.

It was a brutal time. Northern France was occupied, with Paris in the hands of the English and their allies, the Burgundians. France was essentially being choked to death by the encroaching armies and subsequent loss of territory. Joan's father once dreamed he saw Joan with an army. He believed his dream meant she would become a camp follower and instructed her brothers that if it ever happened they were to drown her.

After the stunning defeat of the French army at Agincourt, Charles VI of France (who suffered from an intermittent mental illness) before he died had, in a treaty with the English king, Henry V, basically disinherited his son the Dauphin. The Dauphin, whom Joan would crown as Charles VII, was weak, timid, and had never been properly prepared for leadership. There were rumors, which many believed, that he was not even the son of his father due to the scandalously licentious behavior of his mother, Isabeau. He was, himself, tormented by this doubt. Was he the legitimate king of France? He had never been properly anointed; this seemed unlikely to happen as the traditional location for coronation, Reims, was effectively under Burgundian control. He was short on leadership and money, his men demoralized, defections to the English frequent, the populace in despair. He was the eleventh child—and fifth son—of his father and not expected to succeed to the throne. But the deaths of his brothers thrust the role of sovereign upon him.

Apathy prevailed. Whole areas of France had been reduced in population; wolves sometimes wandered into the streets of the towns. To cap everything, the English had laid siege to Orléans, a critical river city that protected the approaches to the southern regions of France, where the Dauphin had fled to Chinon. If Orléans fell, all of the south, tentatively loyal to Charles, would join the north and make France one great English colony. Only one city gate remained in French control, through which a trickle of supplies kept the city from starvation. The nation watched the siege and hoped for a miracle.

In faraway Domremy, stories circulated of a prophecy that God would send a virgin girl who would save France. Virginity was held in special awe in medieval times, as it was associated with Mary and believed to hold a power that arose from purity. Sometime during her thirteenth year, Joan heard the first whispers within, which increased in the following years. She saw a strange light and heard a voice that told her to be a good obedient girl and to stay close to God and the church. Troubled by these impressions at first, in time she came to trust them and find comfort in them. "I always saw a bright light, and it was always in the direction of the voice. The voice always took good care of me, and I felt very consoled. . . . I was taught how to behave, to pray."[7] Her voices left her with feelings of joy and solace.

Other than these occasional religious experiences, Joan lived the ordinary life of a peasant girl. She said herself that in the crafts of spinning and weaving she did not think anyone could teach her more. Her mother was her source of religious instruction. Other than the messages Joan sometimes received, there was nothing extraordinary about her. She played with her friends, tended the animals, did housework. Yet with the impressions, a growing deeper love for France developed.

"I MUST GO AND I MUST DO IT"

About her sixteenth or seventeenth year, her impressions began to demand action of her, which she hesitated to initiate. She was to go to Vaucouleurs, where she would find Robert de Baudricourt, a royal military commander, and ask him for a protective escort to take her to see the king at Chinon—roughly 400 miles away across enemy territory. Her first visit did not go well. A relative arranged the interview and was promptly told to take Joan home, give her a sound thrashing, and send her back to her father. But she was persistent; there was something compelling about her trusting confidence in her voices and mission. How else would a young girl dare to speak to Baudricourt as though she was his equal?

During her trial, her accusers insisted upon a charge of disobedience as she left Domremy without parental permission. "Since it was God who commanded it," she calmly replied, "if I had a hundred fathers and a hundred mothers, or if I had been the daughter of a king, I would have left."[8]

Her intense belief in her mission gained her the support of Jean de Metz, Baudricourt's squire, to whom Joan appealed, telling him she must save France, though she preferred to stay home and spin wool with her mother. She meant to go to the Dauphin even if it meant she had to walk until "my feet are worn down to my knees."[9] The king would have no help other than through her, of this she was certain. "This is not my proper station," she said, "but I must go and I must do it, because my Lord wills that I do so."[10] As Joan's sincerity won her believers, Baudricourt finally relented and sent Joan with a party of six men as protection. When asked when she wanted to go, she replied, "Better today than tomorrow, better tomorrow than later."[11] Jean de Metz testified that the men's respect for her was so great that none ever dared make any improper advances. For traveling purposes and to conceal her femininity, she cropped her hair, put on male clothing, and departed. This simple precaution would cost her dearly when her life was on trial in Rouen. Traveling mostly at night for safety they covered the distance and sent word to the Dauphin that "the Maid" had arrived and wished to speak with him.

Charles, though deeply religious, was hesitant. Those still loyal to him were troubled by Joan's firm assertion that Charles would have no help except from her. They questioned her, some feeling she was mad, but Charles, indecisive and indifferent as he normally was, agreed to see her. On the evening of her arrival she was taken into the castle, surely an environment of courtly grace alien to a farming girl, but with simple dignity, Joan approached Charles. According to some accounts he was mingling among the lords and ladies of his court to see if she would come to him unrecognized. "Gentle dauphin," she said, "I am Joan the Maid, and the King of Heaven commands that through me you be anointed and crowned in the city of Reims as a lieutenant of the King of Heaven, who is king of France."[12] There was a private conversation between Joan and Charles, which is the cause of some speculation, but in all probability Joan assured him that he was a legitimate son of his father and thus the rightful heir to his throne. She told him a "sure secret that no one knew or could know except God"[13] that had a great impact on the young king. After this conversation, Charles facilitated everything Joan desired to do. But he could not act quickly enough for Joan, for she had announced upon arrival at Chinon, "I shall last one year, hardly more."[14] There was need for haste.

Joan was taken to Poitiers and interrogated by a collection of ecclesiastics. She passed every demanded proof and was sanctioned by the church. At Poitiers she told the churchmen that while watching over the animals at her home, "A voice revealed itself to her, which said that God had great pity on the people of France. . . . Upon hearing that message, she began to weep, and the voice bade her go . . . unto the king and that she should have no uncertainty."[15] So it was not for Charles's sake (who in many ways, as shall be seen, was not worth one of Joan's compassionate tears) that God sent her, but for the war-weary people whose sufferings over the decades of the conflict had been devastating. Joan's own village of Domremy had been raided and her family forced to flee for safety while the ravaging troops destroyed and burned. They asked her if she believed in God, "Yes, better than you,"[16] came the reply. They wanted some proof of the reality of her voices. "I did not come to Poitiers," she affirmed, "to produce signs. . . . But lead me to Orléans, and I will show you the sign for which I was sent."[17]

She displayed no ulterior motive, no desire for personal gain or promotion. She had three things to accomplish: First, assure the king of his legitimacy. This she had already done in their private conversation. Second, lift the siege at Orléans; and finally, see that Charles was anointed with the holy oil at Reims so that all would know he was the rightful ruler of France. She was convincing and her interrogators pronounced her true in faith. The king could send her to Orléans. By believing her, Charles could believe in himself. This infusion of belief in oneself was one of Joan's most compelling characteristics. It was infectious and would spread through the fighting men and over all of France.

CHEF DE GUERRE

That she could attract the admiration and devotion of the common people who were so desperate in their desire for the miraculous is not surprising. That her unadorned faith and straightforward testimony could impress the men of the church is more remarkable. But that she could command the respect of France's aristocratic military leaders, treating them as equals and eventually compelling them to action, may be her most convincing proof. She met the Duke of Alençon, who would become one of her closest friends and whom she always called "my fair duke." Before leaving for battle, Joan promised his anxious wife that she would return him to her safe and alive. She won the confidence of La Hire, a tough, fast-swearing man of war whose prayer is proverbial in France, "I pray my God to do for La Hire what La Hire would do for Him, if He were Captain and La Hire was God."[18] He never swore in Joan's presence, but the pressure was such a frustration that Joan gave him permission to reduce his profane vocabulary to lesser oaths. In spite of her visionary nature, she was still down-to-earth and practical. She counseled with Dunois, leader of the forces seeking to liberate Orléans, who, though treating her at first more as a mascot, came to regard her as a *chef de guerre* [chief of war].

Dressed in a specially fitted suit of white armor, holding her beloved banner designed specifically for her, armed with a unique sword her voices had told her would be found buried in a churchyard near Chinon, and mounted on a jet black charger, the Maid rode at the head of her men at arms to break the siege at Orléans. Her efforts would begin to turn the tide in a war almost lost. She sent letters to the English telling them to leave France, for God would see to it that none of them remained. They could leave alive or remain in graves in France. At the verge of victory, the demands of a paltry girl were seen as the ravings of a witch. The English soldiers shouted back they would one day burn her.

The battle for Orléans is enshrined in French history and filled with the miraculous and the heroic. She entered to the joyful cries of the townspeople believing God had sent them their miracle worker. The story is told of a change of wind promised by Joan, which allowed supplies to move upriver by ship. We read of her unrelenting insistence that the French attack and attack again, each time ending in the dislodging of English positions until finally Les Tourelles, the great fortification which guarded the bridge of the main entrance into the city, fell. An arrow pierced her above the left breast, but after retiring to have the arrow removed, she donned her armor, rushed back to the battle, and led the charge into the English lines.

She wept for the dead, both French and English, including the English commander Glasdale, who had promised to burn her and was drowned in the Loire River. She scolded the men for their soldierly pleasures of profanity, camp followers, and gambling. She forbade pillage. The French, she believed, were fighting in God's holy cause for the liberation of sacred France and should act as *his* soldiers.

As the English withdrew, there was a brief standoff when the two armies stood face to face in anticipatory tension. It was Sunday. Joan announced if the English attacked the men could defend themselves, but the French would hold their positions. Slowly the English turned and marched away. It was a turning point. The survival of France was no longer in doubt. She had completed her second task. Just one remained—crown Charles at Reims. But Reims was in enemy territory and Charles had never been a courageous man.

CROWNING A KING

Joan urged a quick campaign to clear the Loire Valley and open a way to Reims for the anointing and coronation. Others advised caution, but Joan's voices prevailed: "*Fille-Dé* [Child of God], go, go, go; I will be at your aid, go."[19] She had proved herself, and thus Joan convinced the French leaders. A rapid series of battles at Jargeau, Meung, Beaugency, and Patay was initiated and won. It was at Jargeau that Joan encouraged the Duke of Alençon by telling him "act and God will act,"[20] reminding him as well that she had promised his young wife that she would return him safely home. She also warned him to remove himself from a position just before a ball launched by a siege engine struck where he was standing. She would keep her promise to his wife. Felled at one point from a scaling ladder, she rose quickly and encouraged the men to press the attack. Her confidence was never broken, never in doubt. Success was always only a matter of acting.

With these victories, Charles finally relented and agreed to go to Reims, though militarily speaking it was a desperate—bordering on foolish—action. Reims was deep in enemy territory, but Joan would have her way. The town of Troyes refused to open its gates to them, fearing Burgundian reprisals, but Joan promised her troops that they would enter the city within three days. She positioned her artillery and three days later, Charles was welcomed through the opened gates of the city.

It was at Troyes that a fearful monk approached Joan with holy water, making the sign of the cross, perhaps suspecting she was a sorceress after all. But Joan's peasant humor eased the tensions of the moment when she commanded him to draw near, "Be brave and approach, I won't fly away!"[21] When a noblewoman wanted Joan to touch some rosaries, she lightheartedly laughed and said, "Touch them yourselves, . . . your touch will do as much good as mine!"[22] City after city rallied to Joan's banner and the Dauphin's cause until Reims threw open its gates and received Joan and Charles with loyalty and welcome. One man was not so happy to see the Maid and Charles enter Reims: Bishop Pierre Cauchon, who slipped out of the city and made his way to the English. His hatred for Joan would prepare and eventually light the fires of Rouen, but for the moment Joan was at the peak of her influence.

Sunday, July 17, 1429, in the Gothic splendor of Reims Cathedral, Charles was anointed the rightful king of France. The coronation instruments were in Paris, but the holy oil (said to have been brought by divine power for the anointing of the first Christian Frankish king, Clovis, in 496) was in Reims. Joan, riding by the king's side, entered the cathedral and stood next to him with her banner as the anointing took place. Charles was knighted by Alençon, then, according to custom, he was anointed on various parts of his body, symbolizing his total commitment of service to God and the nation of France. The ring that wedded him to the people of France was slipped on his finger. Joan fell to her knees and embraced the king's legs, saying: "Gentle king, from this moment the pleasure of God is executed. He wished me to raise the siege of Orléans and bring you to the city of Reims to receive your anointing, which shows you are the true king and the one to whom the kingdom should belong."[23]

Her three tasks had been consummated. Joan's family was there, two brothers having joined the army that followed her. When asked what Joan would have the newly crowned king grant her, she requested nothing for herself, but asked that her village of Domremy be exempt from taxes. One wonders what her father felt as he watched the ease with which his daughter, whom he had threatened to drown if she came near the army, walked among the nobility and warriors of France. On that day she dictated a letter to the Duke of Burgundy, ally to the English, inviting him to make peace and join with the rest of France in an act of unity that would be the key to ending the horrors of war. "Make a firm and lasting peace with the king of France. You two must pardon one another fully with a sincere heart, as loyal Christians should. . . . I pray you, . . . make war no more on the holy kingdom of France. . . . I commend you to God . . . and I pray

God that He will establish a good peace."[24] Joan was now ready to go home.

CAPTURE

What Joan said after the coronation of Charles VII rings with poignancy. She had done all her voices had commanded. On this day of triumph, she was wistfully sad. "'How much I would desire,' she said to the Archbishop of Reims, 'that it were the good pleasure of God my Creator to allow me to retire and quit the army. I would go and serve my father and mother in watching over their sheep, with my sister and brothers, who would have great joy in seeing me.'"[25] But she had risen too high, created too many enemies, was held in awe by the people, and still had a burning desire to see Charles back in his own capital, Paris. Herein lies the foundation which led to the tragedy of her later life. Yet one wonders if we would know Joan as we do had she returned to farm animals and wool-spinning in Domremy.

Her impact on our memories is ratified and engraved with granite endurance because of the closing events of her life and that awful hour in the Rouen marketplace. Perhaps God, understanding the value of all she could teach us, knew from the beginning how it all would end and allowed events to progress for the greater good her example would inspire down through generations, as long as the world lasts. It seems obvious from even a cursory reading of the Bible that the Lord is more than anxious for us to realize that with his help the weak and the simple can perform wonders. Often there is a cost to be paid: the sealing of those wonders with one's life.

Soldiers began to pour into the French army. It was still a time for action; with quick movement, Paris could be taken. However, Joan had an enemy at court, a powerful noble named La Tremoille, who had opposed Joan from the beginning and had Charles's ear. Into this he now poured doubt of Joan's insistence that Paris could be taken.

There was a two-week truce with Burgundy, which Joan distrusted and opposed because it allowed the English to regroup. Ever a person of action, Joan was impatient with diplomatic maneuverings and backdoor political scheming.

Charles never really intended to win the rest of his kingdom by battle. Word among Joan's supporters was that she would put the king in Paris if he had nothing to do with it. The consistent directing power of her voices also began to diminish at this time. Behind it all, the English were determined to capture Joan and burn her as a heretic. Joan eventually did march on Paris, but a crossbow bolt pierced her thigh while she led the attack. La Tremoille used it as an excuse to convince the always-timid Charles to break off the attempt. Her fair duke, Alençon, was ordered not to see Joan again. The army began to disperse; Joan was directed to the town of Compiegne, largely to get her out of the way.

It was there, while retreating from a foray back to the protection of the city walls, that Joan, guarding the rear, was shut outside the closing gates of the town. Encircled, she was pulled from her horse by the forces of John of Luxemburg, a vassal of the Duke of Burgundy, and taken to his castles at Beaulieu and Beaurevoir. Was her capture part of a greater guiding force? Joan said that she had received the impression from her voices that "I would be captured . . . that it had to be so, that I should not be amazed thereat but that I should take it favorably and that God would aid me."[26]

Under tremendous pressure to surrender the most celebrated captive of the Middle Ages, John hesitated. He was spurred on in his unwillingness to turn Joan over to the English by his wife and the Duke of Burgundy's wife, who saw in Joan nothing but goodness and knew what the English would do to her. He was also waiting for Charles to make a customary ransom offer. No offer came. But English threats prevailed and Joan was eventually sold to the English for 10,000 gold crowns. In one of the most ungrateful concessions of history, Charles made no attempt to contact her, to ransom her, or to intercede in her behalf in any way. She was completely alone—she and her voices!

The Trial

She tried twice to escape, once by prying up the floorboards and lowering herself to the next floor and another time by jumping from a seventy-foot tower. The fall knocked her unconscious; she was recaptured, but not seriously injured. Even these attempts were held against her at her trial, but she simply replied, "God helps those who help themselves."[27] She was chained around the waist and fastened to a beam with her feet in shackles. Her cell was dark, with a latrine at one end. She was harassed almost constantly by her guards and in constant fear of sexual abuse. Five English soldiers were assigned to watch Joan. Three spent the night in her cell with the other two just outside the door. Since she was technically a prisoner of the church, she should have been treated better and under female guards, but her enemies would have none of it.

Her trial was to last months. The charge—heresy! The verdict was determined before the opening questions. She had no advocate, no one to counsel her, and was denied the comforts of her religion. She was never more alone, except for the solace she received from her voices. The English needed the church to condemn her, for then her conquests would be deemed the work of evil forces and the coronation of Charles null. Her trial was laced with illegalities. Her chief prosecutor was Pierre Cauchon, the Bishop of Beauvais, who hated Joan. He had crept out of Reims and hoped to gain certain benefices, including the bishopric of Rouen, by bringing her to the stake. He was aided by Jean D'Estivet, a rancorous, coarse-mouthed friend of Cauchon who delighted in calling Joan every filthy thing his foul mind could invent. Jean Le Maitre of the Inquisition and roughly seventy judges, many from the University of Paris, contributed to the intense grilling Joan endured week after week.

From January 9 to the final days of May 1430, Joan's judges tried to confuse her, bring her to contradict herself, speak heresy, trap her in her words, but through it all this peasant girl from a tiny village held her own. Reading the transcript of her trial is perhaps the truest indication of Joan's resilience and also of divine approval. Some parallels to the trials endured by Joseph Smith and numerous statements made by him while defending his own visionary experiences are easy to see for a Latter-day Saint.

She refused to take an oath that she would answer all questions, as she held her spiritual communications sacred. "I shall willingly swear; but never . . . about the revelations made to me by God. . . . And even if you wish to cut my head off, I will not reveal them, because I know from my visions that I must keep them secret."[28] Her judges' spelling each other off and firing questions in relay fashion forced Joan once in frustration to cry out, "Fair sirs, ask me one after the other."[29]

Perhaps her finest moment came when they tried to trap her with the question, "Do you know if you are in the grace of God?"[30] If she answered yes, they would accuse her of pride; if no, then her actions and voices were of her own inventing. She replied, "If I am not, may God put me there; and if I am, may God keep me there, for I would be the most sorrowful woman in the world if I knew that I was not in the grace of God."[31]

Her voices had instructed her "that I should answer you bravely,"[32] and that is what she did, day after tiring day. Why, they wondered, did God choose her rather than another, but Joan was ready for that question. In words reminiscent of scripture, she quickly replied, "It pleased God to do this through a simple maid, to drive back the king's enemies."[33] Is this not one of the great themes of her life? She sensed martyrdom was coming, for her voices told her, "Take everything serenely, do not shrink from your martyrdom; from that you will come finally to the kingdom of paradise."[34] Perhaps, however, that only meant her present sufferings—not execution. Joan hoped until the end she could escape her destiny. "I do not know if I will have to suffer worse, but I defer in this as in everything to Our Lord."[35] And even if the worst came, she had been granted a calm assurance of her acceptance with God. "I believe firmly what my voices have told me, that is, that I shall be saved, as firmly as if I were already there."[36] There was just no breaking this girl.

Eventually her judges began to interrogate her in her cell, where their presence could be more menacing. She became violently ill through food poisoning—so much so that the English leaders were afraid she would die of natural causes, the Earl of Warwick saying, "The king . . . had bought her dearly, and he did not wish her to die except at the hands of justice and he wished that she should be burned."[37] Toward the end she could only defend herself with pure testimony, which rings from the pages of her ordeal with clarity, grace, and poignancy: "Whatever happens, I will not do or say anything other than what I have said before. I am a good Christian . . . and I shall die as a good Christian. . . . As to God, I love Him, I serve Him, I am a good Christian."[38] At this point she was threatened with torture, but she held her composure. "Truly, if you pull my members apart and make the soul leave the body, I will not tell you anything else, and if I should tell you something, afterward I shall always say that you made me say it by force."[39]

Where did this strength come from? Even some of her condemners wondered at her replies and fortitude. She could return their threats upon them. "You tell me that you are my judge—have a care how you act, for in truth I am sent by God, and your position is one of great peril," she told Cauchon.[40] "Beaupère [an interrogator] asked Joan if the voice had form and features. This the prisoner refused to answer. 'There is a saying among children,' she said, 'that one is sometimes hanged for speaking the truth.'"[41] Perhaps, in spite of her hopes, she knew how it would all end. Yet of one thing she was certain. The English would not have her beloved France, nor would they displace her king—as unworthy as he was of her loyalty. "I know well that these English will have me dead," she told John of Luxembourg in her cell, "because they think after my death they will win the kingdom of France. But were there a hundred thousand *Godons* [French slang for the English] more than there are at present, they will not have the kingdom."[42]

"Least of all Things"

By May, Warwick was running out of patience with Cauchon. He wanted Joan dead and he wanted it soon, but Joan had not yet been broken. "If I were already judged and saw the fire lit, and the bundles of sticks ready and the executioners ready to light the fire, and even if I were within the fire, I would nevertheless not say anything other. I would maintain unto death what I have said in this trial."[43] It was time to lay down their last card, that little matter of wearing men's clothes. At first, she had put them on out of practicality. She kept them on out of necessity while in the hands of her enemies. In the final analysis they had nothing with which to condemn her for heresy so they turned to the prohibition in Deuteronomy that a woman should not wear men's clothes (see Deuteronomy 22:5). Her attitude to this charge is best reflected in her repeated response when this point was pressed. "The clothes are a small matter, the least of all things."[44] Yet upon this "least of all things" would hang her conviction—and even then her interrogators needed entrapment and deceit to make it stick.

On May 24, Cauchon brought Joan into the cemetery of Saint-Ouen for sentencing. Several risers had been set up for the assembled men to sit and witness Joan's burning. Everything was stage-managed to produce terror; the reality of the fire had its effect. Joan, believing she would be delivered to women guards and out of the hands of the English soldiers, signed a paper indicating she was willing to submit to the church. One of those present said later, "I saw clearly that she did not understand this document."[45] There is doubt and debate to this day about what exactly was on the parchment Joan signed, but apparently part of it contained a promise not to wear men's clothes.

There is no question Joan felt that by signing the document she would not have to return to the castle and the former conditions of her imprisonment. She was more than willing to put aside her male clothing, but not in the threatening environment of her jailors. She was given women's clothes, which she put on, but later in her cell, the actions of the guards were so menacing that she returned to her men's attire. (The record is unclear on this point: Either the men tried to "take her by force," or took her dress and threw "her a sack in which were exclusively men's clothes."[46])

When informed of this, Cauchon knew he had her. He reported to Warwick: "Farewell, make good cheer. It is done."[47] Joan was sentenced for being a relapsed heretic and condemned to the stake—all over a matter of a dress. Exhausted by a year of imprisonment, weakened by sickness and wearing chains, menaced daily with sexual assault, isolated from any kindness of humanity, worn down by incessant questions, deprived of hope, cornered, badgered, and hated by the encircling hostility of her foes, the courageous girl's ordeal had come to an end. That she endured for so long is a miracle in itself. "She received Communion 'with great devotion and many tears,'"[48] and went to the fire. Thus the maid from Domremy was brought to the Old Market in the center of Rouen, from there into the soul of the French nation and into ours as well.

After her burning, Warwick ordered the ashes to be gathered and thrown into the Seine so there would be no relics to fuel the fires of French patriotism or martyr veneration. But Joan was triumphant, her faith vindicated. Paris fell to the French in 1436 as she knew it would. The foul-mouthed d'Estivet was found dead in a ditch in 1438. Pierre Cauchon died suddenly in 1442 while being bled by his barber. Rouen was retaken in 1449 as part of the Normandy campaign, Charles VII finally rising to the level of a king. By 1453, the English held only Calais—and that would be lost during the reign of Henry VIII's daughter Mary roughly a century later. In 1455, Joan's mother, Isabelle Romee, entered Notre Dame Cathedral in Paris and pleaded that her daughter's trial and conviction as a heretic be nullified. She ended her moving speech before the assembled bishops with a mother's fervency, "I demand that her name be restored."[49] Joan's trial of nullification took place in 1456, and in the summer of that year the condemnation of 1431 was itself condemned. In an act of dramatic symbolism, a copy of Joan's trial was torn and burned in Rouen where she had been burned.

"If You Really Knew Me"

Nothing really great or noble or worthwhile in the world has ever been accomplished without sacrifice. I do not think it was only for France that God called Joan to the forefront of history, but for a much wider circle. I have thought about her often. I see her listening with first awareness to the voice in the light that told her to be a good girl, or waving her banner before the gates of Orléans, or standing beside her king in the great cathedral at Reims, or chained alone and frightened in the tower prison of Normandy, or parrying questions with the guileless simplicity and common sense that betokens innocence. Above all, I see her calling out to her Savior as the flames engulfed her.

How these images have sometimes chastened me for my overindulgence or concern with petty things! How often they have inspired me to see the grand potential God placed in the hearts and minds of his children. Is there anything we cannot do? We must never limit our God; we must never limit ourselves. He chooses to show us greatness in the meekest of souls that we may know it in our own. I keep reminding myself that Joan was, at heart, just like all of us. Divested of her armor and banner, you would find Joans in every hamlet and high school. When I think of her, I find myself wanting to cry out to the world how grand and magnificent humanity can be! In this instance, exemplified in a girl who never saw her twentieth birthday, but stirred by a cause, lifted by voices from God, motivated by love of country, and touched by compassion for the victims of war's brutality, simply did unbelievable things!

> *If you really knew me, about my life and what I*
> *have done,*
> *You would really want to have nothing to do with*
> *me,*
> *And you would know that you have no reason to*
> *charge or condemn me.*
> *I have done nothing except by revelation from*
> *God.*[50]

To Reveal—the See-ers

For behold, the Lord doth grant unto all nations,
of their own nation and tongue, to teach his word, yea, in
wisdom, all that he seeth fit that they should have.
—Alma 29:8

CHAPTER FOUR

THE CHILDLIKE HEART: MENCIUS, SAGE OF CHINA

China
Fourth Century B.C.E.

A gentleman differs from other men
in that he retains his heart.
A gentleman retains his heart
by means of benevolence.[1]
—MENCIUS

"THIS IS NO PLACE FOR MY SON"

THE CHINESE MOTHER WATCHED her son play, a worried expression shadowing her face. Her house was located next to a graveyard and her son was imitating what he saw, digging and constructing graves. "This is no place for my son," she concluded. She moved so that her son would not grow up near the cemetery. Her new abode was near the marketplace, and soon the young boy was hawking imaginary goods to prospective customers, employing all the right words for making the final sale. "This is no place for my son," she said again. Once more she looked for a new place to live. She settled in a house near a school where the Chinese classics, particularly those of Confucius, were studied. Soon the little boy was imitating the scholars he saw studying. "This is indeed the right place for my son to grow into manhood," the mother said as she smiled. The mother's name is legendary in China. She is Mother Meng, and the child she raised with such foresight became one of the greatest sages in Chinese history. We call him Mencius.

Heaven Is About to Stir

There is no underestimating the influence Mencius's mother had on him—or that of the studies she made sure he pursued. This combination created in Mencius one of the most beautiful minds and open, optimistic hearts I have encountered in my life of studying great people. He lived in a time called the Warring States period, when China was in turmoil after the fall of the Zhou Dynasty. No longer united, each feudal state fought the others for supremacy. The larger ones swallowed up the smaller and then turned on each other in furious battles that brought misery and devastation to China.

Mencius knew man at his worst, for he could, year by year, see and hear of the terrible sufferings of the people. Yet through it all and in spite of evidence to the contrary, he never lost his belief in the inherent goodness of mankind. His example has more than once rescued me when I have seen the cruelties and inhumanities of my own age. To believe in the goodness of remarkable people like Patrick or Joan is one thing, to hold fast to the assurance that man in general—each man—is born to righteousness and mercy is another.

For ages men have been arguing over the true nature of the human race. Are men naturally evil or naturally good? I suppose there is evidence for both, but Mencius came down passionately on the side of humankind's inbred goodness. He would spend his life defending that belief. He spoke of the eyes as revealing the true spirit in man. No one can conceal what they are, for the eyes transmit the spirit. When he looked into the eyes of his fellowmen he saw majesty of soul—except in those who had let their true nature die.

What may be more important than his hopeful, buoyant, and generous assessment of the human species was his instruction on how to help people live up to and tap that goodness in themselves and others. He was not without opposition. In China at the time there was another school of thinkers called the "Legalists." They were convinced that man was inherently evil and could be controlled only by force and harsh laws. Tyranny was the answer to governing the human race. People must be kept in virtual ignorance, requiring only the most basic knowledge. The Legalists agreed that Mencius's beliefs were impractical and idealistic. Thus the lines were drawn and the battle for the soul of China was set.

I grew up thinking the only scriptures on earth were those inspired by the Hebrew prophets of the Old Testament, the words and letters of Jesus and his apostles, and the scriptures of the Restoration. But how could the God I believed was the loving God of all the earth not speak somehow to everyone else? For years I wrestled with this idea. Having now read the Chinese classics, certainly Confucius, but others as well, I believe I have found the scriptural infusion God gave the Chinese nation. Mencius is my favorite, I must admit, and I do not hesitate to call what he bestowed upon the world *scripture*—some of the most optimistic, holy writing the world has. It all started with his mother's decision to change his environment and lead him to the study of China's greatest sages and rulers of the past. Mencius quotes a Chinese ode dating to the earliest dynastic times in China. I wonder if he realized his own life was in the highest sense a fulfillment of it:

> *Heaven is about to stir,*
> *Do not chatter so.*
> —Shi-King, *Odes,* 254.

His father died when he was quite young, but his mother was more than equal to the task of raising her young son. When Mencius was slack in his studies, as boys are prone to be, Mother Meng encouraged him with a remarkable visual lesson. She was weaving when she asked him how he was progressing. When he answered he was pretty much in the same place, she drew forth a knife and cut the threads of her loom, leaving the unfinished cloth frayed and useless. Shocked, the boy asked his mother what she had done. His mother's weaving was part of their livelihood. "Neglecting your study," she responded, "is just like my cutting the threads of the fabric. When you neglect your lessons you will escape neither servitude nor disaster. What difference is there between half a weaving and a boy half educated?"

So the boy learned with great earnestness and mastered all his teachers could offer him. But learning was one thing—changing the world was another. Mencius knew that knowledge unapplied has no real value. So, as his hero, Confucius, had done generations earlier, he set off to find a feudal state that would live according to wisdom and benevolence.

He failed in this, but his life as a teacher ended with a large body of students flocking to him to hear his wisdom. His writings sculpted Chinese thought and gave him in death the victory he was denied in life. Through these writings we gain what we know about Mencius's life. Like the Hebrew prophets of whom we know so little (such as Isaiah), we learn of his heart and mind through the thoughts he recorded, which are studied to this day.

The Mandate of Heaven

The essence of Chinese wisdom, as Mencius learned and extolled it, in one respect should be easy for Latter-day Saints to understand. It is beautifully explained in section 121 of the Doctrine and Covenants. In Liberty Jail, Joseph Smith penned a letter that spoke of many who were called but few chosen. They were not chosen because they could not learn one lesson—that the right to rule in the affairs of men was contingent on the "principles of righteousness." The opportunity to preside is given to man by the powers of heaven, thereby connecting earthly authority to heavenly permission. When the principles of righteousness are neglected, "Amen to the . . . authority of that man" (D&C 121:36–37).

Similarly, in China, this idea was called "the mandate of heaven." The concept was first applied mainly to the emperor and high officials in his court, but Confucius broadened it to include all authority. If the emperor or feudal king was not ruling righteously for the welfare and benefit of the people, they had the right to rise up and replace him—he had lost heaven's mandate. This belief was central to Mencius's thought. We tend to think that rule by consent of the governed is an Enlightenment America–era concept, but it was taught and applied in China centuries before the birth of Christ.

THE GENTLEMAN

In Doctrine and Covenants 121, Joseph Smith listed the principles of righteousness that bring with them moral authority, some of which are persuasion, longsuffering, gentleness, meekness, kindness, and unfeigned love. The Chinese also had an inventory of virtues. These included, among others, courage, propriety, courtesy and respect, doing one's best, righteousness, honest speaking, public service, and the cultivation of the mind through literary and artistic pursuits. One who had achieved these qualities was called, in the closest English translation, a "gentleman." Nobility had nothing to do with birth; it was acquired through education and unselfish service. Nobility was all a matter of character.

The greatest of all Chinese virtues was benevolence, just as Paul taught that the greatest Christian virtue was charity, and the Buddha taught that the greatest virtue is compassion. Mencius believed completely in these virtues and that man was born with them. They did not need to be instilled in humanity; rather, people came from heaven equipped with them. The challenge was to not let these virtues die, but to foster their growth. What made man unique among all of God's creations was his heart, which had moral tendencies placed within it that, if nurtured, would lead all men to wisdom and goodness.

Modern man thinks with his brain, but most ancient cultures believed we think with our hearts. If thought and action were directed by our natural heart, then stability, peace, and goodness would dominate. "Slight is the difference between man and the brutes," Mencius stated. "The common man loses this distinguishing feature, while the gentleman retains it."[2]

Ideally, man would not need to respond to outward commandments issued with prophetic authority or the ethical discussions of philosophers. He certainly did not need harsh, controlling laws such as those trumpeted by the Legalists. One needed simply to look within and one would find innate goodness part of his or her own soul's furniture. Does not the Bible in numerous verses speak of a time when the law will be written within the human heart? Mencius was affirming this truth in China. Proper education would bring man's natural morality out and make it ascendant. If this took place, each man would find himself acting in accordance with the will of heaven. "Given the right nourishment there is nothing that will not grow, while deprived of it there is nothing that will not wither away."[3] Both Confucius and Mencius believed the end product of a moral education was—"the Gentleman."

The responsibility of both the ruler and the gentleman was to set the example, and then the people would follow, just as in a well-known Chinese metaphor: The grass bends when the wind blows over it. "Only the benevolent man is fit to be in high position. For a cruel man to be in high position is for him to disseminate his wickedness among the people."[4] We often quote Paul's phrase, "charity never faileth," suggesting that charity is and always will be necessary, and equally that charity will ultimately succeed. So too did Mencius teach that a man must act consistent with his heart: "There has never been a man totally true to himself who fails to move others. On the other hand, there has never been one not true to himself who is capable of doing so."[5] What we need is already in us, we must simply act in concert with what we already have and know. The teacher, whether a parent, a sage, or the king, accomplished the highest good by helping others do good. There is no greater thing one can achieve. Mencius taught this achievement could be accomplished in five ways:

1. Cause others to grow by nourishing them like rain upon plants;
2. Bring out and encourage their virtues;
3. Help them develop their talents;
4. Answer their questions;
5. Above all, give them an example to emulate.

As a parent, I have often turned to Mencius to understand my role, as his writings reduce it to such basic truths.

Chastening Kings

Mencius was bold in his approach to the rulers of his day, often openly challenging their leadership if it failed to conform to the highest standards. He once asked a king if there was any difference between killing someone with a staff or a knife. When answered there was no difference, he continued by asking if there was a difference between killing with a knife or through misrule. He then drove home his point: "There is fat meat in your kitchen and there are well-fed horses in your stables, yet the people look hungry and in the outskirts of cities men drop dead from starvation. This is to show animals the way to devour men."[6] Another time, Mencius instructed a king on his duty with a few well-placed questions. If a man entrusted his wife and children to the care of a friend while he was away and returned to find the friend had allowed his family to suffer with cold and hunger, what would he do? "End the friendship," came the answer. What if the head of the guards was unable to keep his guards in order? "Remove him from office" was the firm reply. The last question came too close to home: "'If the whole realm within the four borders was ill-governed, then what should be done about it?' The King turned to his attendants and changed the subject."[7]

One king was proud of his humanitarian record and compared himself to other kingdoms that were not as solicitous for the people's welfare, but was mystified about why he still had problems. Mencius asked him if there was any difference between men who, in the heat of battle, retreated only fifty paces versus those who retreated one hundred paces. "There is no difference," came the reply. Though the king did do some things correctly, he still favored war and privileged living. Benevolence was required on all fronts; anything less was insufficient. The king still kept his own interests at the forefront. He was retreating merely fifty paces, but he was still retreating.

Though Chinese tradition is very rigid on what constitutes proper respect, Mencius was clear on the hierarchy of what truly exalted a man. "There are three things which are acknowledged by the world to be exalted: rank, age, and virtue. At court, rank is supreme; in the village, age; but for giving help to the world and ruling over the people it is virtue. How can a man, on the strength of the possession of one of these, treat the other two with arrogance?"[8]

Mencius was persistent and argued persuasively to get the feudal kings and warriors to see the insanity of their ceaseless wars. "Only now do I realize how serious it is to kill a member of the family of another man. If you killed his father, he would kill your father; if you killed his elder brother, he would kill your elder brother. This being the case, though you may not have killed your father and brother with your own hands, it is but one step removed."[9] How often I have thought of this analogy when watching news from the Middle

East, the Balkans, Africa, or any other of a dozen places around the world—the "Warring States" period of world history continues.

The Original Heart

Though Mencius spent a great deal of energy trying to school the kings and rulers of his day, he spent even more defining the qualities of the human heart, which he continually insisted was good. He referred to the moral part of our natures as our "original heart,"[10] or our "true heart."[11] This is the childlike heart with which we are born. "A great man is one who retains the heart of a newborn babe."[12] This is sometimes translated "his child's-heart."[13] No original sin here! As Doctrine and Covenants 93 testifies, "Every spirit of man was innocent in the beginning; and God having redeemed man from the fall, men became again, in their infant state, innocent before God" (D&C 93:38).

Mencius understood that the heart had four purposes or divisions. There was the heart of compassion and benevolence, the heart of shame, the heart of courtesy and gentility, and the heart of knowing right from wrong. To prove men were compassionate by nature, he used the illustration of a child in danger. "My reason for saying that no man is devoid of a heart sensitive to the suffering of others is this. Suppose a man were, all of a sudden, to see a young child on the verge of falling into a well. He would certainly be moved to compassion, not because he wanted to get in the good graces of the parents, nor because he wished to win the praise of his fellow villagers or friends, nor yet because he disliked the cry of the child."[14] All would respond by running to help.

The urge to help is instinctive; therefore, benevolence and compassion are a part of every normal human being. Whoever lost this endowment was no longer human—they had strayed from their true nature. "Benevolence is man's peaceful abode and rightness his proper path. It is indeed lamentable for anyone not to live in his peaceful abode and not to follow his proper path."[15] We live in the house of charity and walk the road of goodness—that is what it means to be human! "Benevolence . . . and wisdom do not give me a luster from the outside," he testified, "they are in me originally."[16] "What is it, then, that is common to all hearts?" he asked, then answered: "Reason and rightness. . . . Thus reason and rightness please my heart in the same way as meat pleases my palate."[17]

We do not practice benevolence and goodness for some benefit, be it a future abode in heaven or an advantage on earth. We live in goodness as fish swim in water: because it is our element. I have always admired Chinese wisdom in that it demands a high level of ethical and moral living without the hope of heavenly reward. Mencius was asking people to be noble and selfless with no other motivation, expectation, or incentive than the action itself would bring. One lived right and practiced benevolence because that is what it meant to be human.

Though the Chinese concept of heaven is not the same as that in the West, Mencius's insight on the true way to understand God is right on center. If we desire to understand Deity, we need look no further than within. Are we not created in His image in matters of the soul as well as those of the body? "For a man to give full realization to his heart is for him to understand his own nature, and a man who knows his own nature will know Heaven. The retention of his heart and the nurturing of his nature are the means by which he serves Heaven."[18]

I have found what we call the "golden rule" in all religions and cultures around the world. Mencius added the insight that living the golden rule generates happiness: "There is no greater joy for me than to find, on self-examination, that I am true to myself. Try your best to treat others as you would wish to be treated yourself, and you will find that this is the shortest way to benevolence."[19] Mencius testified of this three centuries before Christ.

Benevolence had to be extended taking into consideration the dignity of the person one was helping. They too had an "original heart," with the fullest capacity that implied. The way of benevolence was not just giving charity in the manner so often seen in the Western world. Mencius could often be plainly blunt, but when he had finished speaking you knew that you had been told the truth. "To feed a man without showing him love is to treat him like a pig [sometimes translated "domestic animal"]; to love him without showing him respect is to keep him like a domestic animal [sometimes translated "pet"]."[20] Benevolence required more than just the offered help; one had to recognize the mutual humanity of the recipient on its deepest level—the recognition of an innate equality.

GOING AFTER THE STRAYED HEART

Though Mencius expended his major efforts confirming the heart of benevolence, he also touched on the heart of shame. Shame can be a two-edged sword. A great many things in the world are proper and good, but the world tries to make us ashamed of them; there are a great many things people do which once would have been considered the object of shame, but are now openly flaunted and celebrated. For Mencius, shame rightly applied was a sign that the heart was maintaining its original nature: "Only when there are things a man will not do is he capable of doing great things."[21] He focused on a critical problem in our own age by saying, "A man must not be without shame, for the shame of being without shame is shamelessness indeed."[22] We see this emphasis in a statement Mencius made about the three things that made a gentleman happy. First was family, for family was the foundation of the state. The opportunity to teach bright students was the second. But the third was to be able to raise one's head to heaven and to lower one's head in respect to other humans—and to not feel shame in doing either.

As has been seen, Mencius stated that our natural home and road is benevolence and righteousness. Why then do we see so many not living in that house and walking that road? Even more important, what do we do about it? "Sad it is indeed when a man gives up the right road instead of following it and allows his heart to stray without enough sense to go after it. When his chickens and dogs stray, he has sense enough to go after them, but not when what strays is his heart. The sole concern of learning is to go after this strayed heart. That is all."[23] Modern world, stand up and listen! Education throughout Chinese tradition has always been concerned with morality and ethics. It's not about getting a job. It's not about political correctness. Chinese wisdom consists in not only knowing how to reason correctly in an intellectual sense, but also how to act correctly in a moral sense. This is something we have almost totally lost in Western educational tradition.

Mencius continued his illustration of the foolishness of not going after the straying heart with another metaphor we'll have no problem understanding. "Now if one's third finger is bent and cannot stretch straight, though this neither causes any pain nor impairs the use of the hand, one would think nothing of [traveling a great distance to have it fixed] if someone able to straighten it could be found. This is because one's finger is inferior to other people's. When one's finger is inferior to other people's, one has sense enough to resent it, but not when what is inferior is the heart. This is what is called ignorance of priorities."[24] One cannot help but think when reading this truth in Mencius of the over-emphasis in our own society on physical looks and the great lengths people go to maintain them, who are yet often woefully negligent in matters of goodness and decency. "The parts of the person differ in value and importance. Never harm the parts of greater importance for the sake of those of smaller importance, or the more valuable for the sake of the less valuable."[25] "The organ of the heart can think. . . . This is what Heaven has given me. If one makes one's stand on what is of greater importance in the first instance, what is of smaller importance cannot usurp its place. In this way, one cannot but be a great man."[26]

The Legalists criticized Mencius for his high-minded, but in their eyes impractical, ideals. Man needed to be ruled with an iron fist, as he was by nature evil. But Mencius replied that benevolence, courtesy, and righteousness only appeared to fail because they were not strongly enough applied. "Benevolence overcomes cruelty just as water overcomes fire. Those who practise benevolence today are comparable to someone trying to put out a cartload of burning firewood with a cupful of water. When they fail to succeed, they say water cannot overcome fire."[27] Benevolence must be practiced fervently.

Mencius's life was filled with the frustration we see so often in the Bible when the people would not respond to a particular prophet's—or the Savior's—teachings. But he realized that opposition and trial were necessary elements in the creation of the fully developed human soul. He knew enough of the tests of life to understand their value. His words have often reminded me of Joseph Smith in Liberty Jail gaining insight and experience through the things he suffered. "Heaven, when it is about to place a great burden on a man, always first tests his resolution, exhausts his frame and makes him suffer starvation and hardship, frustrates his efforts so as to shake him from his mental lassitude, toughen his nature and make good his deficiencies. As a rule, a man can mend his ways only after he has made mistakes. . . . Only then do we learn the lesson that we survive in adversity and perish in ease and comfort."[28] That is the evidence of a mature mind!

LOOK INTO YOUR OWN . . .

Just as Jesus taught men to look to the mote in their own eye rather than the beam in another, Mencius encouraged his listeners to consider themselves before judging others. He was taught this principle by his mother one day when he walked unannounced into his home and his wife was sitting in a position not respectful for greeting people as taught in the Chinese classics. Mencius was upset at his wife's impropriety until his mother pointed out to him that those same classics he so loved also stated that one must make noise to alert someone they were approaching and give them time to assume the proper position of respect. Looking into himself, Mencius realized she was right and apologized to his wife, taking full responsibility for the embarrassing situation. He never forgot the lesson and from that time forward always looked to himself if others did not respond to him as he expected.

Perhaps our failure to move others to goodness lies in ourselves. "Suppose a man treats one in an outrageous manner. Faced with this, a gentleman will say to himself, 'I must be lacking in benevolence and courtesy, how else could such a thing happen to me?' When, looking into himself, he finds that he has been benevolent and courteous, and yet this outrageous treatment continues, then the gentleman will say to himself, 'I must have failed to do my best for him.' When, on looking into himself, he finds that he has done his best and yet this outrageous treatment continues, then the gentleman will say, 'This man does not know what he is doing.'"[29] This is a very difficult way to live, however, because, as Mencius observed, "The trouble with people is that they leave their own fields to weed the fields of others."[30] Therefore: "If others do not respond to your love with love, look into your own benevolence; if others do not respond to your attempts to govern them with order, look into your own wisdom; if others do not return your courtesy, look into your own respect. In other words, look into yourself whenever you fail to achieve your purpose."[31] If our actions do not bring the response we desire, we ought to examine ourselves. When we have made ourselves correct, the natural goodness in others will turn to us. It is like looking into a mirror—we will see what we are reflected back to us. Or, as the

Doctrine and Covenants teaches, "virtue loveth virtue; light cleaveth unto light, mercy hath compassion on mercy" (D&C 88:40).

LETTING THE SEEDLINGS GROW

Mencius demanded much of his generation, but he was aware that patience both with self and others was needed. Following the road of the natural heart was not always easy. He illustrated the need to allow the soul to develop over time with a wonderful little parable that is one of my favorite passages in his writings. "You must work at it and never let it out of your mind. At the same time, while you must never let it out of your mind, you must not forcibly help it to grow either. You must not be like the man from Sung. There was a man from Sung who pulled at his seedlings because he was worried about their failure to grow. Having done so, he went on his way home, not realizing what he had done. 'I am worn out today,' said he to his family. 'I have been helping the seedlings to grow.' His son rushed out to take a look and there the seedlings were, all shrivelled up. There are few in the world who can resist the urge to help their seedlings grow."[32]

As was the case with Confucius, numerous students gathered around him to be taught. One young man hoped to be given a post in the same city in which Mencius lived so that he could stay and learn at the great master's feet, but the outcome was in doubt; there was a possibility he would depart for his home. Mencius, trusting the natural goodness in all men, sent the young man away with these comforting words: "The Way is like a wide road. It is not at all difficult to find. The trouble with people is simply that they do not look for it. You go home and look for it and there will be teachers enough for you."[33]

BUT CAN YOU RULE IT FROM THE BACK OF A HORSE?

China was finally unified under the Qin (Chin) Dynasty, avid followers of Mencius's antagonists the Legalists. Their first emperor built the Great Wall and produced for his tomb the much-visited Terra Cotta Warriors. They tried to erase Mencius's and Confucius's teachings from the conscience of China by burning all the books they could get their hands on and burying alive the teachers who followed the great sages' truths. Through committed sacrifice and danger, some of the writings were saved. An initial view might bring one to conclude that Mencius was wrong. His focus on the childlike heart with its inherent goodness had not achieved what the harsh regime of the Legalists had—the unification of China. It is from the Qin dynasty that we get the name China. Its founder contemplated that his descendants would rule the empire for 10,000 generations, but it fell apart under the leadership of his son only one generation later.

The people revolted, as Mencius believed they had a right to do and would do, to throw off tyranny. A poor peasant warrior rose to leadership and founded, in true "mandate of heaven" fashion, one of the greatest of all Chinese dynasties, that of the Han, which ruled China at the same time that the Roman Empire was reaching its height in the West. Chinese people today refer to themselves as Han Chinese in honor of this dynasty. When Liu Bang, its peasant founder, was approached by a group of scholars who followed Mencius and Confucius to offer him their services, he replied that he had won the empire from the back of a horse—what did he need of teachers and books? They replied, "Yes, you have won it from the back of a horse, but can you govern it from there?"

Their point was well taken; the new dynasty favored the teachings of Mencius (and others), which never were again in serious doubt in the long years of changing Chinese rule. Under the assumption of man's inherent goodness, China created the longest continual civilization in world history. They experienced no "Dark Ages," no loss of light—just a seamless passing on of the inheritances of the past. In Xian, China's ancient capital, there is a temple dedicated to the great Chinese classics, wherein one finds Mencius's writings engraved on huge stone tablets. Though I cannot read the Chinese characters, I try to always visit and walk down the long rows of engraved granite to pay my respects to a man who has left me so much. His words are worthy of being carved deep into rock. When I enter the chiseled hallways and wander through the stone pages of a book as tall as myself, I cannot help but quote Job's thoughts: "Oh that my words were now written! oh that they were printed in a book! That they were graven with an iron pen . . . in the rock for ever!" (Job 19:23–24).

Looking into the Eyes

"What is man, that thou art mindful of him?" the Psalmist wrote—and then added: "For thou hast made him a little lower than the angels, and hast crowned him with glory and honour" (Psalm 8:4–5). That crowning is not only one of dominion over the rest of creation, but, as Mencius believed, an enthronement of the divine nature, centered in the heart of man wherein he is most like God. As Mencius taught, you can see in the eyes of a person something of their inner self. I recall one year sitting in a class while working on my doctorate at the University of Colorado. C. U. is a liberal school as far as colleges go; I went there a little defensive and somewhat judgmental.

The Lord changed my whole attitude one morning while I was sitting in class by offering me a challenge. "Look into the eyes of every student in this class," the Spirit directed, "and see if you can find one soul in whom the light of their Divine Father does not still burn, albeit dimmed by the world." I looked into the eyes and faces of each of my fellow students and could see the divine spark still there. They were surely the offspring of Deity; a feeling of unity with them was instilled in my very core. That was an important moment and I thanked God for the lesson, but he was not done with me yet. "Now walk the campus. Go into the buildings, pause by the lawns where the students gather and study. Look into the eyes of every person you meet and see if you can find one soul in whom the light of their Divine Father does not still burn, albeit dimmed by the world." I walked for the rest of the morning along all the paths and sidewalks of the campus, into the buildings and onto the lawns and I could not find a single pair of eyes where the spark of divine humanity was not evident.

Since that day I have developed the habit of looking into faces wherever I go. In foreign countries or at home, among those of other religions and cultures or in my own Salt Lake Valley, in the cities and in the countryside, I have looked into eyes as Mencius and the Spirit suggested. I have yet, after years of looking, and hundreds of thousands of faces, to find one in whom I could not see the in-planting of the childlike heart.

Perhaps this is why I love Mencius so much. We need his optimism, his confidence in humanity, his unbending belief in the educability of men and women, of each child, all who were born to goodness. The heart does stray. We all know how far it can stray. There are perhaps those who have killed their original, true, childlike heart and may never be able to retrieve it again. But surely it is the goal of humanity to do all in our power to teach, encourage, and cultivate that which God placed within us. Indeed the childlike heart has, as Mencius instinctively knew, always been within us. Did not Paul testify, "In him we live, and move, and have our being; . . . for we are also his offspring" (Acts 17:28).

I have been to China many times and have learned to love her people, her history, her art, and above all her wisdom. I must admit it was difficult to choose only one Chinese sage to present. There are at least three others who have schooled me as well as Mencius. After one trip, my mind filled with the stories and teachings of China, I was particularly touched with a sense of deep gratitude to the Chinese for the truths they have brought to the world. I had been teaching Chinese history and philosophy accompanied by a delightful young

Chinese guide named Bing. After having spent several weeks with him, on the last day I turned to him, embraced him, and said, "Bing, I want to thank you as representative of the Chinese people for all that your beautiful country has given me. I have been edified, and enriched, and enlivened by your culture, your history, and the wisdom of your sages. I am a better man because of all China has offered me. Thank you. Thank you." He was moved, then, patting my heart, he said: "Chinese! Chinese!"

I believe that is the highest compliment I have ever received; I desire to be true to it. I hope that within the part of my heart that belongs so completely to China the faith and vision of one of her greatest teachers, Mencius, will always be found. His intense witness that our own example of benevolence is the greatest motivator of goodness in others must be our own contribution to God's grand enterprise, that of turning men into gods themselves—to help the childlike heart mature and become the Divine Heart. I pray often that my own life may validate the faith of Mencius as I seek to do good—without need for reward—but simply because it is my nature to do so, for "we believe in being . . . benevolent, virtuous, and in doing good to all men" (Articles of Faith 1:13).

The sage is teacher to a hundred generations.[34]

CHAPTER FIVE

THE KNOT IN THE CORD: KHADIJA AND AISHA, WIVES OF THE PROPHET MOHAMMAD

Saudi Arabia
Seventh Century C.E.

The most perfect in faith amongst believers
Is he who is best in manner and kindest to his wife.[1]
—THE PROPHET MOHAMMAD

HALIMA'S STORY

SHE WAS A POOR BEDOUIN WOMAN, but wise to the ways of the desert's harsh realities. She had barely enough milk to give her own baby, let alone the infant she had agreed to nurse. Her camel's milk had dried up and she was, at best, on the brink of survival. Yet there was something about this child, call it a miracle or not—she had sufficient for both infants, and the camel's milk returned to feed the family. Her name was Halima; the infant she'd agreed to nurse was the son of Amina from Mecca, whose husband had died just before her son's birth. Because of their respect for the heritage of the desert ways, many Meccan families nursed their children with the Bedouins of the desert to give their sons strength.

One day, two men dressed in white, in the power of symbolic vision, came to Halima's tent and took the young child aside. They opened his chest, reached for his heart, and, taking it gently in their

96

hands, washed it with melted snow, removing a black spot from it. Then they kissed him and left. When Halima was told of the heavenly visitors, she rushed to the boy's side to find him sitting on the ground, weak but unhurt.

Somewhat unnerved by the experience, Halima returned the child to his mother in Mecca, who reassured her that her son was destined to greatness. His own grandfather, while presenting him to God in a prayer of thanksgiving at the sanctuary, the Ka'aba, had seen a vision of a great tree growing out of his grandson, whose top reached the sky and whose branches stretched to vast distances. Out of the tree shone a wondrous light. This child's name was Mohammad. He was born in 570 c.e. Halima was just one of a number of remarkable women whose care and devotion would mark his life and help to shape his destiny.

"I Will Make Him a Great Nation"

I once asked a Muslim woman which of all the tales of Mohammad she loved the best. She could speak no English, so we were communicating through her nephew, a close friend of mine. She paused for only a second or two, then answered, "The black spot story." I nodded in affirmation, for I too love this story. It is a wonderful example of a traditional initiatory cleansing of one called of God to be a messenger of his word. I have no doubt Mohammad *was* called of God. To do God's work, he would need a pure heart. This is the theme of Halima's story.

The promise was made to Abraham that through his seed God would bless all nations. Perhaps we are a little too exclusive with this promise, seeing its fulfillment only in Isaac's descendants. Abraham had another son named Ishmael. When praying for this son just prior to sending him and his mother, Hagar, out into the wilderness, Abraham said, "O that Ishmael might live before thee!" To this plea, God responded, "As for Ishmael, I have heard thee: Behold, I have blessed him, and will make him fruitful, and will multiply him exceedingly; . . . and I will make him a great nation" (Genesis 17:18, 20). Three great religions and three remarkable books arose from Abraham's descendants—Judaism and the Old Testament; Christianity and the New Testament; and Islam and the Quran—two of which we as Latter-day Saints share as founding beliefs and books. All have bestowed a level of goodness, truth, and inspiration for billions of people throughout millennia.

I have no desire to enter into the various arguments about the relative merits or abuses of the world's great monotheistic religions. I am a Christian and find an unmatched maturity in the teachings of Jesus of Nazareth, but I understand the power in Islam and the tremendous goodness it has brought to billions of people on the surface of the earth for close to 1,500 years. I will certainly like to meet Mohammad in heaven, but I would equally like to speak with the women who were close to him, two in particular: his first wife Khadija, and then Aisha, often thought to be his favorite wife after Khadija's death. She had equally obtained his heart and perhaps knew him more intimately than any other person alive.

"Al Amin"

Amina, Mohammad's mother, died when he was six years old. His grandfather cared for him until he was eight and then he too died, leaving the young boy in the care of his uncle Abu Talib. Orphaned young, Mohammad was always sensitive to the sometimes tenuous lives of the widow and the fatherless. We have little concrete knowledge of Mohammad's early life. At the time of his birth, there were stories circulating in Arabia that God would send them a prophet as he had the Christians and the Jews. This was the time of the *Jahiliyah*, or ignorance, when the tribes of the peninsula were still worshipping idols. The story is told of a man named Zayd who chastened his fellow Arabs for their form of worship and then, turning his eyes to heaven, he prayed, "O God, if I knew how you wished to be worshipped I would so worship you; but I do not know." That knowledge would soon be revealed.[2]

Mohammad, as a young man, took part in the trade that went south from Mecca to Yemen and north to Syria. While engaged in these activities, he came to the notice of Khadija, an intelligent, wealthy widow running her own trading business. Though she had been widowed twice she was still considered a woman desirable for marriage. As an orphan, Mohammad's own prospects for marriage were not great. He had earlier wanted to marry the daughter of his uncle Abu Talib, but was told he was not in a position to marry yet. Wise and discerning in her decisions, Khadija had engaged Mohammad's services in her caravans and was favorably impressed with his honesty and management of her resources. She sent her trusted servant Maysara with the caravan, who reported both Mohammad's business ability as well as certain signs that indicated a spiritual and moral power.

Mohammad had obtained a reputation for his diplomacy and dependability and acquired the nickname of *Al Amin,* meaning "the reliable" or "the trustworthy one." The story is told (one of my personal favorites) of a quarrel over which clan would be allowed to set the sacred black meteorite stone into the wall of the Ka'aba as they were refurbishing it. The debate went on for days, until it was finally suggested that the next person who appeared would decide and all the rest would submit to his arbitration. Mohammad then approached and was presented with the problem. He thought for a while, then spread a cloak on the ground, laid the precious and sacred stone in the middle, and instructed each family to take a place along the edge of the cloak and lift together. When the stone was in position, Mohammad slid it into place and the contention was over. There is a certain foreshadowing in this event, because it was Mohammad who finally united the tribes of Arabia, teaching them to lift together and forging them into a force that would spread Islam from Arabia to the horizons of Spain and India within a short hundred years.

With an understanding few others had at the time of Mohammad's character, and sensing greatness in him, Khadija proposed marriage, not the other way around. Mohammad, also discerning unique qualities in this woman, agreed, and though she was considerably older than he was (some traditions state as much as fifteen years), their relationship would prove to be very close and their marriage very happy. He was surely thinking of Khadija when he later advised the young on how to choose a companion with the expectation of mutual happiness. "Do not marry only for a person's looks, because their beauty might be a cause of moral decline. Do not marry for the sake of wealth, as this may become a source of sin. Marry rather on the grounds of the person's religious devotion."[3] This was the soundest foundation for love to flourish.

Love would become central to Muslim marriages and interpersonal relationships, with Mohammad and Khadija setting the example. "You shall not enter Paradise until you have faith," he taught, "and you shall not have faith until you love one another. Have loving compassion on those who are on earth, and the One Who is in Heaven will have loving compassion for you."[4] All is concluded in Mohammad's brief testament of the central concern of the building of character, especially in men. He taught, "Marriage is one half of religion."[5] Khadija bore him six children, two sons, who both died young, and four daughters. She had a Christian cousin named Waraqa who had told her from the first that Mohammad would surely be the anticipated prophet to the Arabians. Khadija's discerning eye could see in him the greatness necessary to fulfill that mission.

"At the Feet of the Mothers"

What Mohammad observed as Khadija mothered his six children, and her other influences in his life, are easily seen in many of the "Hadiths" [traditional stories and sayings of the Prophet] regarding women and the high respect he had for them. "Paradise lies at the feet of the mothers," he summarized one day.[6] His concern for even the simplest needs of mothers is reflected in his attitude regarding prayer and women: "I sometimes stand to lead [the congregation] in prayer, intending to pray at length; but when I hear the cry of a child I shorten it for fear that the mother might be distressed."[7] That would be an interesting tradition to apply to an LDS sacrament meeting! In one of Islam's most famous hadiths, Mohammad was asked by a member of the community, "'O Messenger of God, to whom should I be loyal and good?' 'To your mother,' he replied. 'And then whom?' 'Your mother.' 'And then whom?' 'Your mother.' 'And then whom?' Your father."[8]

Mohammad was himself a devoted father. He frequently embraced and kissed his children. He was questioned one day by a man for his public show of affection. "'I myself have ten sons, and have never kissed any of them,' to which the Prophet replied, 'He who has no loving compassion, to him no loving compassion will be shown.'"[9]

"Recite"

With his character fashioned and refined in the tutorial of family, Mohammad was now prepared for the call of God. He had always been a reverent man, but like others in Arabia, he was troubled by the paganism of the peninsula and drawn to the idea of the one God of the Jews and Christians. He retreated to the solitude of a cave on Mount Hira near Mecca and pondered the questions that penetrated his soul. Even Khadija could not calm the seeker within. Mount Hira was a barren place and was—like the wilderness of Judea in which Jesus fasted in for forty days in preparation for his ministry, or the top of Mount Sinai, where Moses communed with God—devoid of distractions. Here a man could be alone with his God, the natural world uncovered and reduced to the barest elements.

Mohammad began to experience dreams that filled him with hope and joyful expectation. They were "like the dawn of the morning."[10] One day the angel Gabriel appeared to him and commanded him to "Recite." Troubled by the vision and command, Mohammad replied that he was not able to do so. The instruction was repeated with the same reply. The angel embraced him tightly, until he thought he could not bear it, and at last he found himself reciting the first *sura* of the Quran. "Recite in the name of your Lord, the Creator . . . Recite! Your Lord is the Most Bountiful One, who by the pen has taught mankind things they did not know."[11]

Terrified by the experience, bewildered and confused, he rushed from the cave. As had so many prophets in the scriptures, such as Moses, Enoch, Gideon, Isaiah, or Peter, he did not embrace his call with confidence and immediate acceptance. He climbed to the summit of Hira in deep agitation. "When I was midway on the mountain, I heard a voice from heaven saying: 'O Muhammad! Thou art the apostle of God and I am Gabriel.' I raised my head towards heaven to see who was speaking, and lo, Gabriel in the form of a man with feet astride the horizon. . . . I stood gazing at him, moving neither backward or forward; then I began to turn my face away from him, but towards whatever region of the sky I looked, I saw him as before."[12] The message was clear—there was no escape from the work God had called him to do.

To whom could he turn in his fear and distress at his encounter? Instinctively, he sought out Khadija and, falling shaking into her arms, asked her to cover him—cover him and shield him from the presence on the mountain. She wrapped him in a cloak, holding him and soothing him until he was calm. As he unfolded his experience on Mount Hira, Khadija assumed another role so critical in his life—that of spiritual advisor and confidant. She was the first to believe, the first Muslim next to the Prophet himself.

Her unshakable confidence and faith in her husband buoyed him up, instilled within him the will to continue, to become, and to do all God was asking of him. When Mohammad wondered if he were possessed of the *jinn*, it was Khadija who recognized this was not something to be feared, but a revelation from God. All the signs of God's election were present. Mohammad had been a good and righteous man. "You are kind and considerate toward your kin. You help the poor and forlorn and bear their burdens. You are striving to restore the high moral qualities that our people have lost."[13] Khadija counseled that they talk to her relative Waraqa, the Christian, who better understood God's ways, and listen to his advice. When he heard the story, Waraqa confirmed Khadija's assessment, assuring Mohammad he was the foretold prophet and that God had a work for him to accomplish.

When the Lord directed section 25 of the Doctrine and Covenants to Emma Smith, he outlined one of the major contributions she would offer in the grand unfolding of the Restoration. He told her that her "calling [was to] be . . . a comfort unto [her] husband, in his afflictions, with consoling words, in the spirit of meekness" (D&C 25:5). It seems that great men who are called of God often have women near them to fulfill this essential responsibility. I think of how often Jesus sought comfort, love and consolation in the meekness and devotion of the sisters Mary and Martha, or Mary Magdalene. Barak would not face the chariots of the Canaanites unless Deborah went with him, and what would Isaac have done without his Rebekah, or Jacob his Rachel?

Mohammad had Khadija; without her, the advance of Islam would have suffered a great loss. As I read of her influence with Mohammad, I have thought often of the loving, reassuring women in my own life who have filled similar roles. We need these women;

I suppose very little of deep import in the moral advancement of the human race has been accomplished without the Khadijas of the world standing nearby with their peaceful voices and confidant arms. Was she any less important than France's Joan who was so much at the forefront? Mohammad named Khadija among the four noblest women who lived; his daughter Fatimah; Pharaoh's daughter (in Islamic lore, Pharaoh's wife); and Mary, the mother of Jesus, completing the righteous four.

"Like the Reverberations of a Bell"

Other revelations followed that often unsettled him. Each time, he would run to Khadija and the solace he found in her arms and calming voice. He described how difficult it was to receive, as Allah wished, the truths he was to teach. Often when receiving the suras of the Quran he would endure violent trembling, sweat, and fevers, having to place his head between his knees. "Never once did I receive a revelation without thinking that my soul had been torn away from me," he explained. "Sometimes it comes unto me like the reverberations of a bell, and that is the hardest upon me; the reverberations abate when I am aware of their message."[14] These were difficult experiences. Even Allah confirmed that the Quran had to come gradually rather than all at once and that its power was sufficient to split a mountain. The Quran in Arabic is poetic in style, much like Isaiah or the Psalms, and deals with a large number of subjects, from the benevolence and mercy of God to the wonders of nature and the rewards of the final judgment. Like the Book of Mormon is to Latter-day Saints, it became the key to Islamic conversion.

For Muslims the Quran is the greatest miracle of Mohammad, who was himself an illiterate man. Its power and poetic beauty was far beyond his ability to produce. It touched people deeply and could turn an opponent into a supporter within minutes of hearing it recited. The story is told of Umar, one of the first great caliphs following Mohammad's death, who, after beating his sister for reciting the Quran, was so ashamed at his violence that he picked up the passage and read it. He was immediately touched; it was Umar who would build the Dome of the Rock at Jerusalem. As does the Doctrine and Covenants, the Quran challenged those who disbelieved it to produce a chapter like it. If they could not, how could they continue to fight it?

After the first few revelations of the Quran were given, the heavens were silent for about two years. This was a period somewhat like the period of Joseph Smith's life between the First Vision and the appearance of Moroni—a period for further maturity, reflection, and moral growth. Mohammad wondered if he had somehow offended God; Khadija's reassurances once more became vital. In time, the messages continued and Mohammad was instructed to begin teaching what he was receiving. His first followers were those closest to him; he was careful about whom he approached, but, in time, others received his message and he taught more openly. Some had dreams that directed them to listen. One saw himself falling into a fire, but felt someone's arms encircling him in deliverance. Looking behind, he saw Mohammad. Another heard a voice proclaim, "Sleepers, awake! For a prophet has come among you." The establishment of Allah as the only God and the overthrow of paganism was the heart of the message. To Allah alone must man submit.

"THE SUN IN MY RIGHT HAND"

Mohammad's teachings split the community of Mecca in two. Eventually persecution became the norm. Some of his own family opposed him, but Khadija's faith never wavered. Mohammad was pelted with a sheep's uterus and had dirt thrown on him. One skeptic crushed a bone in his presence, then blew the dust in his face in mockery of the truth he defended of a final resurrection. Even women hurled insults at him. On one occasion his own aunt tossed a load of thorny firewood at his feet. His daughter wept, anxious for his safety, but he calmed her fears by telling her that her father was in the hands of God and God would protect him. His enemies tried a boycott of the believing families. No one was to sell or trade with them, including food. They huddled together in one section of Mecca for about two years trying to survive. Ultimately, the boycott failed, but persecution continued to mount. His uncle Talib, head of his clan, was not a believer, but protected his nephew as a member of his family. When the pressure became severe, Talib pleaded with Mohammad to not place upon him a burden greater than he could bear, to keep his teachings private at least, but Mohammad, with tears, answered, "O my uncle, by God if they put the sun in my right hand and the moon in my left on condition that I abandon this course, until God has made it victorious, or I perish therein, I would not abandon it."[15]

Talib remained faithful to his nephew until his death, which coincided also with the passing of Mohammad's greatest supporter, Khadija. This is known as the Year of Sadness. She had believed him, spent her resources sustaining him and his followers, comforted, encouraged, and counseled him. Now she was gone and no one would ever replace her. Her absence weighed on him profoundly. The new leader of his clan was his most hostile uncle, and the persecution became unbearable. He sought sanctuary in Ta'if, a neighboring town, but they drove him out with rocks. This was the time of his deepest trials. But several things happened to sustain him.

Often when we reach our lowest points, God compensates with truths and experiences that lift and uphold us. This was the time of Mohammad's famous "Night Journey." He was taken in vision to Jerusalem on a wonderful horse named Buraq who could reach the horizon with every step. There he ascended through the various levels of heaven and met with some of the great past prophets, including

Moses and Abraham, and received instructions regarding the Muslim prayers. He was asked to choose between a cup of water, a cup of wine, or a cup of milk. He chose milk, symbolizing that Islam would trace a middle path. Life should not be lived in constant denial of the body as Christian ascetics practiced nor the continuous pursuit of pleasure. Moderation and balance were needed in all things. He once mildly chastened one of the believers for his severity in fasting and self-denial by reminding him that his eyes, his body, and his family had rights over him also; therefore, he should sleep, and eat, and enjoy the love of wife and children. Mohammad would teach a religion of "milk."

AISHA

Yet another blessing was brought into Mohammad's life. One of the earliest followers was a man named Abu Bakr. He once saved Mohammad at a time when he was being threatened by crying out, "Would you kill a man for saying Allah is my God?" Abu Bakr had a young daughter named Aisha. Though plural marriage was permitted in Arabian society, Mohammad never took another wife while Khadija lived. At her death, an arrangement was made for a future marriage with Aisha, who was just a young girl at the time. A few years later the formal marriage ceremony was performed, but Aisha was still too young and she remained in her parent's house some time longer until she was brought to Mohammad and the marriage consummated.

Though she never replaced Khadija in his heart, his love and need for her became a central strength in his life. He ran foot races with her, laughed in gladness while watching her amusements with her friends, joined in the merriment of her play, and occasionally rebuked her. She sometimes fell asleep in the heat of the Arabian day. Her pet lamb ate the kneaded dough while she slumbered and once, when asked to watch a captive, she became distracted, as young people often are, and allowed him to escape. Mohammad, angry over the neglect, and without thinking, muttered something about her hand being cut off by Allah. He returned later to find her staring at her two hands and, when asked what she was doing, she replied, "I am wondering which of my hands Allah will take." The poignancy of the moment stung him deeply and he apologized. Like all men, prophets or not, Mohammad needed to learn from life. He realized that day how careful he needed to be from then on in every word. There is no question her youth, vibrancy, innocence, and devotion drew her deeply into his love. She was like a cooling breeze on a hot summer day. Mohammad knew a great deal about the heat life sometimes demands that we endure.

Aisha asked him once to "pray for me, that the Most High may also make me one of thy wives in Paradise." He told her to be generous to the poor and not hoard riches, but to keep no more provisions "than a horseman takes with him for a journey."[16] Aisha gave everything away, often when her own clothes were patched. Mohammad once saw a beautiful pearl necklace, part of the spoils after a confrontation with his enemies from Mecca. He gave it to her, then, bothered by his conscience in the night for having taken it before the official dividing of the spoils, asked in the morning that she return it to him. However, she had already given it to the poor.

She was once the object of rumor and gossip when she innocently fell behind the advancing caravan and was brought back alone by a young man. Even Mohammad was moved by the accusations. The stories became so problematic that a revelation clearing Aisha was delivered. That revelation is part of the Quran today; it demands four witnesses for accusations of adultery and a stern rebuke for gossip. Aisha cried for two days. When she finally learned she had regained the confidence of her husband, and her father urged her to go to Mohammad and thank him for the revelation, she told her father she would neither go to Mohammad nor thank him, but would rise and give thanks to Allah alone.

The women of Mohammad's life were certainly not intimidated by him nor reluctant to speak their minds. He was a gentle companion and an understanding husband who assisted his wives with house chores and lived simply. He played with his grandchildren, even teaching at the mosque with a granddaughter on his shoulders, and allowed his grandsons to climb on him as he offered his prayers. As there were difficulties in Biblical polygamous families—such as Jacob's—so there were in Mohammad's. One day Umar, whose own daughter had married Mohammad, decided he would straighten out the wives and strode angrily into the home. The women scattered and hid behind the partition. Umar shouted to them, "O wives of Mohammad, are you more afraid of me than the Messenger of God?" "Certainly," came back the reply, "he is not so rough and severe as you are!" Mohammad only laughed. It was this same Umar who one day asked the Prophet why he could not enjoy a few comforts as the rulers of Persia and Byzantium did. "They have their happiness in this world; I will have mine in the next" was his reply.

FLIGHT TO MEDINA

Mohammad's need for a place of refuge for his people was answered in a visit he had from pilgrims coming to Mecca from Yathrib, which would later be called Medina ("the City"—meaning the City of the Prophet). Quarrels and violent confrontations between factions in the oasis had made life unbearable. Hoping Mohammad could unify the torn community, they invited him and his followers to immigrate. An agreement was made and Mohammad prepared to flee Mecca. He sent the believers in small groups to Medina so they would not attract the attention of his enemies, then prepared himself to flee with Abu Bakr, Aisha's father.

Plots were brewing against him in Mecca, as each opposing family sent a young man to unitedly assassinate Mohammad. In this way, blood vengeance would be hard to exact from Mohammad's clan and they would be forced to take a monetary payment instead. But when the assassins arrived at his house, they heard the laughter and conversations of the women in Mohammad's house and felt it would be dishonorable to kill a man in front of women, so they waited for the morning light. Warned, Mohammad dressed his nephew Ali in his cloak, had him lie on Mohammad's bed, promised no harm would come to him, and then escaped into the desert. In the morning Ali left the house and the would-be assassins discovered, too late, the ruse.

Mohammad and Abu Bakr headed south instead of north to throw off the pursuers and hid in a cave. They were still there when a search party came upon it, but strangely did not enter. A spider had spun a web at the entrance and birds were nesting there. Convinced no one could be inside, they left without searching and Mohammad made his way to Medina. When he arrived, everyone wanted the Prophet to lodge with them. Since the oasis was already frustrated with conflict, the situation was fraught with hostile possibilities. With great diplomacy, Mohammad told everyone that Qaswa (his camel) would decide where he would live and build the first mosque. Then, dropping the reins of his camel, he let her take the lead. The camel walked through the oasis, followed by gathering crowds of people, until she finally stopped and sat down. It was a brilliant dispersing of a potentially volatile moment. Everyone saw the wisdom of their new leader. The Muslim community thrived in Medina, and in spite of frequent raids and battles with Mecca, Mohammad's leadership and new religion inspired continual conversions. He took other wives, many of them to cement ties with other families. One of them would prove invaluable during a crisis among the community of the faithful.

PILGRIMAGE

Mohammad announced that he would celebrate the pilgrimage to Mecca that year. He had seen himself in a dream with a shaven head, dressed in pilgrim white, standing by the Ka'aba with its key in his hand. The right to worship at the Ka'aba in Mecca was a time-honored privilege in Arabia. In spite of any other conflict, this right was held sacrosanct. Followed by a large number of equally eager pilgrims, Mohammad made his way south to Mecca unarmed, but he was forbidden entry. Negotiations were entered into, and an agreement made between Mohammad and the Meccans that many among his followers took to be demeaning to their beliefs and their position of strength. Mohammad had given too much away. They were disturbed by their inability to enter the sacred precinct, which they felt Mohammad had promised them they could do. Had he not seen this in his dream? Was he still the prophet of Allah or not?

Mohammad sensed the dream would have fulfillment, but according to God's own timing. During the treaty negotiations, the wording was changed twice, once by striking out the Muslim opening, "In the name of Allah, the Compassionate, the Merciful," and a second time by removing Mohammad's title of Prophet. Ali, who had married Mohammad's daughter Fatimah, refused to do either, but Mohammad instructed him to change the wording. When he outright refused to strike out the words indicating the prophetic status of Mohammad, the prophet asked him to point out the offending words as he could not read. Then Mohammad himself struck out the words. He was a wise diplomat to the last, and he was patient. All would be well in time; he would not quarrel over words.

When all was over the mood in the camp was not good. This was too much diplomacy for these proud men to swallow. Umar, one of the leaders, would not put his hand to the treaty until Mohammad assured him that he was still God's Messenger and that God would not make him the loser. Patience was required. It was a dissatisfied and mutinous group of pilgrims that returned from the treaty signing. Mohammad told them they could offer the sacrifices and perform the rituals where they were, though it was not within the sacred area. This did not go over well; silence pervaded the camp. Mohammad was at the point of despair. These were moments when he could have used the wise counsel of Khadija.

Repairing to his tent, he asked his wife Umm Salamah what he should do. She had been watching from the doorway of the tent and could feel the tension in the air. His wives rarely failed him in their advice. "Without saying a word to anyone, go and sacrifice your camel in front of the whole body of pilgrims." He did so, and then began to cut his hair. Seeing their prophet perform the time-honored Arabian ritual stilled the animosity, and each man followed suit. It was exactly the right thing to do under the circumstances. When all was over a wind picked up the cut hair and blew it toward Mecca. The men felt God had accepted their offering even though it was not performed within the sacred area. Allah, as Mohammad would often assert, was understanding.

So too was Mohammad understanding. One time a man was brought to him who was guilty of a petty crime. He sentenced him to give alms to the poor. When the man assured him he had neither food nor possessions to give away, the Prophet turned to a large basket of dates that had just been given to him and told the man he could have it and distribute them to the poor. The man assured him there was no one he knew who was poorer than he was, whereupon, Mohammad laughed and told the man that his penance was to go home and eat the dates.

TRIUMPH

In time, the tide in Arabia turned in Mohammad's favor as more and more families and Bedouins became Muslims. Finally in

630, he rode at the head of an army into Mecca largely unopposed. From the back of Qaswa he rode around the Ka'aba, crying "God is Great!"—meaning nothing is greater, and the cry was picked up by 10,000 voices. He smashed the pagan idols and recited a verse from the Quran which says, "The truth has come, and falsehood has vanished away."[17] He was magnanimous in victory, pardoning freely even his most hostile opponents. This was his most triumphant moment.

United now in one common faith, the Arabs of the desert were poised to spread Islam from India to Spain and provide religious truth, comfort, and morality to billions of people for centuries. That terrible things have been done in the names of Islam and Mohammad should not surprise us much, for horrible things have been done in the names of Christianity and Jesus also. We cannot judge a religion on these matters, but must turn to the origins and try to grasp the essence of the men and women who brought it forth and the spirit of its teachings. Within the life and message of Mohammad and the verses of the Quran is sufficient goodness to silence the more militant voices within Islam today. Mohammad did what few have ever accomplished: He founded a world religion. His influence led to the creation of a great empire that represented a high civilization for centuries, while Christian Europe was locked in the Dark Ages and struggled to emerge through feudal times. And he authored a masterpiece of religious literature that continues to inspire millions today.

Mohammad would live to enjoy the mastery of Islam in Arabia for only two more years. He returned to Medina and began to complain of headaches. He one day said that God had given one of his servants the choice between Paradise and this world and that the servant had chosen Paradise. When Abu Bakr heard this he wept bitterly. As Mohammad's health failed he kept asking his wives, "Where will I be tomorrow?" They understood that he wanted to die in Aisha's home and moved him there. He lay there quietly in Aisha's lap and slowly lost consciousness. When he died, Aisha placed his head on a pillow and began to beat her breast and cry aloud in heartfelt mourning. Umar could not bring himself to believe Mohammad was dead, but Abu Bakr came out to the gathered crowd and announced, "If anyone worships Mohammad, Mohammad is truly dead. If anyone worships God, God is truly alive and immortal."

The Measure of a Man's Greatness

One of the ways of measuring a man's greatness is by the devotion of those closest to him. Mohammad had many companions and followers, but I think those who understood him and knew him best were the women in his life, especially Khadija and Aisha. What stories they could tell us! Aisha was the source of many hadiths about Mohammad and continued to be a force in the growth and governance of the Islamic community until her death. Mohammad bore testimony to Khadija's influence when Aisha, somewhat troubled by his continued devotion to her after her passing, said to him, "'It seems there is no woman in the world except Khadija.' . . . 'Khadija had many fine points and my children came from her,'" he answered.[18] Another time Mohammad heard Khadija's sister knock at the door, was filled with memories of his first wife, and became melancholy. Aisha told him, "'How much thou rememberest an old woman . . . and yet the Most High has given thee something better in her stead!' . . . 'The Most High has not given me a better one than she was; she had believed in me at a time when all the people were still unbelievers, and testified in my favour when all the world was denying me; and she assisted me with her fortune when all other people were shunning me; and by her the Most High gave me children.' Aisha adds, 'After this I made up my mind never again to say anything derogatory of Khadija.'"[19]

Khadija had a dream before she married Mohammad in which she saw the sun descend to her house and from there spread light throughout all Mecca. She was the first to accept that light; its continual spreading was helped tremendously by her faithful support and goodness. The dream itself testifies to the confidence God had in her love and dedication.[20] Somewhere behind great men we will inevitably discover inspiring women. Mohammad once had a vision where Gabriel appeared to him with a message for Khadija. "O Apostle of God, Khadija is coming to bring thee a basin full of savoury food; when she has come, give her a salutation from her Preserver and from me, and announce to her the good news that she has a house in Paradise, made of a hollowed-out pearl, in which there is not any adversity or affliction."[21] When she received these words, Khadija simply replied, "Truly, God is peace, and from Him comes peace."[22]

Aisha never replaced Khadija in Mohammad's life, but his love for her was as tender, though in a different way, as that he cherished for Khadija. We see this in some of the more intimate moments shared by husband and wife. Certainly we see it in Mohammad's wish to die in Aisha's lap. There is something beautiful and so very satisfying in those last moments. Aisha liked to anoint her husband's hair with perfume. He never could abide offensive smells and would sweeten his breath and clean his teeth with small pieces of wood. She was also accustomed to drink from his cup. She needed reassurance of his love for her. One day while he was repairing his sandals, she looked up and saw him staring at her with an expression of joy on his face. She told him he looked happy, to which he replied, "O Aisha, may Allah reward you well. I am not as much of a joy to you as you are to me." He rose and kissed her on the forehead.

He was once asked who he loved the most among all the people. He openly answered, "Aisha."[23] Among the men his answer was, "Abu Bakr," Aisha's father.[24] When Aisha asked him how much he loved her, he took a cord, tied a knot in it, and pulled it tight. Showing it to her he declared, "I love thee as the knot in the cord."[25] The intertwining twists were a visual witness of how deeply she was part of his life. From time to time she would ask him, "How is the knot of the cord?"

To which he always replied, "As before. I love thee as much as at first; my love to thee has not changed." Aisha would equally express her love with the words, "My love for thee is unalterable."[26]

The Gift

To some it is given to be the movers of humanity, to exhibit greatness few mortals are allowed. The world is never the same after they have passed through it. But there is another form of greatness. To some it is given to believe in those movers, to be the supports and comforters without whom they could not accomplish their great commissions. This is true of all of us. We all need a Khadija, an Aisha in our lives. They lift us up by their love and their belief in our abilities. They infuse us with confidence and courage. At the passing of my own beloved Laurie, I was deeply touched by a friend's words written in a letter and given to me. "Laurie," she wrote, "tried in every way to be the foundation from which you could soar." How true those words are and how necessary it is that we be reminded of this truth from time to time when we explore the notable lives of the mighty ones of the earth.

I once told a woman in conversation how much I respected and loved the Muslim people and their faith. She replied that she did not know any Muslims. I thought, *How sad!* By and large they are a warm and hospitable and kind people. I would wish that everyone could share friendship with someone of the Muslim faith. On a recent visit to the Middle East, I was exchanging stories about Mohammad with a lovely Muslim woman. She was Bedouin. I told her that of all the places on the earth that I would most like to visit, Mecca would be the number one destination and I would dearly love to witness the Hajj in person. But I will never walk there nor see the masses of the faithful circumambulate the Ka'aba in symbolic acknowledgment of the brotherhood of man and the central gravitational pull God must have in our lives; I am not Muslim. We continued our conversation and parted. The next day I received a small package from her. Within I found a small piece of wood of the kind used by Mohammad to clean his teeth and breath, two tiny vials of perfumed oil, and a set of Muslim prayer beads. These are from Mecca, I was told. She had brought them back when she went on the Hajj years before. She wanted me to have them, for, she explained, "I have seen Mecca and performed the Hajj. You will not have that privilege." When I look at these precious gifts, so graciously shared with me, I think about Mohammad; but, as they are gifts from a woman, I ponder more on Khadija and Aisha who were so much a part of that foundation from which he could soar!

> *We revealed the Torah, in which was guidance*
>   *and light. . . .*
> *And we sent Jesus, the son of Mary, in their*
>   *footsteps,*
> *confirming the Torah that had come before him,*
> *and we gave him the Gospel, in which was guid-*
>   *ance and light. . . .*
> *And we revealed the Book [Quran] to you in*
>   *truth,*
> *confirming the book that came before. . . .*
> *To each one of you we have given a law and a*
>   *path*
> *and, had God willed it, he would have made you*
>   *one people.*
> *But in order to test you according to what he has*
>   *given you [he has not done so]*
> *So compete with one another in good works.*
> *The return of all of you is unto God.*
> *Then he will inform you about that in which you*
>   *have disagreed."*
> *"So strive as in a race in all virtues . . .*
>   —QURAN, SURA 5:44, 46–48

CHAPTER SIX

THE WHEEL-TURNER: SIDDHARTHA, THE BUDDHA

India
Sixth Century B.C.E.

If you find no one to support you
on the spiritual path,
Walk alone.[1]
—THE BUDDHA, *DHAMMAPADA*

UNDER THE ROSE-APPLE TREE

IT WAS A YOUNG BOY OF PERHAPS seven or eight who sat under the rose-apple tree on a warm morning in India. It was the day of the annual plowing festival and the boy's father, Suddhodana, was the king. He ruled the territory of the Sakya clan at the foot of the Himalayas. He would guide the ceremonial plow that opened the earth in hope of good harvests. The boy was drowsy and had been placed in the shade by his nurses, who left to watch the plow cutting through and turning over the rich earth. While others observed the king perform the ritual, the boy noticed the many tiny creatures: the insects, the small rodents, the birds whose homes were being disturbed with the smooth gliding of the plow. He saw the new shoots of grass that had reached for the sun now rolled beneath the soil. Their plight touched him deeply. He was immersed in compassion even for such inconsequential life. Yet in that compassion there was a strange joy, a welcome release, the forgetting of self, a rejoicing in being relieved of the burden of ego. This joy and compassion was innate, something natural abiding within. He could not yet comprehend all of this, but the memory of that bright day remained. He sat motionless as the sun moved through the afternoon sky, lost in empathy, removed from himself. The traditions say that the rose-apple tree's shadow also refused to move; continually shading the child's meditations, for this boy would search for and discover an answer to human suffering. He was called Siddhartha, a name which means "one who attains his purpose." We know him as the Buddha.

The Prophecy

That he was a child destined to greatness was known from his birth. At Siddhartha's conception, his mother, Maya, had a dream that a white elephant came to her while she was sleeping and touched her side—a sign of the purity and significance of him whom she carried. While en route to another city, her pains came. Maya stopped in a grove of trees, reached up to grab hold of a lowering branch, and gave birth to her son. She would not live to see the fulfillment of her premonitions. She died a few days after childbirth, leaving her son to be cared for by her younger sister. The story is told, however, that Siddhartha took seven steps and lotus flowers grew where he walked, further signaling his purity, in a manner similar to the washing of Mohammad's heart. At the ceremonies heralding his birth, a holy man named Asita prophesied that Siddhartha would either become a great king, ruling over vast areas of India, or would renounce his royal heritage and become a truth seeker, wandering the forests searching for spiritual fulfillment.

His father favored the former and decided to do all he could to turn his son to his kingly destiny by giving him all that royal privilege and wealth could provide and by shielding him from the harsher realities of life. Thus he would choose comfort, power, and pleasure—a king's inheritance. He often referred to his early life of ease and indulgence in his later years of enlightenment. Only the softest silk ever touched his skin and only the freshest fruits were presented for his taste. He had ponds filled with lotus flowers, one all blue, one all red, and one all white. Living secluded from the masses outside the palace walls, he never knew disappointment, frustration, pain, hunger, sickness, or loss. In time he was engaged to and married a beautiful young woman named Yasodara, who was as loving as she was lovely. She soon presented him with a son, whom he named Rahula. All had combined in life to bring him joy and well-being. Thus Siddhartha grew into manhood and thus he had lived for twenty-nine years.

He was a man of great intelligence, however, and though he had all in the world to make one happy, he was troubled in soul and wondered about the meaning of life. There was a certain fragility and sense of impermanence in the life he lived. His son's name seems to suggest his unease, for *Rahula* means "fetter." Perhaps we could read in this name the binding of a child to his parent's heart, but there is within the name also a hint of the state of Siddhartha's soul. Life had to be more than he was experiencing. This child so lovely in its innocence and his wife so compelling in her beauty would surely tie him more and more securely to his present life—a life that was beginning to trouble him. Something was missing. In time he wished to see beyond the walls of his palaces to the broader world of humanity outside.

THE FOUR SIGNS

His father wanted to ensure that Siddhartha saw nothing unpleasant when he ventured into the wider world and went to great lengths to clear the road of anything other than beauty. Sooner or later, however, one must confront life, and Siddhartha saw four things that changed him in the profoundest regions of the soul. His long journey to enlightenment would begin. A see-er would soon walk across the stage of the world.

Some versions of Siddhartha's life indicate that the prophecy pronounced at his birth foretold that he would renounce all he had and begin his quest for truth when he saw four signs and that the holy man wept when he realized he would not live to partake of the light that was coming into the world. I can't help but think of Simeon holding the infant Jesus at the temple in Jerusalem and his gratitude that he had seen God's salvation. The four signs would acquaint Siddhartha with sickness, old age, death, and the need to seek for enlightenment as others were doing. They would shake his soul and propel him into a relentless pursuit of an answer to human suffering, hence his father's anxiety that none of these come within his son's gaze. Accompanied by his charioteer named Channa, and in spite of all the precautions of his father, Siddhartha set forth and soon caught sight of a man weak with sickness whose face was drawn in pain. "What is the matter with that man, Channa?" he asked.

"This is disease," came the reply.

"Must all suffer so?"

"Yes, even the wealthiest; even the greatest king can be struck down by sickness." He had seen the first sign. Haunted by the memory of the pale face and sunken eyes, Siddhartha continued. Soon he and Channa came upon an old woman whose back was bent toward the ground. She shuffled slowly along her way, staff in hand. Siddhartha could see the wrinkled lines of her face, her thinned whitened hair, dimming eyes, and skeletal frame. "Is this also disease, Channa?" he asked.

"No, master, this is old age."

"Must all become such as she, even my wife, Yasodara?"

"Age comes to all, great prince, even to Yasodara." Troubled by the second sign, Siddhartha and Channa passed on and soon the third sign appeared. They saw the body of a man who had died and was being prepared for his cremation. "Why does that man not move, Channa, but is stiff like a log?"

"This is death and it reaches us all, the young as well as the old, the sick as well as the healthy."

"This must come upon my son also?"

"Yes, master, even Rahula will come to this end some day." It is not that Siddhartha was totally unaware of these things. His words to Channa were said with resignation, not naiveté. He was beginning to feel a part of mankind in a way he had never experienced before. Turning to retrace his steps to the palace, shaken to his very core, Siddhartha saw a mendicant, a seeker, sitting by the road. His eyes were closed in meditation, the outside world seeming not to touch him. "What kind of man is this, Channa?"

"This is one who has renounced the world to find enlightenment." The fourth sign had appeared and with it the final transformation of the soul of the young prince. He could never return to the former life. He had breathed the air of his fellowmen, of humanity, and was touched at a level beyond mere empathy. He was one with them; the compassion he had once felt so naturally while under the rose-apple tree for the little creatures of the world responded in kind, but now with a much broader reach.

The Burdens of Our Brethren

There is a moment in the life of Moses we might pass over without reflection because it is so casually stated, but I think it is a key to the great prophet's life and also to Siddhartha's. We read, "And it came to pass in those days, when Moses was grown, that he went out unto his brethren, and looked on their burdens" (Exodus 2:11). If we are human, something happens to us at a profound level when we look upon the burdens of our brethren. Siddhartha had so looked and would reach out and seek to find an answer to the human condition, especially human suffering.

I remember how troubling the sight of a homeless man lying under newspapers in the streets of San Francisco was to me when I was about eight years of age. To this day I can recall every detail of that image. The palaces of comfort in Siddhartha's early life may be emblematic of our own blindness to the needs and distress of our fellowmen. Unwittingly we may find ourselves in a form of denial about how so many of God's children pass through mortality. Our own lotus ponds may occupy too much of our thoughts. When we do recognize those needs we often do not know what to do or how to help. Neither did Siddhartha at first, but what is remarkable about him was his unrelenting pursuit of any kind of answer, any form of relief more permanent than just alleviating the immediate need.

Until we open ourselves up to others, we will never fully develop the godliness that lies within. We will remain spiritually immature in a world that asks us to see with compassionate eyes. We cannot close our hearts to the sorrow around us. This is what Isaiah meant when he described Christ as "a man of sorrows, and acquainted with grief." Yet he did not turn away from this but "hath borne our griefs, and carried our sorrows" (Isaiah 53:3–4). I think we often interpret these words as almost exclusively describing Gethsemane, but Jesus had this awareness throughout his life. Siddhartha was coming to a similar discovery.

Most Western religions begin from the premise that sin is the great problem that religion seeks to address and solve. Mankind must be saved from sin. Jesus was therefore sent to atone and bring cleansing and forgiveness. He is sin's conqueror; we can all conquer and find eternal joy in the presence of our Father in Heaven through his mercy and sacrifice. Likewise, he came to bring the resurrection and end death's sting. Sin and death overcome by the great plan of mercy is the center of Christianity.

In India, the focal problem was that of suffering and, in an ironic way, of continuing to live. Suffering and repeating lives were the great dilemma. This is the foundation from which Hinduism and then Buddhism would spring: there must be an answer to human suffering and its continuance. It must be remembered that in the religious beliefs of the subcontinent one would pass through numberless rebirths. The necessity to find the solution to suffering was compounded by a belief in reincarnation. You did not face suffering in only one life which ended with death—life repeated continually!

This was the law of *samsara,* which means "to keep moving or to continue." In life each person generated *karma*—every action produced a consequence. Cause and effect being the natural law of life, each life produced karma that would propel the individual into a new life and thus continue into a ceaseless cycle of lives. One faced not only the challenges, pains, and sufferings of one mortality, but would continue to do so over and over again. Good deeds could improve one's lot in the next life just as evil deeds could worsen it, but eventually life would be faced again. No evil actions merited eternal punishment, just as no acts of righteousness deserved eternal glory.

Siddhartha needed to find a way for his fellow creatures to get off this eternal wheel so that suffering could cease and peace be attained. He was not aiming at an eternal consolation, but a solution for this present life, or each repeating life. In the LDS hymn "Abide with Me," we sing "change and decay in all around I see."[2] As he witnessed the four signs, Siddhartha's deeper awareness of that change and decay sent him on a journey he was determined not to abandon until he found relief—not only for himself, not only for Yasodara and Rahula, but for all creation.

The Seeker

When Siddhartha returned to the palace, his father could see something had shaken him. Fearful of the result, he tried to distract the troubled reflections of his son by entertaining him with all the comforts at his command. He brought the finest musicians to play for him while lovely girls danced, but when the music ceased and all within the palace were asleep, Siddhartha still lay awake, musing on the great questions of life. There in the darkness he made his decision. He would "go forth," as others in India were doing, to seek enlightenment. Fearing that if he saw his wife and son his love for them would weaken his resolve, he dared not approach too closely. Gazing at them from a distance as they slept, he turned from their doorway into the darkness of the night.

Mounting his horse, Kanthaka, and accompanied only by the charioteer Channa, Siddhartha left the palace and rode into the forest. Once there he cut his hair, symbol of his royal past life, bid goodbye to his friend and horse, removed his silken clothes, replaced them with plain, saffron yellow robes, and began his search. For six years he studied meditation and renunciation with the best teachers, mastering all their techniques until his control over mind and body was complete, but each time he turned away. The answer was not here. Yet he had learned to master his mind, to focus it on one thought and hold it there, and to control his emotions. He turned now to the ascetic life and practiced self-denial to a greater extreme than others, subjecting his body to every type of mortification in his desire to release spiritual power and free himself. He was joined by five other ascetics; together they tried to achieve detachment from this temporal world of change and decay, all to no avail. Though he was living on only a few grains of rice a day, his efforts only resulted in losing energy and his mind's focus. His meditations lacked depth of concentration. He was destroying not only his body but also his meditative powers. One did not end suffering by forced bodily suffering. There had to be another way.

Some traditions say that the futility and reality of his situation rose in his awareness when he heard a musician teaching a young student how to play a lute. He would use this illustration later in his life. "If you tighten the strings too tight, they will break; if you leave them too loose, they won't play," he heard. Here was wisdom—the starving, emaciated man realized the strings of his life were too loose during his time in the palace, but now they were so tight he could break. Severe austerity was not the path he should walk. He needed to find a middle way, much as Mohammad chose milk over water or wine when he ascended into heaven. Others say he remembered that moment when he was a young boy sitting under the rose-apple tree and found release in his compassion for the little creatures whose lives were being destroyed by the furrowing plow. He had felt joy and peace then, the release of self-forgetting, but that release arose from compassion and the stilling of his mind. This was naturally within him. With his reflections confirmed, Siddhartha reached a turning point. He had not found his answer, but he did understand his present attempts were not the way, and that is usually an important step in learning.

FLOATING UPSTREAM

Rising, Siddhartha bathed and was met by a village girl named Sujata carrying a bowl of rice, which she offered him. Looking at the simple meal, he realized all that he had renounced, not just the pleasures of the palace, but life itself with its many joys. Now a young girl was presenting him with a return to living represented by the white grains held out to him. She offered the gift with innocence and kindness; he could not refuse. He took the bowl, smiled in gratitude, and ate his first meal in years.

Sensing that he had made progress, but unsure if there was an answer, he placed the empty bowl in the river and said, "If I can reach enlightenment, let this bowl float upstream." He released his hold and allowed the bowl to turn in the swirling water. Then slowly, but without doubt, he watched it begin to float against the current and move upstream. What was true of the bowl could also be true of him. He could go against the forceful currents of self—we all can! It was a significant symbolic moment in the history of the world, one easy to understand and hold in the heart: It is God's will that we all float against the current.

When his five companions saw him breaking his severe fast, they chastened him, believing he had abandoned his search, and left him alone. With an inner serenity, surely guided by a greater power than his own, he traveled to a place, now called Bodh Gaya, near Benares, and positioned himself underneath the Bodhi tree. His strength had recovered and his mental command was restored. He directed his mind into deep meditation and vowed, "I will not remove from this spot until I have reached enlightenment and found an answer." It was spring; a full moon shone in the night sky. He was close now. A supreme moment in the history of man was about to take place.

Yet just as Moses faced the adversary as recorded in Moses 1, just as Jesus faced Lucifer during his preparatory fast before he commenced his mission, and just as Joseph Smith wrestled with Satan in the Sacred Grove, Siddhartha faced opposition. In Hindu belief, the forces of chaos and evil are represented by a personality named Mara. Mara is all selfish passions, all delusions, the totality of ignorance and darkness. He now appeared to turn Siddhartha from his state of deep contemplation. Mara tempted Siddhartha first with his daughters, women of unknowable beauty, but Siddhartha remained still and focused. Sensual desire having failed, Mara tried fear, attacking Siddhartha with visions of massive armies arrayed against him. But cowardice, doubt, terror, retreat could not move him. He delved deeper into his meditations, remaining always calm, always searching his life experiences for the solution.

In a last desperate attempt, Mara himself appeared and challenged Siddhartha. Who was he to think he could escape this world's desires? Nothing was sufficient to overcome the demands of the self. That was a current too swift to swim against. There was no freedom from those enchaining words: "I want . . ." Who would bear Siddhartha witness? All of life, all of history: man's incessant, persistent desires for self stood against Siddhartha's confident probing for the answer. This was Mara's world, and no one could free themselves from its demands. Siddhartha called as his witness the earth itself, reaching down and touching it. Creation bore testimony that individual enlightenment could be reached; the fires of desire could be extinguished in the selfless surrender of compassion. Let the earth itself, the stage of so much pain and sorrow, witness that Siddhartha's meditative wisdom and active compassion are greater and more powerful than Mara's delusions and insistence that the self must remain the center of one's focus. At this, Mara departed and left Siddhartha descending deeper and deeper into that level of consciousness where ego surrenders and one becomes fully awake. He was no longer Siddhartha; he was the Buddha, a title that comes from a Sanskrit word meaning "to be awake."

NIRVANA

He had found the way, the joy of turning away from himself. He had reached nirvana. *Nirvana* means "to blow out" or "to extinguish." What is being blown out? Not existence, but all thoughts, actions, and desires that center on self. Nirvana is not the Buddhist equivalent of heaven; it is not a place. Rather, it is a state of being where one has extinguished the fires of all human negatives: lust, greed, selfishness, anger, hatred, pride, envy, and others. These cause so much human suffering. When one reaches nirvana, there are no more "I wants." Desire centers on others. There is only love and compassion for all living things. Nirvana is insight into the fundamental truth of the unity and oneness in the universe. Therein one finds joy, the wonderful joy of releasing selfishness.

Nirvana is an unchaining, of which we get only glimpses in our life from time to time. Those hints, however, promise the liberation Siddhartha would offer to the world: How can I suffer when I am not thinking of myself? It is a simple question, but the mind puts up all kinds of defenses to deny its reality. In the cultural thinking of Siddhartha's time, karma ceases to generate. The law of cause and effect has been surmounted. Now all cause seeks as its effect is goodness for others. It produces no karma for itself. The cycle of rebirth ceases, for the essential lesson of life has been learned. Siddhartha said: "I have seen the builder of this house. . . . I have shattered its ridgepole and its rafters; that house shall not be built again. I have found the deathless, the unconditioned; I have seen life as it is. I have entered nirvana, beyond the reach of sorrow."[3]

The heart is lost in kindness, in pity, in understanding for others. There is no thought of "my rights," or "my needs," or "my expectations," or "my pains." Siddhartha would still experience sickness, old age, and eventually death, but nothing would disturb his inner peace. He would live in "coolness." He had discovered a stormless harbor, an inner haven of tranquility, where one could remain joyful even in the midst of pain. It is almost impossible for any of us to conceive of a life completely devoid of the demands of ego, but Siddhartha under the Bodhi tree reached this land, just as Jesus had lived within its boundaries all his life. Siddhartha was once somewhat cynically asked, "What have you gained through meditation?" His reply was ironic. "Nothing at all," he said, "Let me tell you what I lost."[4] Siddhartha faced one final temptation. He could remain in his state of blissful un-desiring or rise from his place and teach others the way. Mara returned to offer his last enticement. "'You have awakened to nirvana,' he whispered, 'and thus escaped from my realm. You have plumbed the depths of consciousness and known a joy not given even to the gods. But you know well how difficult it has been. You sought nirvana with your eyes clear, and found it almost impossible to achieve; others' eyes are covered with dust from the beginning, and they seek only their own satisfaction. Even in the midst of sorrow, do you see anyone throw the toys of the world away? If you try to teach them what you have found, who do you think will listen? Who will strive as you have? How many will even try to wipe the dust from their eyes?"[5]

These thoughts troubled Siddhartha more deeply than Mara's previous attacks. Could others really forget the self and believe that love always begets love, that all desire other than desire for others ultimately ends in suffering? "Charity . . . seeketh not her own," Paul wrote (1 Corinthians 13:4–5). Is it truly conceivable that people can believe and fully live by that brief truth? Resisting one last time, Siddhartha saw the deception. If he failed to teach, he would still be thinking of self, of Siddhartha, and all he discovered would end in the subtle hypocrisy that Mara suggested. No! Compassion should reach out in action. To know truth is to offer it to others. Even though there would be few who could even comprehend or try to attain the control of mind and heart he had achieved, there would be some who would clear the dust from their eyes and see without delusion. For those who would listen, he would teach the *dharma,* a word that means "truth" or "doctrine" or "way."

THE DHARMA

He pondered his message; how could he make it understandable to others? He would teach them the Middle Path, the strings neither too tight nor too loose. Having found his way, he arose and entered the deer park in Varanasi, where he found his five former companions still lost in the delusion that austerity could bring release. Here he taught his first sermon—the Turning of the Wheel of the

Dharma. The teaching he set in motion would prepare the way for people to reach a new level of humanity. He was the wheel-turner. The image is similar to the way we think of Daniel's interpretation of Nebuchadnezzar's dream of a stone cut out of the mountains without hands that would roll forth and fill the world.

Siddhartha taught his former companions the Four Noble Truths:

1. In life we experience suffering.
2. Selfish desire creates that suffering.
3. Selfish desire can be extinguished.
4. The way to extinguish selfish desire is by walking a road Siddhartha called the Eightfold Path. This consisted of:

Right Understanding—The acceptance of the Four Noble Truths; and the realization that to overcome ego with its accompanying selfishness is to find happiness.

Right Resolve or Motivation—The willingness to make the conquest of self the central object of life and our most vital interest.

Right Speech—Never hurt another with words such as gossip or slander; always speak truth, in season, to another's profit, and with kindness.

Right Action—Live in harmony with the rest of life. Act for the joy of others; never harm another creature. Actions such as adultery, stealing, and taking life must cease.

Right Livelihood—Obtain your daily bread in a manner that causes no injury to others. Do not support yourself at the expense of another's well-being.

Right Effort—The constant endeavor to maintain, foster and develop qualities of goodness and to reduce, eliminate and overcome all negative characteristics.

Right Mindfulness—Being always aware of what motivates us and what is going on in our minds. Learn to focus the mind on one thing and hold it there. The mind like a monkey jumps from thought to thought. One trains the mind to stay still.

Right Concentration—The ability to control the mind in such a way that all thoughts, emotions, and attitudes are pure, complete with compassion, and what you wish them to be.

None of these will seem earth-shattering to discover. Yet, like the Ten Commandments or the Sermon on the Mount, they need no justification or defense. They stand alone, self-evident, self-proclaiming, self-proving. They are absolutes. They don't change with circumstances, cultures, or cycling time. We accept them because at their foundation they are already engraved upon our hearts. It would be difficult to add to them. There is no question the world would be a vastly different place if we all tried to live them.

Though these truths appear to be quite ordinary, what Siddhartha presented in the deer park was the hope, the assurance, and the conviction *that it could be done—man could master himself.* He had done so. He was not suggesting that people walk a path that could not be walked. No one had yet taught that. Jesus would come six hundred years later to demonstrate with his own life the truthfulness of the selfless and sinless life.

We notice, in addition, that there is a natural relationship and progression in the Eightfold Path that Siddhartha taught. Without the acceptance of the first two, there can be no real progress. We can also see that the last two require the greatest maturity. To speak right, act right, maintain oneself without harming others, and strive to foster goodness and eliminate evil in our characters are mostly matters of behavior, but focusing the mind and controlling our thoughts and emotions requires a much deeper commitment and power over self. Yet therein lies the deepest serenity and the key to correct behavior. "For as he thinketh in his heart, so is he" (Proverbs 23:7).

THE MASTER TEACHER

The Buddha would spend the next four decades traveling across the Ganges Plain, teaching and gathering disciples. Like Jesus and Mohammad, he wrote nothing down. What we know of him and his teachings was passed down by oral transmission initially and finally, in written form, drawn from the memory of monks. He was not interested in theology, but stayed the course of bringing those who listened to him into a life of selfless compassion.

The battle he chose to fight was the battle with suffering, with selfishness. A man once asked him a series of theological or doctrinal questions, expecting an answer before he would commit to the life Buddha presented. Is the world eternal or not eternal? Are the soul and the body the same or are they different? What exists after death? Similar questions about the nature of God and Christ ripped Christianity to pieces in the early centuries; religious wars were fought and heretics burned in doctrinal controversy down through the centuries. How would the Buddha respond?

He asked a question. Would a man, wounded by a poison arrow, before he would allow someone to extract it, ask ceaseless questions about the man who shot it? What was his name, what was his caste, was he tall or short, what kind of bow did he use, and on and on? No, he would die before learning all these things. Selfishness is a poison; its conquest does not depend on metaphysical answers. Let one stay focused on the task at hand. Nobody will argue about the necessity of kindness, loving our neighbor, or the elimination of hatred, greed, and ignorance in the flowering of compassion.

Hounded by this kind of question on another occasion, Siddhartha reached for the branch of a tree, took a handful of leaves, and showed them to those surrounding him. Compared to the many leaves still on the tree he held very few. Those in his hand were his teachings. Those in the tree were all the truths and answers he had not taught. Why had he not taught them? Because they were not necessary to the task of self-conquest! They were not "useful," "helpful," "skillful"—"it does not profit." He used various examples and parables throughout his life to negate the arguments and dissensions religious debate often creates. "Always remember what I have explained and what I have not explained," he said, "and why I have not explained it." These were questions that far too often led to contention and not to edification. He could stay on task.

He taught his disciples to live like the lotus, whose waxy petals repelled even the filthiest water; they could grow and give beauty even in a ditch. His disciples were to live in a world of selfishness, hatred, bigotry, envy, and greed without letting these things disturb their peace or their constant quest for the serenity of selfless compassion. Their lives as well as their words would be their message. A king and queen once approached him seeking wisdom. He asked them who was dearer to themselves than any other. They answered that no one was dearer to them than they were to themselves. Then he counseled, "If you find this to be true about yourselves, then all selves must feel the same. Hence, a person who truly loves himself should never harm another." He told a group of young men in search of courtesans that it was better to search for yourself, your noblest self, than to seek pleasure.

Across the Ganges Plain, in the cities and villages of India, and in the forests people flocked to him and heard him affirm: "Our life is shaped by our mind; we become what we think. Suffering follows an evil thought as the wheels of a cart follow the oxen that draw it. Joy follows a pure thought like a shadow that never leaves."[6]

In a world of war, animosity, vengeance, and slaughter he taught men that "hatred can never put an end to hatred; love alone can.[7] We hear echoes of the Savior's Sermon on the Mount in these simple words. Yet there was a greater enemy than even those who hate and a greater friend than our closest family members. He quietly schooled his disciples by asserting: "More than those who hate you, more than all your enemies, an untrained mind does greater harm. More than your mother, more than your father, more than all your family, a well-disciplined mind does greater good."[8] Since the source of all action rests in the mind, there we must focus our most intense efforts. The greatest challenges and the highest triumphs were not won on battlefields, but in the silent struggles of the soul. Victory there was success indeed. "Be victorious over yourself and not over others," he said. "When you attain victory over yourself, not even the gods can turn it into defeat."[9]

In the spirit of his earliest rose-apple tree reflections, he urged his followers to live with all creation in harmony, for every life on earth had value. "The wise live without injuring nature, as the bee drinks nectar without harming the flower."[10] In our present world of environmental decay and threatened ecosystems, his words will remain forever relevant.

We are not really different, no matter what nation or culture or religion we belong to, therefore "if, hoping to be happy, you strike at others who also seek happiness, you will be happy neither here nor hereafter. If, hoping to be happy, you do not strike at others who are also seeking happiness, you will be happy here and hereafter."[11] Let the common aspirations and hopes we all share govern our responses to others. We have the measure of how to treat each individual already nesting in our own soul. This is the power behind what we call the golden rule. It was a backbone principle in the Buddha's teachings.

As the Buddha learned from his last temptation offered by Mara, it is not sufficient to gain truth and goodness for one's self. We need to turn outward to instruct, inspire, elevate, and edify others. Ezekiel testified, "Woe be to the shepherds of Israel that do feed themselves! should not the shepherds feed the flocks?" (Ezekiel 34:2). Those truths we gain must be shared, freely offered to others. Life is simple, really. We just need to "learn what is right; then teach others."[12] If we do so, there will be joyous reunions in our life to come, for not only will we be greeted by those we have loved and lifted, but "as your family and friends receive you with joy when you return from a long journey, so will your good deeds receive you when you go from this life to the next, where they will be waiting for you with joy like your kinsmen."[13]

In truth, Siddhartha testified, the perfect man or woman, striving for nirvana, "never asks what life can give, only 'What can I give life?'"[14] "[They] have reached the end of the way; they have crossed the river of life. All that they had to do is done: they have become one with all life."[15]

FINAL RELEASE

Siddhartha died in Kusinara after more than forty years of living without thought of self. He sensed the end was near. The final factor was a meal offered in kindness which, however, made him grievously ill and probably gave him food poisoning. Having forgiven the provider of the meal, he gave final instructions to his closest disciples, lay on his side, and died peacefully. His last words were: "Be a refuge unto yourselves. . . . Be a lamp unto yourselves. . . . Hold fast to the dharma as your lamp, hold fast to the dharma as your refuge, and you shall surely reach nirvana, the highest good, the highest goal, if that is your deepest desire."[16] Alma the Younger taught that we all receive what we truly desire (see Alma 41:5–6). In later centuries, C. S. Lewis would strongly testify to this same truth,[17] taught in India centuries before the birth of our Savior by one of the greatest men who ever lived, who chose to end his forty-five-year ministry witnessing its validity.

Siddhartha returned to his home once and was reunited with father, wife, and son. These had been hurt the most by his plunge into the forest to seek enlightenment. How could he compensate them for the distress he had brought them? He told his father that if he allowed the ties of love that had given him grief over the loss of his son to be extended to all men's sons and daughters, he would receive a greater joy than he would have had Siddhartha become a great king. He told Yasodara and Rahula that he could not give them an earthly inheritance or perishable treasures which were always accompanied by care, but he had found something of far greater worth. He would bequeath to them the joy of a holy life, spent in serenity and compassion, a happiness that would never be lost. He would leave them truth. He would leave them peace. It seems that we receive no deep insight or knowledge without sacrifice. This sacrifice was a difficult one for Siddhartha as well as his family.

Compassion's Broadest Reach

I have studied the Buddha's life and teachings for a long time. Though I have not mastered his level of compassion and meditative powers, I have been enriched by his example. He seemed to have found the right combination of heart and head and attended to both. I have particularly pondered that history-changing night under the Bodhi tree. A moment in the life of Enoch captures the essence of the Buddha's epiphany under the full moon and explains better than anything else why Siddhartha was such a remarkable human being and why my admiration for him reaches such a high mark. This moment occured just after Enoch witnessed God weeping over the miseries of "the workmanship of mine own hands." God had asked his children to simply "love one another, . . . but behold, they are without affection." He wanted compassion, but "they hate their own blood." The Lord explained to Enoch that not only will He weep, but "the whole heavens shall weep over them, even all the workmanship of mine hands; wherefore should not the heavens weep, *seeing these shall suffer?*" (Moses 7:32–33, 37; emphasis added). We must note that it is their suffering more than their wickedness which is so distressing to God. Remember that to Siddhartha the central concern was not sin, not wickedness, but suffering, though the two are closely connected. Enoch opened his heart and mind as Siddhartha tried to do and gained an understanding of God few ever achieve. This transforming moment in his life has been my favorite verse of scripture since the first time I discovered it. Its power sent Enoch onto the path that led to the creation of Zion—the society of those who were "of one heart and mind" (Moses 7:18).

"And it came to pass that the Lord spake unto Enoch, and told Enoch all the doings of the children of men; wherefore Enoch knew, and looked upon their wickedness, and their misery, and wept and stretched forth his arms, and his heart swelled wide as eternity; and his bowels yearned; and all eternity shook" (Moses 7:41).

Shook means to overflow. What did eternity overflow with? What was so broad, so all encompassing, so full that even the farthest reaches of eternity could not contain it? It spilled over! The answer is not hard to realize. All eternity overflowed with compassion— with mercy, forgiveness, longing, empathy, love. This was essentially the Buddha's experience, and we might add, that of the Savior in Gethsemane, though Jesus' was on an infinite scale. That overflowing is the most powerful force in creation; it has no boundaries. It was in recognition of this power that Siddhartha touched the earth, asking it for a confirming witness.

After their witnesses of this overflowing of compassion, both Enoch and Siddhartha devoted all their energies to the creation of a community that could overcome selfishness and live in compassion and oneness. I cannot help but interject here how completely I am impressed time and time again with how closely Joseph Smith's writings align with the great minds and souls of antiquity. I am deeply moved by the thought that much of what I once believed was unique to the revelations of the Prophet Joseph Smith has been granted to other minds in other places throughout the world, whether it be the close tie to foundational Chinese thinking of Doctrine and Covenants 121 or the twin experiences of Enoch and the Buddha.

THE IMMEASURABLES

Attempts to explain exactly what happened under the Bodhi tree will always be insufficient. Some say that Siddhartha remembered all his previous lives. The symbolic mystery in this belief is not to be taken too literally. We do not believe in reincarnation, but the idea being presented is that Siddhartha somehow connected with many different aspects of creation and could understand other forms of life and people because he had walked their paths and breathed their air. Above all, he affirmed that the moral and joyful life is one lived essentially for others. This was a crucial insight.

Buddhists believe that the Buddha's meditations reached different and ever-deepening levels. These levels would be taught later, called the "Immeasurables." They are still part of Buddhist practice to this day. These levels are immeasurable because one can never reach the height, depth, or breadth of them. To this Enoch could also testify. Siddhartha first directed his mind to a feeling of friendship with and benevolence for all things. There were no real enemies. There could be no hatred or anger, no enmity. This is the first immeasurable. He progressed to deeper compassion, striving to feel the pain, the distress of others, imagining what their sorrows were and allowing their grief and anguish to become his own. This is the immeasurable of pity. He entered the meditation of joy next, delighting in the happiness of others without comparison, without envy, grateful for their elation and gladness as if it were his own. This is the immeasurable of sympathetic joy. As the night passed, he entered into a state of mind where there is total equanimity towards all of life, all experiences, where all is complete serenity, a state of disinterested tranquility. All personal preferences are abandoned in favor of impartial benevolence. The self was forgotten. There was only oneness. This is the immeasurable of serenity and equanimity. When these four are actively cultivated in a soul they begin to root themselves within us and, in time, unconsciously become habitual, dismantling the ego and turning the view always outward.

Jesus taught that in order for us to find ourselves we must first lose ourselves. We might add, with the Buddha's teaching in mind, that we lose ourselves through compassion for those around us. Surely this is what Jesus meant. We do not embrace a religious life—regardless of which we choose—to obtain something, though most speak of eternal rewards. Rather, we engage ourselves in a religion to lose ourselves. I can go to church expecting the talks and lessons to offer me something and be disappointed when they don't, or I can go with the hope that I can lift someone and be of service. If I in return receive something, that is a bonus, but I am mainly there to give.

To expect anything else of our faith is to fall short of the mark and miss the main objective. This is true of all religion. I have often heard people say, "I really don't need church. I don't get anything out of it." Whether we get anything out of it has never been the question. What *we* need is not the central concern. We are needed! The critical question is, "Will I respond to that need and strive to fulfill it?" God is giving—or he would not be God. It is inconceivable that these crucial truths should be granted only to men and women of the Savior's time, and then only in the Middle East and subsequent Christian lands. If God is a god of love he would want such essential knowledge to be disseminated throughout the world. In India, Siddhartha, whose very life proclaimed the necessity of all he verbally taught, would be his major messenger.

Siddhartha was once sitting under a tree in the serenity of meditation when a Brahmin, the leading priestly caste in India, approached.

There was something about this man under the tree that drew his attention. There was a radiance, a holiness that could not be missed.

"Are you a god?" he asked. "Are you a saint, a spirit? Are you more than a man?"

"No," came the reply, "I am awake!" May we all so awaken!

> *The good shine like the Himalayas,*
> *Whose peaks glisten above the rest of the world*
> *Even when seen from a distance.*[18]
> —THE DHAMMAPADA

To Discover—the Seekers

I gave my heart to seek, and search
out by wisdom concerning all things that are
done under heaven.
—Ecclesiastes 1:13

CHAPTER SEVEN

THE BOY ON THE *BEAGLE*: CHARLES DARWIN

South America
Ninteenth Century C.E.

I think he was the only man I ever knew
against whom I never heard a word said;
and as people when shut up in a ship for five years
are apt to get cross with each other,
that is saying a good deal.[1]
—VICE ADMIRAL ARTHUR MELLERSH

AN "INSATIABLE LONGING TO DISCOVER"

H<small>E WAS A CAMBRIDGE STUDENT</small>, but the bulk of his studies were uninteresting to him. What he really was after were beetles, so his heart began to pound when he tore the bark off an old tree and spotted two rare beetles that would grace his growing collection. Quick as lightning, he grabbed the two different species and triumphantly held them up in his hands. The old tree, however, had even more delights. When he looked down, a third completely different beetle began crawling away. What to do? Without thinking, overly anxious to have three new additions, he popped one of them into his mouth to free a hand and reached for the new prize. The beetles had their own defenses, however. As he later described, the one in his mouth, not eager to be swallowed, "ejected some intensely acrid fluid, which burnt my tongue so that I was forced to spit the beetle out, which was lost, as was the third one."[2] The student was Charles

Darwin, one of the most controversial personalities to appear on the pages of history, often viewed by people of faith, such as an acquaintance of mine, as "the enemy."

When I tell friends that Darwin is one of the people I would dearly like to meet, they are usually mystified, if not troubled, by my desire. A few years ago I would have been puzzled myself, but in preparation for a boat trip along the same route as that used by Darwin in the 1830s, I was induced to examine the man more closely. Whether or not we agree with his conclusions, I feel fairly confident in asserting that all of us would have liked Charles Darwin—and liked him intensely and deeply. Everybody who met him did! With the exception of a few professional rivals, he endeared himself to all. I have come to admire the man very much for the depth of his humanity, his commitment to family, and the inborn goodness of his heart, but largely because of his remarkable love for this wonderful planet and all its forms of life. Having been born with a fascination with this earth also, I can imagine myself popping a beetle into my mouth in a rash moment of collecting frenzy.

Nothing in creation bored him. The smallest and most inconspicuous life form held a world of discovery within it. He studied everything from earthworms to insect-eating and climbing plants, from barnacles to the facial expressions of his children. He was humbled in the presence of so grand a thing as this world we share with its myriad varieties of life. His curiosity was vast; his delight in nature was contagious. His friend Alfred Wallace said he had an "insatiable longing to discover" everything "presented by living things"; this was coupled with "the restless curiosity of the child," which seems "never to have abated its force."[3] He approached nature with enthusiasm, joy, and reverence. Though he remained uncertain about God's role in the natural world most of his adult life, I assume the Grand Creator himself smiled frequently as he watched this child of his own heart relish even the tiniest details of "the workmanship of mine hands" (Moses 1:4). Much can be forgiven one who never lost his sense of wonder.

"A VERY ORDINARY BOY"

Darwin's love for and sympathy with living things began when he was very young. He grew up in an environment where the upper and middle classes of England were deeply engaged in the discovery of their world. Science was on the rise. He was born in 1809. His father was a prosperous doctor and his mother the daughter of Josiah Wedgwood, the famous pottery founder. She died when he was eight, which contributed to his strong attachment to his father. "My father . . . was the kindest man I ever knew and whose memory I love with all my heart."[4] The family was close; his elder brother Erasmus ("Ras") was his dear friend, as were his sisters. He spent a great deal of time with his cousins and would in time marry his first cousin Emma Wedgwood.

Collecting was fashionable and Charles took to it zealously, amassing shells, coins, minerals, insects (especially beetles), and bird eggs. He found it difficult to enjoy more formal education. "I have been told," he wrote in his autobiography, "that I was much slower in learning than my younger sister Catherine, and I believe that I was in many ways a naughty boy."[5] "I was considered by my masters and by my father as a very ordinary boy, rather below the common standard in intellect. To my deep mortification my father once said to me, 'You care for nothing but shooting, dogs, and rat-catching, and you will be a disgrace to yourself and all your family.'"[6]

Darwin was also very humane; he could never abide seeing things suffer. He enjoyed hunting and fishing, but was relieved when his uncle Josiah Wedgwood II told him he could kill the worms with salt water and end his feelings of guilt when putting them on the hook. "From that day I never spitted a living worm."[7] After a conversation with his sister, he tried to only collect already-dead insects, as he wondered about the morality of killing them just to admire their beauty or uniqueness. When older he once casually tossed a rock in the direction of a bird, killing it. It so distressed him he could not talk about the incident for years. Dogs sensed his friendship and in no time he would win them over—even above their own masters.

He could walk tirelessly in nature and dreamed of exotic lands. He had a copy of a book titled *Wonders of the World*; it instilled in him a desire to see remote countries. Later the travels of Humboldt in South America would stir his wanderlust. He and "Ras" became fascinated with chemistry, conducting experiments while at school in a garden shed late into the night from which he received the nickname "Gas."[8] He was a voracious reader and remained so throughout his life, enjoying particularly the plays of Shakespeare. He wrote to his sister that in the Bible, he liked the Gospels the best.

"Any Man of Common Sense"

Darwin's father hoped Charles would follow him into the medical profession and sent him to Edinburgh, but Charles found the lectures extremely dull. All thoughts of being a doctor ended when he watched an operation on a child, rushing from the room unable to bear the pain he was witnessing, this being before chloroform. The memory haunted him for years after.

Darwin developed instead a fascination with the inhabitants of tide pools; he would spend hours wading among the creatures of the shore. While probing the tide pools, he shared a discovery he had made with a professor whom he thought would be enthusiastic, but to his mortification he was confronted with a hostile and protectionist attitude. How dare Charles interfere in an area he himself was studying? This encounter stayed with Darwin all his life. He never could understand why everyone would not want to share truth without becoming territorial. His daughter Henrietta commented on her father's memory of this episode, saying, "This made a deep impression on my father, . . . and he has always expressed the strongest contempt for all such little feelings—unworthy of searchers after truth."[9] I have spent a good part of my professional life in a university setting; having seen similar postures in that world, Darwin's openness is compelling. Later in his life, he shared his life's work and most important conclusions with the much younger Alfred Wallace while working on *The Origin of Species.* "What wretched doings come from the ardor for fame," he said. "The love of truth alone would never make one man attack another bitterly."[10]

Edinburgh and medicine proving a failure, Darwin's father decided, with a somewhat dubious Charles assenting, that he should go to Cambridge and study to be a clergyman. In a country parsonage he would have much free time to study the natural world that so dominated his thinking. It was at Cambridge he met one of the great friends of his life, John Henslow, a professor of botany. The two hit it off immediately and were soon tramping the fields together. Darwin picked up the title, "the man who walks with Henslow."[11] His voracious interest in everything soon had him also immersed in geology. He took a field trip to Wales with another future friend, a geology professor named Adam Sedgwick.

Henslow would set in motion the definitive experience of Darwin's life. He was just twenty-two and returning from his weeks with Sedgwick when he received a letter from Henslow offering him the opportunity to apply for the post of naturalist on the *Beagle,* a surveying ship that would chart the coasts of South America and then continue around the world on a voyage lasting about two years. The *Beagle*'s captain, Robert FitzRoy, a young man about Charles's age, needed a traveling companion who would serve also as naturalist. Dr. Darwin, Charles's father, disapproved and squashed his son's enthusiasm. Charles would never go against his father's wishes, but his father held out a thread of hope. He said that if Charles could "find any man of common sense who advises you to go I will give my consent."[12]

Charles visited the Wedgwoods, who enthusiastically endorsed the idea. His uncle Josiah agreed to pen a letter refuting all of his father's objections. Josiah ran a very successful pottery; he would surely pass the test of being a man of common sense. Dr. Darwin was true to his word—Charles was given permission to apply. His first meeting with FitzRoy did not go too well. The good captain, versed in the Victorian "science" of phrenology, was discomforted with Charles's nose, which he thought forebode a lack of energy and determination—and the Darwins were of the opposition political party. However, Darwin's affable character, eagerness, and enthusiasm soon won over the reluctant captain and Charles was granted the position. The voyage that would last five years, not two, became the foundation of all Darwin did and thought for the rest of his life and marked the future of the biological sciences.

The Flycatcher and the Abolitionist

The *Beagle* was a small vessel, only ninety feet long, with a crew of seventy-four men. Charles suffered terribly from seasickness. His quarters were small; his hammock hung over the chart table. In this tiny room were his books, personal belongings, and countless specimens of fossils, insects, birds, marine animals, minerals, and more. In order to stretch out his six-foot frame, he removed the top drawer of his cabinet at night and slept with his feet in the drawer frame.

He was soon the favorite of all on board. He endured the hazing associated with crossing the equator with good cheer and learned all the ins and outs of the ship. The crew gave him pet names of "Flycatcher" and "Philosopher." FitzRoy wrote of him, "Darwin is a very sensible, hard-working man and a very pleasant mess-mate. I never saw a 'shore-going fellow' come into the ways of a ship so soon. . . . Everyone respects and likes him. . . . And a child with a new toy could not have been more delighted than he."[13] A friend,

remarking on Darwin's long voyage on the small ship without confrontation, assessed the situation accurately by simply saying, "Yes,
but who could quarrel with Charles?"[14] He was good-natured, congenial, and preferred to see not only creation with admiring eyes, but
also people, anticipating the best in others. He remained positive even
through receiving a heart-wrenching letter from England announcing
the marriage of Fanny Owen, the girl he loved and had hoped would
wait for him. He so wanted to please that any hint of criticism could
devastate him. His temperament was such that he would not defend
himself, contention being an emotion he could not abide. "I do so
hate controversy."[15] Huxley, a great defender of Darwin and close
friend, said, "Dear Darwin never could nor would defend himself."[16]
An acquaintance once remarked after spending only a short time with
Darwin that there was "something almost pathetic in his simplicity
and friendliness."[17]

Tension between Darwin and FitzRoy developed only once, on
the issue of slavery. Darwin was a fierce abolitionist and could not
understand FitzRoy's defense of so repugnant an institution. Once,
when the captain remarked that he had asked the slaves of a Brazilian
owner if they wished to be freed, they all responded with "no."
Darwin merely asked FitzRoy if he felt the answers of slaves in their
master's presence were worth anything. FitzRoy exploded, much to
the surprise of Darwin, and banished him from their friendship—but
no one could stay at cross-purposes with Darwin very long. He was,
within hours, back in the cabin after having been offered quarters by
nearly every other officer on the ship.[18] It was in Brazil that Darwin
had experienced a troubling moment with a slave that he never forgot,
using it as ammunition in his abhorrence of slavery.

"I was crossing a ferry with a negro. . . . In endeavoring to make
him understand, I talked loud, and made signs, in doing which I
passed my hand near his face. He, I suppose, thought I was in a passion, and was going to strike him; for instantly, with a frightened look

and half-shut eyes, he dropped his hands. I shall never forget my feelings of surprise, disgust, and shame, at seeing a great powerful man afraid even to ward off a blow, directed, as he thought, at his face. This man had been trained to a degradation lower than the slavery of the most helpless animal."[19]

His intense interest in everything he saw and experienced sustained him through years of separation from his loved ones and the unpleasantness of constant seasickness. "It has been for me a glorious day, like giving to a blind man eyes.—he is overwhelmed by what he sees & cannot justly comprehend it," he wrote in his diary early in the voyage. This enthusiasm would continue throughout the five years he was gone.[20] Everything fascinated him. "I am at present red-hot with spiders,"[21] he wrote Henslow. Seeing a tropical rain forest in Brazil for the first time caused him to write in his journal, "The delight one experiences in such times bewilders the mind. . . . The mind is a chaos of delight, out of which a world of future & more quiet pleasure will arise."[22] On the subject of the rain forests of Brazil and Tierra del Fuego, he wrote: "Both are temples filled with the varied productions of the God of Nature:—no one can stand in these solitudes unmoved, and not feel that there is more in man than the mere breath of his body."[23]

While reading Darwin's descriptions of all he saw during his years on the *Beagle,* I have often thought of Joseph Smith's reveletory comment on the power of creation to move the human soul: "Yea, all things which come of the earth . . . are made for the benefit and the use of man, both to *please the eye* and to *gladden the heart* . . . to strengthen the body and to *enliven the soul*" (D&C 59:18–19; emphasis added). The progression of the three verbs—"to please," "to gladden," and "to enliven" are so powerfully linked to "eye," "heart" and "soul." It is one of the best descriptions I know of what the beauties of creation do for those who look. Even in the drier areas south of Buenos Aires, Darwin found things to marvel at. "If your view is limited to a small space, many objects possess beauty," he wrote. He also commented that "the smaller birds are brilliantly coloured" and the ground "ornamented by dwarf flowers."[24] All in all, South America was like a dream to the avid collector. "The brilliancy of the scenery throws one into a delirium of delight, and a beetle hunter is not likely soon to awaken from it."[25]

GAUCHOS AND BOLAS

Darwin was equally charmed by the many people he met, assuring any future traveler that "he will discover, how many truly kind-hearted people there are, with whom he never before had, or ever again will have any further communication, who yet are ready to offer him the most disinterested assistance."[26] Of course, Darwin's amiable personality made assisting him a very easy task. His insatiable need to learn took him on long exploring trips into the interior of South America, traveling many thousands of miles on foot and horseback. He climbed the Andes in Chile and camped with the gauchos of Argentina, whose carefree way of life appealed to him. He loved their "moustaches and long black hair curling down their backs. With their brightly coloured garments, great spurs clanking about their heels, and knives stuck as daggers . . . at their waists."[27] He became one of them, eager to try every aspect of their rough-and-tumble existence. They were expert with the bolas; Darwin, ever ready to any adventure, gave them a try, much to the amusement of his gaucho friends. "One day, as I was amusing myself by galloping and whirling the balls round my head, by accident the free one struck a bush; and its revolving motion being thus destroyed, it immediately fell to the ground, and, like magic, caught one hind leg of my horse; and the other ball was then jerked out of my hand, and the horse fairly secured. . . . The Gauchos roared with laughter; they cried out that they had seen every sort of animal caught, but had never before seen a man caught by himself."[28]

He traveled for weeks on end, through the dangers of the road, among revolutionaries and bandits, his open disposition winning him friends among all types. "You cannot imagine what merry work such a wandering journey is," he wrote his sisters, "in the morning we never know where we shall sleep at night. Carrying, like snail, our houses with us we are always independent; when the day is over we sit round our fire & pity all you who are confined within houses."[29] The open, unabashed inclusion of "we" in this description is typical of Darwin's sense of human equality and acceptance of other cultures. He was distressed profoundly at the inhumane treatment of native peoples by his supposedly civilized society. Cruelty was something he could never understand; his questioning lament echoes to this day: "Who would believe in this age that such atrocities could be committed in a Christian civilized country?"[30] His experiences with man's inhumanity to man were part of what caused his deep doubts about religion and God. How could a good God allow it?

His observations and budding theories formed throughout the *Beagle* voyage. Fossils, lifting land masses with sea shells at dizzying heights, varying adaptations of life in the Galápagos, Darwin's famous finches and ride on a giant tortoise are topics for other works. But those five years reveal a young man in love with life, amazed at creation, desirous of more than surface answers, one who felt that no human being, even the primitive Yahgan Indians of Tierra del Fuego, should be considered alien or unworthy of his deepest friendship. In these areas, perhaps, he was closer to the heart of God than most of us. Regardless, without the voyage there would have been no Charles Darwin, for he would not have uncovered the idea of natural selection without broad experience among innumerable life forms over a wide swath of the earth.

"I Think You Will Humanize Me"

When Darwin arrived home, he was amazed that he had become somewhat of a celebrity through the mass shipments of specimens he had sent back over the years. He was considered one of the best field scientists of his time. Marriage was on his mind; his heart settled on Miss Emma Wedgwood, his first cousin. He was considered a good catch, in the female jargon of the day, a "shootable."[31]

His systematic mind and playful sense of humor are seen in a list he drew up stating the pros and cons of marriage. In the *Not Marry* column, he mused, "Freedom to go where one liked—choice of society & little of it. . . . Not forced to visit relatives, and to bend in every trifle.—to have the expense and anxiety of children—perhaps quarreling—Loss of time. . . . less money for books . . ." In the *Marry* column, he noted, "Children—(if it please God)—Constant companion, (& friend in old age) who will feel interested in one,—object to be beloved & played with—better than dog anyhow.—Home, & someone to take care of house—Charms of music & female chit-chat.—These things good for one's health." Certainly with a little romance in his eyes, he also imagined "a nice soft wife on a sofa with good fire . . . and music perhaps." It is obvious he is having fun with his own quandary and where his strongest inclinations lie. He concludes his list with "It is intolerable to think of spending one's whole life, like a neuter bee, working, working, and nothing after all,—No no won't do."[32] He knew the positive effect Emma would have on him and told her, "I think you will humanize me, and soon teach me there is greater happiness than building theories and accumulating facts in silence and solitude."[33] Their children noticed the tender feelings of Charles for Emma and commented on it years later, remembering that "all the sympathy and tenderness of his nature came out. . . . Rejoicing in all that gladdened her, and feeling with her in any sorrow or anxiety."[34] In return, Emma understood clearly what kind of man and father he would be. "He is the most open, transparent man I ever saw, and every word expresses his real thoughts. He is particularly affectionate and very nice to his father and sisters, and perfectly sweet tempered, and possesses some minor qualities that add particularly to one's happiness, such as not being fastidious, and being humane to animals."[35] (Darwin once called in the authorities to stop a neighbor from harnessing a horse with sores on its neck.) On another occasion, Emma wrote to her aunt that Charles was "as warmly affectionate as ever. . . . It is a great advantage to have the power of expressing affection, and I am sure he will make his children very fond of him."[36] Which he did!

His marriage and family were one of the constant joys of his life. Emma and Charles would have ten children, three dying in childhood. The death of their daughter Annie was especially distressing to him. He was a solicitous father and devoted husband and had the rare ability to show unconditional love. The house was a cheery bedlam, with children everywhere: "The only place where you might be sure of not meeting a child was the nursery."[37] Music, games, stories, and general merriment were the order—there was even a rope attached to the ceiling in the upstairs hallway on which the children could swing. Charles had an outside path, nicknamed "the Sandwalk," made so that he could pace when his mind raced with ideas, but generally he continued work within the boisterous activities of the house. "My father," his daughter Henrietta reminisced, "took an unusual delight in his babies, and we have all a vivid memory of him as the most inspiriting of playfellows."[38]

Darwin passed on to his children, almost unconsciously, his sensitivity to the beauty all around them. I have hoped that in my own way I too have bequeathed to my children an appreciation of all the splendor that God has placed in our mortal schoolroom. Darwin's son Francis commented fondly on this invaluable gift. "I used to like to hear him admire the beauty of a flower; it was a kind of gratitude to the flower itself, and a personal love for its delicate form and co-lour. I seem to remember him gently touching a flower he delighted in; it was the same simple admiration that a child might have."[39] A daughter also drank in Darwin's refining gratitude and joy in lovely scenery, remembering a carriage ride with her father while visiting Wordsworth's Lake District near his home at Grasmere. "The perfect day and my father's vivid enjoyment and flow of spirits, form a pic-ture in my mind that I like to think of. He could hardly sit still in the carriage for turning round and getting up to admire the view from each fresh point."[40]

"Everything That Concerns You Concerns Me"

His growing alienation from religion gave Emma anxiety, but did not affect her love or their relationship. His father, knowing of the growing doubts and questions swirling in his son's mind, counseled him to keep them from Emma, but he was too honest to do so. He opened his heart to her about a week into their engagement, holding nothing back. She let it sink in and wrote him a letter a few days later. "When I am with you I think all melancholy thoughts keep out of my head but since you are gone some sad ones have forced themselves in, of fear that our opinions on the most important subject should differ widely. My reason tells me that honest & conscientious doubts can-not be a sin, but I feel it would be a painful void between us. I thank you from my heart for your openness with me & I should dread the feeling that you were concealing your opinions from the fear of giving me pain." She then asked him to read the Savior's final words to the apostles at the Last Supper as recorded in John. "It is so full of love to them & devotion & every beautiful feeling. It is the part of the New Testament I love best."[41] She was every bit as remarkable as her hus-band, whom she loved deeply. She was afraid his waning faith would keep them from being together eternally after death.

They were married in January of 1839, and Emma wrote Charles another letter in February. In it she suggested that he was devoting so much of his thought to his scientific inquiries that he was not "able to give your whole attention to both sides of the question. . . . It seems to me also that the line of your pursuits may have led you to view chiefly the difficulties on one side, & that you have not had time to consider & study the chain of difficulties on the other, but I believe you do not consider your opinion as formed. May not the habit in scientific pursuits of believing nothing till it is proved, influence your mind too much in other things which cannot be proved in the same way, & which if true are likely to be above our comprehension." She was asking him to be intellectually honest and apply the same strenuous thought to both sides of the debate, which of course is very difficult for most people to do. She counseled with her head in this part of the letter, but the poignancy of their relationship is revealed later when she wrote, "I know you will have patience, with your own dear wife. Don't think that it is not my affair & that it does not much signify to me. Every thing that concerns you concerns me & I should be most unhappy if I thought we did not belong to each other forever. . . . I cannot tell him [Charles] how happy he makes me & how dearly I love him & thank him for all his affection which makes the happiness of my life more & more every day." The letter moved Darwin profoundly; he kept it always. At the end he added his own thoughts, penned at the bottom. Whether he shared these with Emma is unknown. "When I am dead, know that many times, I have kissed & cryed over this. C.D."[42]

I have reflected on Charles and Emma's relationship a great deal and been touched by its poignancy. We may learn from this remarkable couple that, though differences may divide two people, love may yet abide between them if they remain mutually respectful, nonjudgmental, and focused on those things that unify them. Near the end of Darwin's life, he tried to express some of his misgivings about religion in his autobiography. Emma did not want them published, as she felt he had never really, as she had suggested so early in their relationship, applied his probing mind to the subject of God. To her, his thoughts on religion were "not worthy of his mind." Part of what bothered him was the pain of animals, but he had been sensitive to this from his early childhood. Man might receive moral improvement through suffering, but what of the rest of creation? "What advantage can there be in the sufferings of millions of the lower animals throughout almost endless time?" He confessed that the majesty of life and the wonder and order he saw in everything he studied led him to believe in a "First Cause having an intelligent mind . . ." Therefore, he concluded, "I deserve to be called a Theist." And that's where they left it![43]

ORIGIN

His health was always an issue, but the causes of Darwin's chronic ill health are still debated. He wrote in *The Voyage of the Beagle* of an attack of insects while in South America: "At night I experienced an attack . . . of the *Benchuca* [Vinchuca], . . . the great black bug of the Pampas. It is most disgusting to feel soft wingless insects, about an inch long, crawling over one's body."[44] These insects transmit a parasite which, in all likelihood, gave Darwin Chagas disease. Some speculate that he suffered from anxiety due to stress. Both theories are likely. He worried continually about his growing perception that species evolve over time. This was a constant source of both scientific interest and emotional stress. At night he found it difficult to shut down his brain, being "troubled . . . by the activity of his thoughts, and would become exhausted by his mind working at some problem which he would willingly have dismissed. . . . Anything which had vexed or troubled him in the day would haunt him."[45] In a letter to a friend he stated, "I am almost convinced (quite contrary to the opinion I started with) that species are not (it is like confessing a murder) immutable."[46] When overworked, his symptoms increased and he would be floored for some time. His son said later of Charles that his father never knew a day of good health for forty years. His life was one long struggle against weariness and strain. In spite of his large family and continual ill health, he explored the world around him passionately, publishing book after book on the natural world. If it was part of creation, Darwin wanted to know everything about it! From atolls to orchids, earthworms to volcanoes, all came under the scope of his scrutinizing mind. There was so much to learn, to explore and be amazed at that "a man who dares to waste one hour of time, has not discovered the value of life."[47]

The idea for *The Origin of Species* had been with him since his *Beagle* days. He was working laboriously on having his research published, but held back because of the reaction he suspected he might receive and because he was also a thorough researcher. He was launched into writing the book by the reception of a letter and treatise by Alfred Wallace, a young naturalist who had been collecting in both South America and Indonesia, suggesting the adaptation of species over time, the very theory he was exploring. Unnerved by the thought that another might present his own theories before he was ready to do, he pondered the correct response to Wallace. Rather than being threatened, remembering his unpleasant experience in Edinburgh, he followed the advice of friends and a joint presentation of papers was offered. Thus a warm friendship between Darwin and Wallace began. A situation that in most circumstances would have been confrontational became congenial, even collegial. Wallace later said of Darwin's gracious inclusion of the younger man's ideas, "I was then . . . the 'young man in a hurry': *he,* the painstaking and patient student. . . . It was really a singular piece of good luck that gave to me any share . . . it was only Darwin's extreme desire to perfect his work that allowed me to come in."[48]

He could be brutally honest with himself. At the completion of

The Origin of Species he wrote, "I have at last as good as done my Book. . . . So much for my abominable volume, which has cost me so much labour that I almost hate it."[49] He revised it continually, remarking once, "Upon my life, my dear fellow, it is a very good book, but oh! my gracious, it is tough reading."[50] He wrote down every opposing view to his theories and examined them meticulously, ever ready to adapt where he felt others had made a valid point. Responding to a friend's comment that he should hesitate about making general conclusions about species until he had mastered at least one life form, he spent eight years in an intense study of barnacles. At the end, he humorously though honestly wrote, "I hate a Barnacle as no man ever did before, not even a sailor in a slow moving ship."[51] He recognized the need to doubt your own affirmations and that the longer one held a view, the more likely one would be closed to alternative explanations. He observed in his autobiography, "What a good thing it would be if every scientific man was to die when sixty years old, as afterwards he would be sure to oppose all new doctrines."[52] Unfortunately this is true in many other areas of life. This maxim he applied strenuously to himself: "The truth . . . will not penetrate a preoccupied mind."[53]

A workaholic from the beginning, he lamented his inability to relax and knew it took a toll on his ever-patient Emma. "The word 'holiday' is written in a dead language for me, and much do I grieve it."[54] But work was the one thing that enabled him to survive the health problems that plagued his life after his return from the *Beagle*. He also regretted that his all-encompassing need to know and observe the natural world dulled his once-enjoyed understanding of the humanities, especially literature, music, and art, and spoke of the "lamentable loss of the higher aesthetic tastes."[55] He offered us a bit of advice on becoming too preoccupied with only one focus of knowledge, especially the scientific or technical: "If I had to live my life over again, I would have made a rule to read some poetry and listen to some music at least once every week; for perhaps the parts of my brain now atrophied would thus have been kept active through use. The loss of these tastes is a loss of happiness, and may possibly be injurious to the intellect, and more probably to the moral character, by enfeebling the emotional part of our nature."[56] There may be in this confession also a partial understanding of the fading of his religious sentiments. It is a lesson from the life of a brilliant man I am grateful to receive. We must try to remain well-rounded.

A Little Darwin in Us All

Darwin was accepted in his own day as a notable scientist and never ceased exploring the world around him until his death in 1882 from angina. As he sensed the end was near, he told Emma, "I am not the least afraid of death. . . . Remember what a good wife you have been to me."[57] His son Francis summed up her influence on him best perhaps with the simple words, "In her presence he found his happiness, and through her, his life."[58] For a man who loathed contention, it is ironic that he is still counted among the most controversial personalities of the modern world. He was given one of the greatest honors an Englishman can receive, burial in Westminster Abbey. His face graces the British ten-pound note, but it is the face of an older, bearded Darwin, which has been much parodied and caricatured, not the young man I picture when I think of him. For me, he will always be the boy on the *Beagle* reveling in the glories of nature. That is the deeper Darwin, the one I would have others reflect upon. I have been fortunate enough to have explored Darwin's *Beagle* voyage from the Canaries to the Galápagos. I recall standing in the rain forest along the Brazilian-Argentine border surrounded by butterflies. The climate was very humid; we were all perspiring. A beautiful yellow butterfly landed on my hand and I have to admit my little-boy excitement and fascination with living things lit up inside. I too caught, labeled, and displayed dozens of insects in my youth. By holding still and with a little encouragement, I was able to attract six different species to my hand at the same time, each colored with unique patterns, one with the number 88 perfectly reproduced in vivid detail on its wings. A small crowd gathered and watched with delight the lovely winged insects crawling across my hand, their long curled tongues drinking up the moisture. It was a pure "Charles" moment. As I listened to the eager, excited amazement of those around me, I thought, "There is a little Darwin in the heart of us all!" God forbid that we should lose it. My mother taught me the love of God through such simple moments by briefly asking me each day when I returned from my forays into the world of tiny living things, "Which of Heavenly Father's little creatures did you bring home today, son?"

ENJOYING "ETERNAL FELICITY"

I've sailed to the Falklands, up the Beagle Channel in Tierra del Fuego, along the Chilean coast, and once made it out to the Galápagos—all Darwin territory. The islands pulse with the heartbeat of creation's mornings. The "days" are all there, the first dawning of light, the second day's wonder of painted clouds and lifting waves, the third's division of sea and rising rock, then the spreading green cloak of vegetation. The night sky, unhampered by electric neon, is a carpet of stars and moon-paths reaching across the water—fourth-day glory! Then the fifth and sixth days, with their motion of fish and fowl—the brightly striped and spotted swimming schools, the flying finches, the swarming scuttles of red crabs, the black marine iguanas, the giant tortoises Darwin rode—all the flying, swimming, creeping things! And there in the midst I stood, as Darwin had stood, the whole spectacle of life crowned by thinking humans who could wonder at the splendid glory of it all. I could understand how these islands would cause Darwin to ponder the earliest sources of life with its amazing ability to adapt, survive, and thrive.

In all his searching through the wonders of nature, Charles never found God; more is the pity. Perhaps when Darwin met his Creator at the end of his life, after an apology for placing in doubt His engineering of the world, the two might have been lost in conversation about a thousand and one things with Darwin posing question after question. Did not the Father offer to Moses, "Look, and I will show thee the workmanship of mine hands; but not all, for my works are without end"? (Moses 1:4). Who can resist the hungry student? Darwin was one of the hungriest ever to walk the earth. Perhaps some formal religion alienated him too much from God, for so many things he disapproved of, such as slavery, were often justified by religion. This created too much doubt and tension in his mind, especially in light of all he observed in the natural world. The death of his children—especially his daughter Annie at the age of ten—further gnawed at his dwindling faith. He was a man who wanted truth regardless of where it led him, yet never applied his keen mind to questions about God. But then, such questions cannot have the certitude he craved, as his wife knew, which religion far too often, in its sometimes too-literal interpretation of scripture, believes it can provide. He knew he had not given the question adequate thought and avoided as best he could talking about it, feeling he was not "equal to deep reflection, on the deepest subject which can fill a man's mind."[59]

That life adapts and changes with the environment cannot be disputed. It is one of the miracles God placed in his creations and it enhances Divine intelligence rather than diminishes it. How much?—I will let others wrangle over that question, with the hope that civility will prevail. Darwin would have wished it so. Strangely, if more were like him there would not have been the fierce and sometimes tragic disagreements and doctrinal debates that have marred the face of Christianity for centuries. He was not a fighter; differences of thought were not something to become hostile about. Men could hold widely divergent opinions and still be united in goodness, in their probing desire for truth, in their love of humanity, and in friendship. We must see the value in others. We can disagree with their ideas, conclusions, or beliefs and still love and admire each individual soul for the unique qualities of their mind and personality. This I have learned from Darwin.

Joseph Smith revealed that all the myriad "classes of beings in their destined order or sphere of creation" would receive "the enjoyment of their eternal felicity" (D&C 77:3). The Father we worship is lovingly concerned with "the happiness of man, and of beasts, and of creeping things, and of the fowls of the air" (D&C 77:2)—even finches! This being so, all of us, Darwin certainly included, will maintain our sense of wonder, worlds without end. Won't it all be joyous fun!

> It has been my greatest comfort to say hundreds of
>   times to myself that
> "I have worked as hard and as well as I could,
> And no man can do more than this."[60]
>   —CHARLES DARWIN

CHAPTER EIGHT

"By Endurance We Conquer": Sir Ernest Shackleton, Polar Explorer

Antarctica
Early Twentieth Century C.E.

We had seen God in his splendors,
Heard the text that Nature renders.
We had reached the naked soul of man.[1]
—SIR ERNEST SHACKLETON

"Not to Yield"

THREE MEN STRUGGLED FORWARD, their faces all but concealed in the warm protection of hoods drawn tight to shut out the Antarctic cold of the Ross Ice Shelf—the Great Barrier. The ice-blasted wind drove like piercing needles into every fold and crevice of their frozen clothes. Warmth was only a distant memory. Wilson and Scott pulled the sledge. The third man, weakened beyond exhaustion by weeks of stinging cold and the creeping spread of scurvy, fought off death. The lining of his lungs was torn by microscopic ice crystals. Each step forward brought them closer to their ship and survival. They were naïve and inexperienced, pursuing the wildly impossible dream—considering their preparations—of being the first to conquer the South Pole. Fighting snow blindness, hunger thinning their stomachs, the sledge dragging heavier and heavier against ice that gripped like sand, the three men pushed on in the nightmare of white.

It was a stumbling slow race for life. The third man coughed constantly, couldn't sleep, was disoriented and dizzy, fighting off incoherency, dreaming of food flying past him just out of reach. His companions, facing despair themselves, felt he couldn't remain alive for long. Huddled in their tent with a wind-howling blizzard outside, the fading man, passing in and out of delirium, heard the other two talking. Wilson, the doctor, told Scott he didn't think their companion would last through the night. The words came like a blow through the fog of his misery. He vowed to himself he would prove them wrong and outlive them both. Somehow he survived the racking coughing of the night and rose the next morning. It took him twenty minutes to stumble out of the tent and make it to his feet. Speechless, he headed north. Quoting Tennyson's *Ulysses,* he found inner resources and stayed on his feet, letting the words substitute for his wasted condition:

> *That which we are we are;*
> *One equal temper of heroic hearts,*
> *Made weak by time and fate, but strong in will*
> *To strive, to seek, to find, and not to yield.* [2]

And he did not yield! He was born with a will baptized in optimism and endurance. Was that not his family motto? "By endurance we conquer!" A few more days of agony and two figures suddenly, mirage-like, approached with rescue—the ordeal was over. In typical understatement he wrote in his diary, "Very nice to be back again; but it was a good time." [3] It was February 3, 1903, and they had been alone on the ice for ninety-four grueling days. They had bagged the record for the furthest south latitude—that was something, but not enough for these men. Not for Earnest Shackleton—the third man. He had to take the Pole!

The White Wilderness

Antarctica is silent, wild, untamed, a splendidly beautiful place in spite of the Spartan demands its blizzards, debilitating cold, and harsh terrain require. It is nature in the extreme—magnificent, haunting, a place you never forget. There is no environment more hostile to human life than where temperatures dip scores below zero. Yet once you've seen it, you can't get it out of your mind. Black pinnacles of rock shoot up from the sea, their heads capped with overhanging ledges of snow. Glaciers pour through the valleys, wedged between mountain walls that bear their tremendous weight. Here is the constant, grinding, buckling, tearing struggle of ice and stone. The whitest white that nature can bring forth reflects in the bright sunlight where the pure air magnifies the distance, giving everything within eyesight a translucent clarity and deceptive distance. Pristine waters rise and fall in the ocean swell, where the light plays upon the surface of cathedral icebergs displaying blues that put the sky to shame and inviting a dozen new shades into the wheel of color. Whales breach in the waters. Flocks of penguins leaping like skipping stones through the calm sea show their own joyful appreciation of their southern home. Seals sleep on the bergs without a care in the world and albatross skim the surface of the waves, grateful for the gift of effortless flight and unmoving motion.

There are few places on earth I have enjoyed more, so I understand how the pull of this part of the world would draw men such as Shackleton like a magnet. But there was more—he was a child of the last great age of exploration, and the South Pole was one of the final frontiers a number of daring men wanted to plant with their nation's flag. We can comprehend, then, how he felt when the commander of the British Expedition, Robert Falcon Scott, invalided him home after their ordeal on the Ross Ice Shelf. When the ship heading back home to England pulled away from the ice, Shackleton broke down and wept.

The Dream and Emily

Shackleton was outgoing, magnetic, naturally optimistic, confidently persuasive, a charismatic and open friend to all, one who inspired among men a sense of camaraderie and equality. He was born to lead and he always led by example, showing at the same time a sincere deference to his men. He was born with the need to see new and changing vistas. Full of enthusiastic energy, willpower, charm, and congeniality, his men affectionately called him "The Boss."

Shackleton was born in Ireland in 1874 and had something of the Irish romantic spirit about him. His mother believed he was a perfect baby. His eight sisters, whom he laughingly called his "harem," adored him. Adept at teasing and playful jokes, he was at the center of any gathering. He was highly intelligent but not suited to the restrictions of formal education, though he loved literature, especially poetry, which he memorized, quoted, and harvested like grain. He took to sea like a bird to flight at the young age of sixteen. Afraid of being mocked for reading his Bible and praying, he did so anyway, and his example and goodwill soon had much of the crew doing the same.

He mastered the ways of a ship through a succession of voyages to distant parts of the globe, but being a sea captain was not sufficient for his ambitions—especially when he met Emily Dorman, a captivating young lady six years his senior. She fired his inbred determination to do something great. While on the deck of a ship and staring out to sea he told a friend, "I think I can do something better. In fact, really, I would like to make a name for myself . . . and her."[4] That "something better" became an obsessive desire to reach the Pole. Shackleton spoke of a dream he had while at sea: "It was a simple dream. I seemed to vow to myself that some day I would go to the region of ice and snow and go on and on till I came to one of the poles of the earth, the end of the axis upon which this great round ball turns."[5] After that he never had any doubt that sooner or later he would go on a polar expedition.

He won Emily to his love; the story is told of his coming to an auction at the Dorman home and being asked what he was planning on getting out of the old man. "A daughter, I hope," he replied. Shackleton's own daughter later remarked that her father wanted to lay the world at Emily's feet and entered Scott's polar expedition in great part because of her. With all this in mind, we can understand Shackleton weeping when he was sent home from Antarctica. But he would be back! Had not his dream told him he would go on and on until he reached the pole? Besides, once he had seen the white wilderness of the "last place on earth," he would forever have snow and ice in his veins. He tried to explain once to his sister what it felt like to walk over places no human had ever walked. It was a commanding emotion. Emily understood her man completely, once explaining he was "a soul whipped on by the wanderfire."[6]

He returned to England shaken but not defeated. He had made an invaluable friend in Frank Wild, who would accompany him on both future attempts for the Pole. Shackleton's seven-year courtship came to an end when he and Emily were finally married, but he could not settle down.

"We Have Shot Our Bolt"

He had seen the white wonder of the South and it would not let him out of its grip. With sheer determination, calling upon all his persuasive powers, he raised enough money to supply his own polar expedition and purchased an old sealing ship named *Nimrod*. In July 1907 he set sail for Antarctica. Though dogs and skis would prove to be the best means of polar travel, the British seemed to prefer man-hauling. Shackleton, however, decided to try Manchurian ponies. He had planned to establish his base camp in McMurdo Sound, where his nearly fatal attempt had been made earlier, but a critical letter from Scott, who claimed priority, forced him to seek another jumping-off point. Unable to find one, he reluctantly went back to McMurdo Sound, but ice conditions forced him twenty miles farther from the Pole. Too late to lay critical supply depots the summer before making the attempt, all efforts would be concentrated on one season. The ponies began dying from eating sand covered with salt spray. Before Shackleton and his men could discover the cause, the ponies were reduced to four. Shackleton had counted on at least six for the journey. There were more than 1,700 miles to go round-trip, a climb of roughly 12,000 feet to the polar plateau, and only four months to complete the journey. It would be a race against the steady approach of winter and into the unknown. But Shackleton was never one to retreat from demanding challenges. They would adapt and adjust—and endure.

He took three men with him, including Frank Wild, his friend from the first attempt with Scott. Other team members laid depots with fodder, fuel, and food for the out-and-back journey, then left the four men on the ice barrier. They carried food for ninety-one days; four ponies would do the majority of the pulling. Blizzards, snow-blindness, crevasses, and rough ice slowed them. It became obvious ninety-one days would be insufficient. They cut food rations. They passed the furthest southern point, advancing steadily, and the mountains leading up to the plateau loomed into sight. They were the first humans to see the Transantarctic Mountains at the end of the Ross Ice Shelf. One pony died and was cut up for food. They scouted a glacier leading up through the mountains and began the ascent. It was about 100 miles long and would be tough climbing. Two more ponies died. They pushed on and narrowly escaped disaster when the remaining pony broke through a snow bridge over a crevice and was lost from sight, almost pulling Wild with him. He and the sledge were only saved because the swingletree broke, leaving them on the rim. Shackleton remained determined, perpetually cheerful, and full of hope. Wild gave him the nickname "The Boss" at this time.

Just after Christmas, they reached the top of the glacier. The plateau stretched south before them like a highway. Only 250 miles to go and the Pole was his! But hunger, man-hauling the sledges, the extreme cold, and icy winds were taking their toll. They lightened their load and cached supplies. The altitude was giving them severe headaches. The nights were an agony of stiff, iced sleeping bags, growing ever heavier with their frozen breath. Their core temperatures dropped a few degrees below normal. Shackleton and his team were exerting every resource of strength and sheer willpower. He knew they were not making sufficient time to reach the Pole and return safely. Unwilling to concede defeat, they pushed on, Shackleton pulling like two men. They ate rations meant for the ponies, grinding the coarse grain between two rocks. Thirst was a constant agony as precious fuel had to be carefully guarded, but the only water they had came from melting ice. Shackleton read Shakespeare to the other three to keep their minds focused and away from negative brooding thoughts.

They were just over 100 miles from the Pole, but the end was in sight. Shackleton decided to make one last push to try to get within a hundred mile radius of the Pole, but a blizzard blew in and they had to hunker down in the tent. Precious hours mattered now. Leaving everything behind, the four men marched five hours, then finally stopped. With disappointment too deep for words, they took one last longing look south then turned and headed back to their supplies and shelter. Shackleton took his final latitude reading. They had reached 88 degrees 23 minutes—ninety-seven miles too short, but it was a victory of sorts: they had penetrated the one hundred-mile radius. It was January 9, 1909.

Men's lives always mattered most to Shackleton. In this he was a true leader. His decision to admit defeat is certainly one of the most courageous admissions in polar exploration. Those lacking clear wisdom go willfully on, sometimes to their death. All four men felt one more hour south would have meant their demise. The truly courageous know when it's time to face failure. Yet was it failure? Shackleton knew they had battled with the strongest forces of nature. "We have shot our bolt," he wrote as he turned north toward the waiting safety of the ship. It was deeply disappointing, but to remain longer could mean a cold death on the ice. "Whatever regrets may be, we have done our best." He had also promised Emily he would not do anything rash for the pole. If tempted, he would think of her and make the correct decision. She meant more than a flag in the snow. As he jokingly said to her when he returned, "I thought you'd rather have a live donkey than a dead lion." But to miss it so closely!

"Difficulties Are Just Things to Overcome"

They were not home yet, though, and a long dangerous journey still lay ahead. Rigging a sail to the sledge, Shackleton took advantage of a north-blowing wind and made good time. Descending the glacier was as difficult as the climb. They fell so many times into the heavily creviced ice that dangling over hundreds of feet of darkness became as habitual as tripping on the sidewalk. They battled dysentery, storms, poor food—suffered, prayed, starved, living from depot to depot on cached pony meat, once going over forty hours without food. Shackleton marched again across the Ross Ice Shelf, thoughts of his last near-collapse weighing on his mind.

But they persevered. Extreme hardship seemed to awaken in him reserves of courage, willpower, and resilience. *Hopeless* was not a word registered within his mind. "Difficulties are just things to overcome after all," he had said earlier.[7] As they approached the end, one man was too weak to go on. Shackleton and Wild raced on alone to find help, arriving at their base camp in the evening of

February 28. Shackleton had left instructions for the ship to sail on March 1 if they were not back. When the two exhausted men arrived they found a note telling them the ship had weighed anchor and left with everybody on board on the twenty-sixth from fear of being iced in. They had missed salvation by only two days! "To give way to despair," Wild later related, "was not possible for Shackleton," so they lit fires in hope the *Nimrod* would see the smoke.[8] If that failed, Shackleton was already planning an open-boat journey to New Zealand. To their immense relief, they saw the ship reappear, pushing through the ice floes to pick them up. Their joy was only muted by the need to answer the question that was eagerly asked by their rescuers: "Did you reach the Pole?" He had no time for self-pity; there were two men still on the ice; Shackleton felt it the leader's responsibility to bring them in. In a few hours he was heading back and did not rest until all were safe.

For a second time Shackleton had narrowly missed disaster and death, but his clear thinking, resolute optimism, and concern for the lives of those who trusted his judgment brought them to the very brink of life, but no further. They had accomplished much. He had discovered hundreds of miles of Antarctica, gathered a great deal of scientific data, found a way through the mountains, and had been the first to walk the Polar Plateau! He had come so close, but missed the final goal by less than a hundred miles. Would he try again?

Victory and Death on the Ice Shelf

He returned to England and Emily and a hero's welcome. No one had ventured as far south; he was knighted for his efforts. The restlessness remained, but, as he had indicated, he had shot his bolt and he had more than once told Emily this was it. Emily sensed, however, that his restlessness would send him again. "How could you keep an eagle tied in a backyard?" she remarked. Scott tried next in 1911–12, his British team locked in a race with the Norwegians under the leadership of Roald Amundsen, the first man to sail the Northwest Passage. Each country vied for the coveted first-to-plant-the-flag prize. Amundsen used skis and dog teams and, though he had to chart his own new route to the Pole, beat the British by a month, all the time making the whole journey look like a cross-country ski trip in the hills near Oslo. Scott, with the advantage of Shackleton's proven route, died tragically on the Ross Ice Shelf after the bitter disappointment of seeing the Norwegian flag flying where he had wanted to plant the Union Jack. He was only eleven miles short of his main depot of food on the return when frostbite and scurvy won the day. In the Antarctic crucible, hours at times mattered critically. Scott's four-man polar team perished with him, including Wilson, who had remarked he did not think Shackleton would survive the night on their previous expedition. Dogs and skis had proved the crucial key. Shackleton would use them the next time he went south.

All this was prelude to Shackleton's greatest achievement, which ironically was also his greatest failure, for he would not even step on the continent, let alone sledge to its center. His destiny seems to have been to teach us how to lead, for he would never reach the Pole after three attempts. Yet the story of his third trip is one of the greatest in the heritage of survival, daring, cool judgment, and undaunted courage. In his story I have grown to love the poetry-quoting Irish explorer and learned immense lessons for my life. To comprehend that schooling, it is necessary to put his last attempt for the Pole against the backdrop of his two previous disappointments. He would be driven to succeed, but fate would decree otherwise.

THE LEADER

I became an avid admirer of Shackleton the first time I went to Antarctica. I read all I could get my hands on. I was serving in a leadership position in the Church at the time, training other leaders. Shackleton completely fascinated me. I made a list of his leadership qualities as I studied his three attempts on the Pole and had to agree with the almost unanimous assessment of the men he led. As one indicated, he was simply the greatest leader God had ever placed on earth. I'm not sure he is *the* greatest, but I think we would search a long time before we found one greater. Perhaps there is no finer testimony than Frank Wild's. Shackleton asked him while on their return journey, in the midst of their misery, if he would join him in another attempt. Frank recalled that so great was his admiration and trust in Shackleton's leadership that he immediately said yes. And he did! There was something in Shackleton that inspired confidence both in his leadership and in oneself. He never lost his cheerfulness, his sense of humor, or his solicitous concern for his men. I have kept the list I made of his leadership qualities and referred to it as I've pondered various roles and responsibilities. Here are some of my observations:

- Stay visible and personally involved with all.
- Remain optimistic, but grounded in the reality of each situation.
- Communicate honestly—manipulation of another's emotions or hopes is unacceptable.
- Be uncompromisingly just and fair and insist on the same in the interactions between those you lead, thus minimizing status.
- Grant autonomy through delegation and respect each individual's unique contribution, granting all opportunity.
- You can learn from whomever you lead—so listen!
- Never allow contention, conflict, or personality to destroy unity—maintain it at all costs!

- Find the delicate balance between acceptable risk and overall safety.
- Remain focused on your objective, but be flexible and adaptable to new circumstances.
- Discouragement is not allowed and must never be demonstrated—control your own anxiety.
- The primary leadership idea is to keep genuine concern for others central in all your thinking.
- Never forget that leadership is a responsibility, not a privilege—you exist for them, not them for you!
- Private ambitions or dreams must never cloud your decision-making.
- Be foresighted and prepared to the highest degree, then trust to Providence for the unseen contingencies—there is no such thing as luck!
- Be clear-minded about what you desire. This is often more critical than how you will achieve it.
- Always work for higher purposes than celebrity status, power, or wealth.
- Expect the best out of people while allowing for human frailty; be forgiving without lowering the standard of performance demanded.
- The past is the past—always look ahead.
- If you must call upon outward symbols of authority or position, you have failed. In the final analysis it is you they follow, not "the mantle."

One man described Shackleton's leadership by stating simply, "The power was in himself, . . . it was not outside."[9] Shackleton once drew up a list of qualities he believed an explorer needed. Optimism, then patience, led the list. Courage came in last at number five. "Few men are wanting in courage," he said, "but optimism nullifies disappointment and makes one more ready than ever to go on."[10] He would need all of those skills on the third attempt.

"Proceed"

When Scott died on the Ross Ice Shelf, he became a national hero, but British morale also took a hit. With the Norwegians first to the South Pole and the Americans first to the North, there was really only one major challenge left undone—a complete crossing of the Antarctic continent with the Pole attained mid-journey. This became Shackleton's new central drive. Once again, with personality, persuasive charm, cheerful confidence, devotion, and appeals to Britannic pride, Shackleton mustered the funding for an assault on the entire continent. Two teams would work from both ends, with Shackleton leading the crossing from the Weddell Sea, opposite the Ross Ice Shelf he had previously conquered. He christened his ship *Endurance* in honor of his family motto, hand-picked a team of twenty-seven (including Frank Wild) to accompany him, and prepared to sail for the South Georgia whaling station, the last outpost of civilization before entering the South Atlantic and the Weddell Sea. He was returning to the land of his most intense suffering, but he was not one to give up on his dreams. World War I broke out and the whole enterprise was in danger of being canceled. Shackleton offered his ship and men to the war effort. He received a one-word telegram from Winston Churchill, at the time Lord of the Admiralty: "Proceed."

They sailed south, this time with dog teams, and arrived in South Georgia, where the whalers told them the ice pack was particularly heavy that year and farther north than normal. Shackleton felt he had no choice and that he could squeeze through along the east coast where the wind and drift blew the ice in a circular pattern toward the west. In addition, the *Endurance* was specially built with a thick hull capable of pushing its way through and cracking the ice. Hopes were high; all went well until they encountered substantial ice floes in the Weddell Sea. For weeks they battled the ice pack, picking their way through open leads and patches of water. One good run with engine or sail would take them to Vahsel Bay, their final destination, but the ice closed round tightly. They had come more than 12,000 miles, the last 1,000 wrestling with the ice.

Now they were trapped, roughly 60 miles short of the goal. Days of abnormal cold and wind from the wrong quarter plagued them. They cut the engines to preserve coal in the heavy slush and bergs. In spite of every effort to pick their way through leads and open water, they were iced in. Numerous attempts to cut channels through the frozen sea to open leads proved futile. Barely perceptible in the distance was the looked-for landing site. They were agonizingly close, but would face the total darkness of an Antarctic winter drifting slowly back north. It was essential that spirits be kept high. Without showing the slightest sign of disappointment, remaining serenely calm, Shackleton told the crew they would have to winter in the ice, but would try again the following summer and ordered preparations to be made. The tremendous forces of nature would decide otherwise.

CRUSHING OF *ENDURANCE*

They waited the long, dark, cold months entertaining themselves with theatrical performances and working with the dogs. Month after month, *Endurance* floated slowly north with the ice, moving closer to the Antarctic Peninsula to the west. Shackleton kept their hopes high and focused on preparations for the sledging journey they still anticipated to run. He knew each man's limitations better than they did, met each one on their own ground, trusted them, praised all efforts, engaged each man in little intimate talks, and worked ceaselessly to save them from their own anxieties.

His own anxieties he kept to himself, but he knew "what the ice gets, the ice keeps." With warmer weather, the ice began to break up and move. Tremendous pressure built against the sides of the ship as the giant bergs and floes ground against each other, piling up in ridges taller than the ship. They could hear the timbers groaning and buckling in protest. Ice breaking even miles away sounded like gunshots. *Endurance* survived a number of pressured squeezings and releases, but time was on the side of the ice. Eventually the ship decking rose and snapped, the rudder tore away, and the ship began taking on water. Exhaustive efforts to pump her free were futile. Shackleton ordered the men to prepare to abandon their wooden home and camp on the ice. Taking as many supplies as they could, the men moved to the tenuous safety of a floe floating among thousands of others in a sea of white pack ice over many fathoms of water—ice that would slowly melt as summer advanced and the pack circled to the north.

The following days brought the slow death throes of *Endurance*. When she finally sank, all knew they faced a journey for survival against tremendous odds. They were 1,200 miles from even the merest outpost of civilization. No one could save them. Shackleton had to inspire them with the will to survive and the belief that they could. They were completely on their own. "The Boss" would face the test of his life—return with every man alive. He wanted no repeat of Scott's tragedy. Nor was he free from the memory of the Franklin disaster a generation earlier in the polar regions of the north. Franklin's entire ship, a crew of more than a hundred men, perished in the biting cold of northern Canada. There is a statement made by Edward Priestly about the three most famous South Pole explorers, Amundsen, Scott, and Shackleton. Priestly had served with the British teams and knew Shackleton well. "For scientific leadership give me Scott; for swift and efficient travel, Amundsen; but when you are in a hopeless situation, when there seems no way out, get down on your knees and pray for Shackleton."[11] The prayers of twenty-seven men were about to be answered.

"A Man Must Shape Himself to a New Mark"

They brought onto the ice with them three lifeboats, which they all knew would, in time, be the deciding factor between life and death. These boats, packed with supplies, would need to be pulled on runners across the ice. There was some comfort in seeing them, but they looked pathetically small in the vast stretch of white that reached to every horizon. Shackleton paced that night with the men sleeping in tents pitched a few tenuous feet above the deep fathoms below. His dream of the Pole was once again lost in "the white warfare of the south."[12]

It was in these circumstances that he said something which has provided for me a treasured lesson from his so-very-instructive life: "The task now was to secure the safety of the party, and to that I must bend my energies and mental power and apply every bit of knowledge that experience of the Antarctic had given me. The task was likely to be long and strenuous, and an ordered mind and a clear program were essential if we were to come through without loss of life. *A man must shape himself to a new mark directly the old one goes to ground.*"[13]

So often in our lives, the dreams, goals, and aspirations that mean so much to us may seem like the shattered wreckage of the *Endurance.* This was his third failure! It is easy to sit on the ice and mourn the loss, to constantly churn the "what ifs" in our minds. When these moments come to me, and they have, I think of those oh-so-powerful words of Sir Ernest. We must shape ourselves to a new mark—and we must do so "directly." Life demands the "ordered mind." There is no room for continuous depressing reflection on the past—what we wanted, what we lost, what we should have done better. Too much is at stake. Living requires our "energies . . . mental power . . . and experience." We find the new mark, shape ourselves to it, and move forward. Out of the ashes of the old dream the phoenix of continued living must arise. For me, Shackleton's articulating of that life theme was worth all the sufferings of three successive endeavors to reach the Pole.

That night the ice cracked, and there was a scramble to get everything and everybody onto the remaining larger floe. It was a foreshadowing of what lay ahead. Shackelton, needing to inspire his men, knowing better than any the trials of polar survival, knowing that the journey ahead would reach for every last reserve of their strength, knowing there was fear and doubt of survival in his men's minds, knowing they all must abandon personal belongings, which would require sacrifice, emptied his pockets of gold coins, dropping them in the snow, and tore a page from the book of Job which read, "Out of whose womb came the ice? and the hoary frost of heaven, who hath gendered it? The waters are hid as with a stone, and the face of the deep is frozen" (Job 38:29–30). God had made the ice; God could get them across it. He also kept Psalm 23. He left the Bible on the ice and said simply, "So, now we'll go home!" So brief a statement, so casual, and so full of confidence.

ORDEAL TO ELEPHANT ISLAND

They could each take two pounds of personal gear. They would head for Paulet Island, where Shackleton knew a cache of food remained from a previous rescue effort. They and the dogs pulled the sledges and lifeboats, cutting passages through the ice ridges. The labor exhausted them. They made so little progress it became apparent they could not cross the ice in a run for the safety of land. They would again have to wait while the circling push of the ice pack would carry them further north. When it began to break up, they would take to the boats and row for safety. Months locked in the grip of the ice aboard *Endurance* now turned into months floating on the ice in various camps—one of which they named "Patience Camp."

Patience they certainly required. "Put footstep of courage . . . into stirrup of patience," Shackleton reminded himself.[14]

They shot seals and penguins for food, which kept them free of scurvy, and blubber served for fuel. They had to be cautious along the edge of the ice as it could calve without warning. Ten-foot sea leopards (a predatory seal), thinking they were penguins, would leap upon the ice and try to drag them into the slush-filled sea. In the daytime, the sun melted the surface of the floe into a watery mush. At night everything froze. They had only eighteen sleeping bags, so some had to make do with blankets alone.

As they continued to drift they realized Paulet Island was now out of reach. New destinations and new hopes were formed and abandoned in the constant drift of the pack, but no break-up occurred. Once two icebergs came crashing through the floes, driven by the wind toward their position and creating a chaos of ice in their path. The bergs veered off just before reaching the stranded men's solitary floe. The excitement was, at least, a change from the months of waiting. Then they began to feel the slight swell of the sea and knew they were close to more-open water. They were past the furthermost tip of the finger of land reaching northward from the continent. There were only at best two isolated islands they could make for, Clarence or Elephant; if they failed to obtain either, the open sea and certain death awaited. When would the ice separate and open water sufficient for the three boats appear?

The pack slowly opened. The floe they were on continued to split and grow smaller. Yet they hesitated to put to the boats, as the colliding bergs and "growlers" could crush a small lifeboat like matchwood. The continual swell of the sea separated the ice; Shackleton felt he could wait no longer. Their five-month-long ordeal on the ice was over. They had christened the three small boats after donors to the expedition: the *Dudley Docker,* the *Stancomb Wills,* and the *James Caird,* the last being the largest. Twenty-eight men divided themselves and their dwindling supplies into three boats and cast off. They had no idea that seven days of hell awaited them.

Dodging bergs and rolling ice, rowing in the sleet and spray that froze onto their clothes and pinned their hands to the oars, laboring without sleep or a decent meal, they endured under Shackleton's constant encouragement and fierce determination. A night camp on a floe almost ended in disaster when it broke under one of the tents. Shackleton had just enough time to reach into the water and save one of his men before the floe snapped together again. They suffered frostbite, debilitating thirst which could only be alleviated by chewing raw seal meat, and seasickness. Killer whales surfaced within yards of the boats. Men became so cramped with cold and rowing that they could not move, their muscles locking into position like a jackknife. Saltwater boils broke over their skin from the constant chafing of wet clothes.

Lying in each other's arms for warmth, the crew scanned the horizon, searching for Elephant Island, their desired and final hoped-for chance of safety. Finally it came into view. Facing stiff headwinds, bucking currents that took them in the opposite direction, chipping encrusted ice from the boats, enduring ever-present seasickness, they rowed for their lives. The wind threatened to sweep them past the island and into the open sea, but in one final, desperate effort they braved the dangerous surf and landed. Their joy was short-lived, however, as high-water marks on the cliffs of the small beach showed the entire area was often inundated by the surf. So to the boats they took again, finally discovering a small beach roughly 150 yards long by 30 wide with fresh water running off a melting glacier and a penguin colony for food. It was hampered by "williwaws," brief spurts of tempestuous winds which picked up anything not firmly tied down—but they had survived and were on land again. Their joy was tempered by the knowledge that no one, not even whalers, ever came to Elephant Island. They were the first humans to set foot on it. Someone would have to brave the Drake Passage, the most treacherous seas on the planet, and try to reach South Georgia to get help.

Over the Sea

Shackleton chose five to go with him. Among them was a navigator named Frank Worsley and a former expedition member named Tom Crean. They would need to outfit the *James Caird,* the largest of the boats at only twenty-two feet, to make her more seaworthy. The ship's carpenter, with the help of some canvas, sledge runners, and wood from crate lids, put a top on her to at least give the impression that she could face the storms of the crossing to South Georgia. The *James Caird* was essentially a lifeboat and not meant to sail in rough waters, but they would make do.

The seas that surround Antarctica are circled almost constantly by low barometric pressure. Since there are no real land masses to temper the fierceness of the winds, the seas are treacherous, perpetually circling the continent. They are the most turbulent, furious seas on earth. Shackleton and his five-man crew would be crossing over 800 miles of this stretch of water. They would aim for a tiny island. If they were off by more than a nautical degree, they would miss their mark completely and sail on into the South Atlantic until they died of exposure and hunger or sank. Not only were the lives of these six men at stake, but also the twenty-two who would remain at Elephant Island in the hope that somehow Shackleton would get through and return with a rescue ship.

Shackleton sailed into the Drake Passage, drawing on all his experience at sea. Their journey is one of the most unbelievable feats of navigation and seamanship in seafaring history. Shackleton treated it like an adventure, infusing the other five men with more than hope. Despair was a weight they could not afford to carry. The six men spelled each other in four-hour watches day after tiring day. Gale after gale hit them. They bailed out the *James Caird* two to three times per watch while trying to sleep in shifts on the rocks laid in the bottom for ballast. Every other wave soaked them. Hit by a rogue wave one hundred feet high, they battled to stay afloat. Shackleton said in twenty-six years experience with the sea he had never seen one like it. Freezing spray and rain burdened the decking, sometimes accumulating ice to a density of six inches, making ropes as thick as a man's thigh. The ice had to be chipped off, or they would sink under its weight. So, clinging to whatever tenuous grip they could, they hacked away at the ice in pitching seas.

Shackleton cared for them like a hovering mother, offering them hot milk and food. They steered by the stars and sun when they could see them, occasional sextant readings, a single chronometer, and a compass. They relied on dead reckoning and navigational intuition. For seventeen days they fought the ocean, taking critical position readings in the pitching sea. Running out of water, the little they had contaminated with salt seepage, they existed on a quarter of a pint a day. Denied sleep, worn to the breaking point with exhaustion, and ever fearful that they would miss, or had missed, the tiny spot of land that meant the difference between life and death for twenty-eight men, they battled forward until straight ahead the peaks of South Georgia came into view through a lifting fog.

A final hurricane-force storm threatened to hurl them onto the rocks. Remaining off the coast, battling the wind for another day, delayed their landing and almost sunk the boat, but half-dead, and in spite of near disaster among the breakers, they pulled into a secluded bay and crawled to safety. They had not drunk any fresh water for forty-eight hours, their rudder was gone, but they had done it! There was no triumph in their hearts, just gratitude and immense relief. The sheer magnitude of what they had suffered and accomplished would come later. They crawled to fresh water running off a glacier and drank their fill.

OVER THE MOUNTAINS

Feasting on a dinner of baby albatross, they surveyed their situation. True, they had reached South Georgia, but the whaling station was on the other side and the *James Caird* was too beat-up to manage another 150 miles of water to circle the island. Besides, Shackleton felt some of the men could not take any more of the sea. South Georgia had never been crossed. Its interior was a maze of glaciers, mountain ridges, plunging cliffs, snow slides, and deep valleys. They were weak from months of privation, had no climbing gear, no map, just a chart with the coasts roughly drawn and the interior a blank. None of them had any experience in technical climbing. In addition, winter was approaching. Three of the men were too weak for the climb.

Shackleton, Crean, and Worsley, with screws from the boat inserted into their shoes as crampons, took an adze for an ice ax, a small length of rope, enough food for three days, and began the ascent. They had no sleeping bags and no tent. They would risk all for speed rather than protection. A storm would have doomed them. A team of highly skilled climbers who recently retraced Shackleton's footsteps across South Georgia took three full days using the highest quality of gear. Yet Shackleton made the climb in thirty-six hours, without a known route. Fog obscured their views and false leads caused them to re-climb heights they thought they had already overcome. On one occasion, while high on a mountain ridge with the cold of night coming on, knowing he had to drop in elevation or freeze, Shackleton coiled the rope, had all three men sit on it, and tobogganed into the unknown two thousand feet down the mountainside. It was a risk he felt he had to take. The exhilaration of the rapid slide soon found them laughing like schoolboys.

They plodded on, sinking knee-deep in the snow with each fatiguing step, walking by moonlight. When his companions fell asleep in the snow, he let them sleep five minutes then woke them up, telling them they had slept thirty. Sleep in the cold and snow meant death; Shackleton knew it, but was also aware they needed the encouragement even such a ruse could offer. Continued hope and endurance was provided with frequent stops for food and brief rest, but they were suffering from dehydration. Shackleton turned mentally to memorized poetry for strength, quoting Robert Browning's "Prospice": "I was ever a fighter, so—one fight more, / The best and the last! . . . For sudden the worst turns to the best to the brave, / The black minute's at end, / And the elements' rage . . . / Shall dwindle, shall blend."[15]

There came a moment just before seven in the morning when Shackleton hushed them into silence. If they were near they should be able to hear the steam whistle at the station. As seven o'clock ticked into position they heard the distinct whistle rising up the slope. They had found their way. A rapid descent, cutting steps in the glacial ice, and a rappel down a waterfall where they had to abandon their last bit of rope finally brought them into the outpost. A gale whipped up a short time later. Had they attempted the crossing that night they would not have made it.

Shackleton went to the station master's home. He was filthy, his face blackened from months of sitting near a blubber-fired stove, hair long and dangling, and a full beard. "Who the hell are you?" boomed the whaler.

"Don't you know me?" Shackleton asked.

"I know your voice," came the doubtful response.

"My name is Shackleton."

His first question concerned the war. When had it ended?

"'The war is not over,' he answered. 'Millions are being killed. Europe is mad. The world is mad.'"[16] They had come home, indeed. While armies were slaughtering each other halfway around the world, Shackleton had spent all to save the lives of his men. Life's ironies are never simple.

"We're All Well!"

The three men still waiting on the other side of the island were picked up, the valiant little *James Caird* also placed on board the whaling ship; it can still be seen today in England. In less than seventy-two hours, Shackleton was on a ship headed for Elephant Island. The ice around the island was unyielding. He could not get close enough for the rescue, but he kept trying. It would take four attempts by four different ships to reach the stranded men. On a day four months later, the weary men saw a ship pulling toward them. They scrambled out of the makeshift refuge they had fashioned out of the overturned remaining two lifeboats and rushed down to the shore. A whale boat was rowing toward them with a man in the helm. Then across the water they heard the voice of "The Boss." He was counting faces.

"Are you all well?" he cried.

Wild shouted back, "All well! We're all well, Boss! We're all well!"

Wild had kept them all alive. He had learned well from Shackleton's leadership. Every day he told the men to get their things ready, for the "Boss" may come today. Hope of rescue had never died. It had been four months since the *James Caird* slipped into the Drake Passage on that never-to-be-duplicated trial of courage and daring. He had saved them all. "Not a life lost and we have been through Hell," he wrote Emily. "Soon I will be home and then I will rest."[17]

The Fourth Man

I have seen Elephant Island and can't imagine a more forlorn, lonely, or foreboding place on earth. I have made the Drake Passage six times. Just thinking about them is enough to give one nightmares of marooning and shipwreck. How did he do it? Perhaps Sir Ernest helps us answer that question with a passage he included in his own narrative of the *Endurance* Expedition. Remember, his creed was to do everything you could and trust to Providence for those things over which you had no control.

"When I look back at those days I have no doubt that Providence guided us, not only across those snow fields, but across the storm-white sea that separated Elephant Island from our landing place on South Georgia. I know that during that long and racking march of thirty-six hours over the unnamed mountains and glaciers of South Georgia it seemed to me often that we were four, not three. I said nothing to my companions on the point, but afterwards Worsley said to me, 'Boss, I had a curious feeling on the march that there was another person with us.' Crean confessed to the same idea. One feels 'the dearth of human words, the roughness of mortal speech' in trying to describe things intangible, but a record of our journeys would be incomplete without a reference to a subject very near to our hearts."[18] They were four! I never read Shackleton's account of the fourth companion without thinking of Luke's account of the Savior walking with two of His disciples on the road to Emmaus.

"That's My Death Knell"

Though he had written to Emily at the end of the *Endurance* Expedition that he would come home and rest, his temperament would not allow it. He was restless anywhere but in the wild, facing enormous challenges. She understood her husband all too well; Shackleton would attempt one final assault on the South Pole. This time, however, he died of a heart attack in South Georgia. He surely would have wanted it that way. One of the men recalled that Shackleton, listening to the rather mournful sound of a harbor buoy ringing as they left Plymouth, had said, "That's my death knell."[19] He was always suspicious about the condition of his heart and had never let anyone examine it. He was just shy of his forty-eighth birthday. When he was young, an old nurse had told him he would die at the age of forty-eight. He believed this omen, and it had haunted him during his life. Perhaps that is why he drove himself so furiously to explore and accomplish something worthwhile.

They were going to bring his body back to England, but Emily knew his heart and instructed them to bury him on South Georgia among the icebergs, snow-encrusted peaks, and wild beauty he so loved—those places of courage and suffering, of failure and triumph. Instead of burying him facing east, they faced him south—and I'm sure he would have approved.

We learn the true mettle of men when they are placed in crisis situations that require all that is within them. Shackleton faced those moments three times in his life: once on the Ross Ice Shelf when his companions thought he would not make it through the night; once on the Polar Plateau when he turned from his dream just ninety-seven miles short; and once in the Weddell Sea, the Drake Passage, and South Georgia when he shaped himself to a new mark and saved the lives of his twenty-seven men. Each leg of this last incredible story of endurance, determination, and human spirit alone would have been remarkable, but the united force of them acting together will not be repeated in human history. If it had been presented to us as dramatic fiction we would have felt our credulity had been strained too far.

I have enjoyed reading of exploration, of survival, of the wilderness as long as I can remember and love the feeling of isolation when the wilderness closes around you. I take such pleasure in learning of the heights of human courage demonstrated by men and women such as Lewis and Clark on the American frontier, Fridtjof Nansen as he crossed Greenland and the North Polar Sea, Cabeza de Vaca traveling from Florida to the Pacific, and Isabel Godin on her long, heartbreaking journey down the Amazon. These and numerous other friends in history have motivated and inspired the best in me.

But none have offered me so much life instruction as Sir Ernest Shackleton. He never gave up his dream, but knew when to turn from it to higher causes. He redefined our understanding of success and failure. Though he never reached the Pole, no one would suggest that his three attempts were not triumphant celebrations of the human spirit. He taught us the meaning of the verb *to lead*. His endurance is a witness that whatever life demands from us, we can be equal to it. For me, I will be forever in his debt, if for no other reason than that one moment when he shaped himself to a new mark because the old one had gone to ground. In every way he lived up to his family's motto: "By endurance we conquer." This legacy he leaves to each of us. May we so endure in the Antarctic challenges of our own lives, as he did in his.

> *He had his faults & knew it, too,*
> *And he expected perfection in no man;*
> *But he was quite willing to overlook what was bad*
> *And just remembered the good in everyone.*
> *He had a way of compelling loyalty.*
> *We would have gone anywhere without question*
> *Just on his order.*[20]
> —LEONARD HUSSEY OF THE *ENDURANCE* EXPEDITION

To Love—the Sharers

Beloved, let us love one another:
for love is of God; every one that loveth is born of God,
and knoweth God . . . ; for God is love.

—1 John 4:7–8

CHAPTER NINE

LOVE RIGHT THROUGH: GEORGE MACDONALD

Scotland
Nineteenth Century C.E.

What is the whole system of things for, but our education?
Does God care for suns and planets and satellites,
For divine mathematics and ordered harmonies,
More than for his children?[1]
—GEORGE MACDONALD, FROM *UNSPOKEN SERMONS*

THE VOICE IN THE BOOK

HE STOOD ON THE LEATHERHEAD Station platform that October evening unaware that his life was about to change dramatically. He had a brilliant mind; his soul was equally alive to the world of human imagination. Oxford was his home and teaching literature his profession as a don at Magdalen College. He had long ago given up his belief in God and did so with a sense of relief. A voracious reader, he turned now to the bookstall nearby and picked up a book in a dirty jacket titled *Phantastes: A Faerie Romance*. That night he began to read.

"It is as if I were carried sleeping across the frontier, or as if I had died in the old country and could never remember how I came alive in the new. . . . I did not yet know (and I was long in learning) the name of the new quality, the bright shadow, that rested on the travels of Anodos. I do now. It was holiness." He had turned a corner that would rekindle his faith and make him the leading Christian writer of the twentieth century, the creator of Aslan and Narnia, the voice of Screwtape, and author of *Mere Christianity*. The man on the platform that October evening was C. S. Lewis, now a household name.

But the name on the cover of the book that led to it all was George MacDonald. "It was as though the voice which had called to me from the world's end were now speaking at my side. . . . It seemed to have been always with me; if I could ever have turned my head quick enough. . . . That night my imagination was, in a certain sense, baptized; the rest of me, not unnaturally, took longer. I had not the faintest notion what I had let myself in for by buying *Phantastes*."[2]

There are few men, even godly men, who can speak with the heart and soul of divinity like MacDonald could. His was a loving voice, a voice that reached deep into the mind and the heart, the voice of a father, but then is that not what we call God?

The Constant at the Center

In *A Man for All Seasons*, Sir Thomas More says, "only God is love right through,"[3] meaning He is motivated in all His dealings with us purely by love. Of all the wonderful people I have read about (outside of scripture) throughout my life, George MacDonald comes closer to this divine perspective than anyone else. He simply was infused with the heart of God, and thus could speak with the voice and soul of the Father and Son in so many ways. It's fair to add that had there been no MacDonald, there also would have been no C. S. Lewis, at least not the Lewis we have come to love. Lewis acknowledged this indebtedness when he wrote, "I have never concealed the fact that I regard him as my master."[4] There certainly would have been no Aslan, that magnificent lion who teaches us so very much about the personality and heart of the Savior we love.

In Lewis's *The Great Divorce*, it is MacDonald who traverses the mountains of heaven to meet Lewis and guide him through the celestial landscapes, teaching and explaining. In truth, the whole concept of *The Great Divorce*—that the door to hell is locked from the inside—is MacDonald's. This truth was also taught by Joseph Smith in Doctrine and Covenants 88: 32–33, where hell is called your "own place," one which people willingly "receive" (in great irony) and "enjoy." It is a unique perspective.

MacDonald's central focus on God's character as the prime need in any religious system shaped Lewis's multifaceted understanding of Christ's and the Father's attributes. And it was MacDonald's open desire to listen to all and center his life's work in the commonalities of faith—the foundational solidity of shared middle ground—from which Lewis would grasp the understanding translated into his most famous Christian apologetic, *Mere Christianity*. Neither Lewis nor MacDonald wanted to engage in contentious debates or condemnatory judgments. They stuck to the essentials. Like MacDonald, Lewis wrote from the romantic perspective of fantasy and children's stories as well as formalized, well-reasoned, and thoughtful expositions of religious understanding. Neither the rational nor the mythic were superior to the other. Both were pathways to goodness and insight. Through it all was one constant—*The* Constant!

MacDonald found the center of the center point, the compassionate, forgiving, and inviting nature of God. There he planted his fixed foot and never moved it. We find Lewis there also. He influenced the thought of other deeply spiritual men, such as G. K. Chesterton, who wrote, "The passionate and poetical Scots ought obviously, like the passionate and poetical Italians, to have had a religion which competed with the beauty and vividness of the passion, which did not let the devil have all the bright colors, which fought glory with glory and flame with flame."[5] To Chesterton, MacDonald was the "St. Francis of Aberdeen."[6] We have much to learn from George MacDonald! Yet his is a life few have heard of, but in his day he was a household name.

A Father and His Son

George MacDonald was born in Huntly, Scotland, December 10, 1824, in a Calvinist family. His grandmother was a dominant force, full of fiery suspicion of anything that could lead to sin; she once burned her son's violin, suspecting it was leading him away from the Lord. MacDonald never forgot his uncle's distress. George's mother died when he was a child, leaving him to his father's care. George Senior was a loving parent and colored his son's view of God. How could an earthly father be better than the divine one? Their relationship was tender, trusting, and filled with patient solicitude and open communication. His father had lost a leg to tuberculosis when George Jr. was only one and, like the young Joseph Smith, had refused alcohol and would not cover his face when the doctor amputated it. God was still good in spite of loss and suffering. The young boy idolized his open-hearted and faith-filled father.

But the church preached predestination and a wrathful God. The two faces of religion—one perceived from the gentle care of his father and the other formalized into the creeds and stern instruction of schoolmasters and ministers, alongside his grandmother's watchful intensity on the possibility of sin—created a severe conflict in the boy's soul.

He was born good-natured and nourished a healthy sense of humor. He shared Francis of Assisi's love of beauty as found in nature. Here was another face of God, one which matched that presented by his father. Silence and scenery penetrated to his core and left their impressions of calm and serenity. He could not get enough of sea walks, sunsets, cool river pools to swim in, animal life to wonder at, or the stark mountain awe of the Scottish highlands. He once wrote of the loveliness of childhood, certainly thinking of his own, but tempering it with more mature and deeper reflections. "For innocent animal delights I know of nothing to match those days—so warm, yet so pure-aired—so clean, so glad. I often think how God must love his little children to have invented for them such delights! For of course, if he did not love the children and delight in their pleasure he would not have invented the two and brought them together. Yes, my child, I know what you would say: 'How many there are who have no such pleasures!' I grant it sorrowfully, but you must remember that God has not done with them yet; and besides, that there are more pleasures in the world than you or I know anything about. And if we had it *all* pleasure, I know I should not care so much about what is better, and I would rather be made good than have any other pleasure in the world, and so would you, though perhaps you do not know it yet."[7]

He would often lie for hours on the back of his mare Missy while she grazed, lost in thought or buried in a book. And he was forever thinking—always questioning, entertaining each doubt. Pensive, introspective, mystical, brooding sometimes on life's deepest questions, he had to have truth. He sensed when he found it there would be radiant meaning and pulsating joy. Like Joseph Smith, he hungered for it, pondered his place and direction in the world, and meditated long hours, searching the New Testament for answers. What was God really like? An inherited faith was not sufficient. He was troubled by his doubts, but came in time to value them as avenues to higher truths. He compared them to hammers thrown through the windows of preconception and accepted tradition, which could then let in clarifying light.

"OUR SOULS MAY BE WEDDED ETERNALLY"

After years at the University of Aberdeen, he decided to enter the ministry and spent three more years in London at a Congregationalist college honing his skills, particularly preaching, the Protestant mainstay of worship. Here he met and loved Louisa Powell. Years of courtship only confirmed his love, and she became his dearest friend throughout their life together. Loving this woman further expanded his heart and taught him more about the love of God. During their engagement, he once wrote to her, "Is love a beautiful thing, dearest? But who created love? Let us ask him to purify our love to make it stronger and more real and more self-denying. I want to love you forever. . . . Oh Louisa. . . . If there is anything beautiful in this our dreamy life, shall it not shine forth in glory in the bright wakening consciousness of heaven?"[8] As a wedding present he composed a poem he titled "Love Me, Beloved," which further hinted at his growing belief in the eternal nature of family relationships, especially husband and wife.

> *And thou shalt be mine, my spirit's bride,*
> *In the ceaseless flow of eternity's tide,*
> *If the truest love that thy heart can know*
> *Meet the truest love that from mine can flow.*
> *Pray God, beloved, for thee and me,*
> *That our souls may be wedded eternally.*[9]

These elevated thoughts, so consistent with Latter-day Saint theology, would deepen into certitude as MacDonald matured. He chose to end his first series of *Unspoken Sermons* with this affirmation. The love developing within his marriage, toward his children, and the family that raised him was too Godlike to cease its loving pull after the grave. "What!" he wrote, "shall a man love his neighbor as himself, and must he be content not to know him in heaven? Better be content to lose our consciousness, and know ourselves no longer. What! Shall God be the God of the families of the earth, and shall the love that he has thus created towards father and mother, brother and sister, wife and child, go moaning and longing to all eternity; or worse, far worse, die out of our bosoms? Shall God be God, and shall this be the end? Ah, my friends! What will resurrection or life be to me, how shall I continue to love God as I have learned to love him through you, if I find he cares so little for this human heart of mine, as to take from me the gracious visitings of your faces and forms?[10]

"It Is Just So Good It Must Be True"

Long walks by the sea in contemplative intensity occupied much of his time at Aberdeen, but the questions could not be ignored. He was not searching so much for dogma, theory, or doctrine, but for the personality of God and his relation to that Being. He needed to know how he was to live his life. Like many who doubt, he could not simply throw everything away because of the inconsistencies he saw. Doing so would be intellectually dishonest, a mentally lazy act disguised often in the dress of objectivity. He must know, and know with certainty. He had met too many people who were fiercely content in proving their own positions as certain rather than openly searching for truth. As Joseph Smith once wrote of his own searching, many "were equally zealous in endeavoring to establish their own tenets and disprove all others" (Joseph Smith–History 1:9).

Eventually his conflicts resolved and he emerged from the dark, confusing days of doubt with a liberating view of his Father in Heaven and insight into His character matched by few on either the intellectual, spiritual, or the emotional level. It was born out of his own warm, dear father's personality. Surely God was like his own father magnified. He would later teach his own children the positive release and wonder of the goodness of God by saying, "It is just so good it must be true!"[11] Herein I have learned how important it is that we as earthly fathers reflect as well as we can the face of the divine Father. I wish I had discovered MacDonald earlier; I believe I would have mirrored this goodness better.

I have often said, after reading MacDonald, "I want to be judged by George MacDonald's God." Certainly it is his portrait of God, so consistent with so many of the Psalms and the personality of Jesus, to whom I pray. This loving God was the God of all. His compassionate commitment was for all. MacDonald sensed this from his childhood, which he came to trust, as children so often see into the heart of things with such clarity. This child's heart he maintained to his death. "I remember feeling as a child," he wrote late in his life, "that I did not care for God to love me if he did not love everybody: the kind of love I needed was essential to my nature . . . the love therefore that all men needed."[12]

Discovering God's nature led naturally to MacDonald's intense desire to teach what he discovered. Everything that deeply enters our life ultimately creates the desire to share; the ministry offered this opportunity. But even as he was studying to preach, some of his views attracted attention as bordering on the heretical. In the Congregational system, each assembly was free to choose their own minister. Clearly this path would not be easy to follow. He accepted a post at Arundel in southern England and with Louisa began his family and his ministry. All went well until his challenges to live what Jesus actually taught came a little too close to home for some in his congregation. If this was not enough, MacDonald, drawing upon his deeply held conviction of the love of God for all his children, began to suggest that a loving Father in Heaven would provide redemptive hope even for the heathen, the non-Christian, after death. These He would not condemn out of hand without the possibility of eventual salvation. The merciful hand of God would be held out continually, certainly to those ignorant of his Son's Atonement, but also to the sinner. He suggested that the phrase "life eternal" referred to the quality of a shared life with God, not a never-ending duration of time. Neither was the concept of hell necessarily infinite. Its purpose was redemptive, not punitive. Suffering was to bring one to Christ. Once that was accomplished, there was no need of its continuance. Christ had come to destroy sin, not merely punish it. My faith is always buttressed when

I see MacDonald perceiving what Joseph Smith confirmed through revelation (see D&C 19:6–12).

It didn't take long before the deacons of MacDonald's congregation launched a campaign against their new young minister. They tried to force him to resign by reducing his salary from 150 pounds a year to 115. This he accepted, not understanding their reasoning fully. When told of the real motive behind the offer he asked for a meeting of the entire congregation. The official record of the charges against him read in part, "We do sympathize with those who were dissatisfied with the statement from the pulpit 'that with the Heathen the time of trial does not (in his, the Revd. G. MacDonald's opinion) cease at their death,' which certainly implies a future state of probation. And this Church considers such a view is not in accordance with the Scriptures. . . . If on reflection he continues to hold and express such an opinion it is evident that it will cause serious difficulties in the Church."[13] Serious difficulties were what he wished to avoid if he could, but to deny what his soul told him was true was impossible.

Unable to alter his views of the mercy and justice of God and fearing his continued role as minister would cause divisions among the people of Arundel, MacDonald resigned and moved to Manchester. He wrote to his father in frustration, wishing that the meek, yearning, and inviting spirit of Christ in the Gospels would dominate in the interpretation of verses in the Epistles so often used to substantiate doctrines alien to a merciful and compassionate Lord. He knew he was straying from established doctrine, but was he moving farther or closer to the heart of God?

"AT THE GREAT WORLD'S CORE"

The next years were difficult for George and Louisa. Manchester was only a temporary home. They would move many times in the coming years, landing in places that included Algiers, a long stay in

London, and eventually Italy, where the warm air was healing for both himself and their children. His health was always tenuous at best. He suffered from lung problems endemic to his family that pushed him to the edge of death several times. The warm air of Italy beckoned and he found relief there in the last years of his life, but Italy also saw the death of some of his beloved children—Mary, Maurice, then Grace. He comforted himself with God's love. "It is well to say 'The Lord gave and the Lord hath taken away,' but it is not enough. We must add, And the Lord will give again. . . . He takes that he may give more closely—make more ours."[14] For all of us who have lost dear ones who are so interwoven into our souls, these words soothe with healing peace.

He tried tutoring, lecturing, substitute preaching, and finally writing. During these years of poverty the family (which in time included eleven children) often survived on the generosity of friends and last-minute gifts. The stigma of being removed from the pulpit was strong, but those years taught him which medium he should use for spreading the truths which continued to stir and grow in his heart. If the pulpit would not receive him, the printing presses were more neutral. He poured out his beloved truths in poetry, short stories, novels, fairy tales for children and adults—and "unspoken sermons." And the public responded! He dedicated one of his earliest works to his father for showing him through his gentle love what God was really like, augmented only by his own deep feelings for his own children:

> *Thou hast been faithful to my highest need;*
> *And I, thy debtor, ever, evermore . . .*
> *Yet most I thank thee, not for any deed,*
> *But for the sense thy living soul did breed*
> *That fatherhood is at the great world's core.*[15]

There was holiness, an awareness of the highest Fatherhood of all, in his writing that touched chords within. He awoke worship, lifted men's sights to nobler views. It was this inherent spiritual "goodness" that attracted C. S. Lewis a generation later and started him on his road from atheism to becoming the great defender of Christianity. Lewis called it "the sweet air blowing from the 'land of righteousness.'"[16] It was MacDonald's spiritual infusion into the land of imagination that would later blossom into Narnia and Middle Earth. "I know hardly any other writer who seems to be closer, or more continually close, to the Spirit of Christ Himself," Lewis wrote.[17] High praise from a man whose very name speaks of Christ's gentleness!

The known writers of the day became MacDonald's friends: Dickens, Lady Byron, Tennyson, Mark Twain, Longfellow, John Ruskin, and many others. Lewis Carroll had Louisa read to the MacDonald children the adventures of a young girl named Alice and received the family's enthusiastic encouragement. As the years rolled by, his lectures were packed, invitations constant, his books lauded, stressful years of poverty overcome. He was even invited to America, where he lectured to full houses until he dropped from exhaustion. In America, he was offered the opportunity of becoming the pastor of a church in New York for a salary of $20,000 per year, a considerable sum at the time, but he turned it down. He could not limit himself to one religious system. He had already seen what that did. His Father in Heaven's work was being done in other ways. He had found his voice!

Letting in Pure Light

MacDonald once wrote to a woman who was concerned about what she considered his loss of faith. He replied, "With all sorts of doubts I am familiar, and the result of them is, has been, and will be, a widening of my heart and soul and mind to greater glories of truth—the truth that is in Jesus. . . . For doubt is the hammer that breaks the windows clouded with human fancies, and lets in the pure light. . . . To Him I belong heart and soul and body, and he may do with me as he will—nay, nay—I pray him to do with me as he wills: for that is my only well-being and freedom."[18]

It is not doubt or questioning that is so damaging to faith, but what we do with them. MacDonald tuned the inner melodies of his mind and drew out of his deep pondering the profoundest truths about God. He could not conceive of a God who would cease speaking to his children, for how could love so respond? Therefore, the Bible was not the only word of God to his children. "A thousand questions will arise to which the Bible does not even allude. Has he indeed nothing to do with such? . . . No. Questions imply answers. He has put the questions in my heart; he holds the answers in his. I will seek them from him. I will wait, but not till I have knocked. I will be patient, but not till I have asked. I will seek until I find. He has something for me. My prayer shall go up unto the God of my life. Sad, indeed, would the whole matter be, if the Bible had told us everything God meant us to believe. . . . There is more hid in Christ than we shall ever learn, here or there either; but they that begin first to inquire will soonest be gladdened with revelation; and with them he will be best pleased."[19] Joseph Smith would agree! "God hides nothing. His very work from the beginning is *revelation*—a casting aside of veil after veil, a showing unto men of truth after truth. On and on, from fact to fact divine."[20]

MacDonald pondered about the commonly taught dignity of God, the monarch on high, almighty judge, creator of worlds, enthroned in majesty, but found his God in the images of the New Testament. "How terribly, then, have the theologians misrepresented God. . . . Brothers, have you found our king? There he is, kissing little children and saying they are like God. There he is at table with the head of a fisherman lying on his bosom, and somewhat heavy at heart that even he, the beloved disciple, cannot yet understand him well. The simplest peasant who loves his children and his sheep were . . . a true type of our God."[21]

This was a God one could approach in prayer and not only be listened to, but one who took our own desires and thoughts into account in his grand purposes and designs. This was a God who shared decisions with his children, cared about all their troubles and nourished their growth—decided nothing independent of them, wanting them to be part of the great work. He is omniscient, certainly, but omniscient in wisdom, omniscient in his openness to every possibility— knowing how to bring about all his ultimate designs, yet able to adapt to each child's prayer! "Anything large enough for a wish to light upon, is large enough to hang a prayer upon: the thought of him to whom that prayer goes will purify and correct the desire. . . . He lays no plans irrespective of his children; and, his designs being that they shall be free, active, live things, he sees that space be kept for them: they need room to struggle out of their chrysalis, to undergo the change that comes with the waking will, and to enter upon the divine sports and labors of children in the house and domain of their Father. *Surely he may keep his plans in a measure unfixed, waiting the free desire of the individual soul.*"[22]

MacDonald's God was a sharing God, perpetually inviting us to be part of his sweeping plan for the happiness of all children. Our prayers and hopes for each other were part of his plans. We were allowed to play roles in the drama of each other's souls and lift, with God at our sides, their lives and spirits. "But how if the eternal, limitless Love, the unspeakable, self-forgetting God-devotion, which, demanding all, gives all, should say, 'Child, I have been doing all I could; but now you are come, I shall be able to do more! Here is a corner for you, my little one: push at this thing to get it out of the way'! How if he should answer, 'Pray on, my child; I am hearing you. . . . I help and you help. I shall have you all safe home with me by and by!'"[23]

MacDonald was certain that one day we would address our Father in Heaven in open realization that we understood his giving heart so little. "Our God, we will trust thee. Shall we not find thee equal to our faith? One day, we shall laugh ourselves to scorn that we looked for so little from thee; for thy giving will not be limited by our hoping."[24] Yet there would be times when he could not grant, because we had no place to put what God desired to bestow. "There are good things God must delay giving until his child has a pocket to hold them—till he gets his child to make that pocket."[25]

"I Want to Get Good"

There was too much guilt in the world, too much unnecessary self-inflicted sorrow. This was not the will of the "cherisher of joy, the lord of laughter."[26] Straining for perfection was a rejoicing effort. MacDonald knew where to find solace that bloomed into gladness. "Come, then, sore heart, and see whether his heart cannot heal thine. He knows what sighs and tears are. . . . Brothers, sisters, we must get rid of this misery of ours. It is slaying us. It is turning the fair earth into a hell, and our hearts into its fuel. There stands the man who says he knows: take him at his word. Go to him who says in the might of his eternal tenderness and his human pity, 'Come unto me, all ye that labor and are heavy-laden, and I will give you rest.'"[27] Perfection was a mighty summit to climb. We must throw off the added weight of our own self-judging souls. What relief is here!

There was salvation in our efforts alone, for God takes all into account, and will judge us even "according to the desire of [our] hearts" (D&C 137:9). "No man can do yet what he tells him aright—but are you trying? *Obedience is not perfection, but trying. . . .* He takes the will in the imperfect deed, and makes the deed at last perfect."[28] It is often said the road to hell is paved with good intentions. This is probably true, but so is the road to heaven. We must walk it with gladness.

In MacDonald's God there was mercy sufficient for all, a mercy that could reach into the darkest regions of hopelessness and cry out for the return of the prodigal. Even hell itself would be emptied of all save those who utterly refused in the end to respond to his mercy. Referring to the Savior's last painful hours, his forgiving words from the cross, the unfeeling crowds, the mocking soldiers, even the betraying Judas, he wrote: "Here was sin dreadful enough surely—but easy for our Lord to forgive. All that excuse for the misled populace! Lord Christ be thanked for that! That was like thee! But must we believe that Judas, who repented even to agony, who repented so that his high-prized life, self, soul, became worthless in his eyes and met with no mercy at his own hand—must we believe that he could find no mercy in such a God? I think, when Judas fled from his hanged and fallen body, he fled to the tender help of Jesus, and found it. . . . I believe Jesus loved Judas even when he was kissing him with the traitor's kiss; and I believe that he was his Savior still."[29]

This level of mercy MacDonald knew intuitively and experientially through his own fatherhood. The imperfections and needs of eleven children taught him much. "How the earthly father would love a child who would creep into his room with angry, troubled face, and sit down at his feet, saying when asked what he wanted: 'I feel so naughty, papa, and I want to get good!' Would he say to his child: '. . . Go away, and be good, and then come to me?' And shall we dare to think God would send us away if we came thus, and would not be pleased that we came. . . . Would we not let all the tenderness of our nature flow forth upon such a child?"[30]

"BE THYSELF, AND ALL IS WELL"

MacDonald spent the last years of his life in the warm sunshine of Italy and finally went back to England. He buried another child, his oldest, Lilia, and then his own true Louisa. He wrote almost continuously until he was stilled by a stroke that took his speech. His silence lasted five more years, but he was not fearful of the final homeward journey nor of his Lord, who would greet him at the doorway. "God will be better to us than we think, however expectant we be,"[31] he once wrote to Louisa as a birthday greeting.

MacDonald knew instinctively that his Father in Heaven was easy to please, though he would not be satisfied until his children were all he desired them to be. We too often fail to understand this about God, focusing instead on the need to satisfy with personal perfection at the expense of the joy of pleasing in everyday obedience. His faith was as true as his words, for in his pondering on the nature of God he realized we could not imagine a God greater than He is. This he once prayed: "I see in my mind's eye, the little children clambering up to sit on the throne with Jesus. My God, art thou not as good as we are capable of imagining thee? Shall we dream a better goodness than thou hast ever thought of? Be thyself, and all is well."[32] These are the words of a faith tempered by life and polished to radiance by long years of reliance on the strength of unfailing love. He was God's child. God had been and always would be his Father; the Son had come to reveal that to us all. John, who knew so instinctively the soul of Jesus, simply testified, "God is love" (1 John 4:8).

There is poignancy in the years of his silent living, for always in his eyes there was a waiting look of expectation. When the door opened into his room, he would look up brightly for a moment, realize it was not Louisa, then return to his quiet inner world. When would she and his Lord come for him? He lived to see the turn of the new century, dying in 1905. What reunions awaited him only the power of his own rich imagination could describe, but we come close to understanding that moment of joy and what it must have meant to him in a letter he wrote later in his life: "There is a live heart at the centre of the lovely order of the Universe—a heart to which all the rest is but a clothing form—a heart that bears every truthful thought, every help-needing cry of each of its children, and must deliver them. All my life, I might nearly say, I have been trying to find that one Being, and to know him consciously present; hope grows and grows with the years that lead me nearer to the end of my earthly life; and in my best moods it seems ever that the only thing worth desiring is that his will be done."[33] The life search was over, the center found, the "one Being" now known in deepest intimacy—"Thy will be done," the grand echo of his life, the loving heart at the center of all things resting peacefully in the depths of his own.

I believe that God has always done,
Is always doing his best for every man;
That no man is miserable because God is forgetting him;
That he is not a God to crouch before,
But our father,
To whom the child-heart cries exultant,
"Do with me as thou wilt."[34]

CHAPTER TEN

"If I Leave All for Thee . . .":
Elizabeth Barrett Browning

London, England, and Florence, Italy
Nineteenth Century C.E.

It is nothing to me that my whole life
Shall be devoted to such a woman,—
Its only happiness will consist
In such a devotion.[1]
—Robert Browning

"Bro"

S HE HAD ONCE LOVED THE SEA. Reminiscences of quiet walks along its shore brought healing and serenity. Now she couldn't stand the sight or the sound of it. She had been brought from London to Torquay on the warmer coast of England for her health, which had been tenuous for years. In light of the present tragedy she only wanted to return to the house on Wimpole Street. The years at Torquay had been the hardest of her life. Her family called her "Ba," short for Baby, though she had been christened Elizabeth—Elizabeth Barrett Moulton Barrett. She signed her letters simply EBB.

The Barrett children were a close family, sufficient within themselves, exchanging endearing nicknames in their childhood. There was "Addles" for Henrietta, "Stormie" for Charles John because he had been born during a storm, "Sette" and "Occy" for Septimus and Octavius, names indicating the seventh and eighth child (and

Roman emperors). Poor Alfred was for some unknown reason called "Daisy," and George she teased with "Pudding." Arabella was simply shortened to "Arabel." All in all there were eleven children. Just plain "Sam" was full of fun and laughter and a perennial favorite, but Ba's closest, preferred, and most beloved of all her siblings, Edward, she just called "Bro." They were the two oldest and had relied on each other from their earliest years.

Bro was not just one of her brothers, all of whom she loved deeply, he was *the* brother. Now he was dead. The sea had taken him, and she felt it was her fault. Elizabeth had not wanted him to return to London without her and she could not depart until her health improved. "And once *he* held my hand," she recalled years later, "how I remember! & said that he 'loved me better than them all & that he *would not* leave me—till I was well.' . . . Ten days from that day the boat left the shore which never returned; never—& he *had* left me! gone! . . . And I was grateful to [my father] for not saying aloud what I said to myself in my agony, *If it had not been for you!*"[2]

"God Knows What Is Within"

Elizabeth was already acquainted with the separation that death brings to family members. Her little sister Mary had died when Elizabeth was of the impressionable age of eight. After having given birth to her twelfth child, Elizabeth's mother, Mary, who showed no signs of ill health, just a gradual weakening, died suddenly. Her mother's passing turned Elizabeth even more firmly toward Bro and her father. Sam's merry laughter was silenced by a fever while tending to the family's Jamaica plantations in February of 1840. In July 1840, only a few months later, Bro was gone.

He was sailing with his friends when a squall hit. No one knew exactly what happened, but a passing yacht saw the boat go down. Arriving on the scene a short time later, they saw nothing on the surface of the water, no sign of any life or debris. For days, hope lingered that Bro and his friends would return. Perhaps they swam to safety or would be found floating and still alive, but when the bodies washed up on the shore a few weeks later all the family fears were confirmed.

To love is to place the heart in a vulnerable position, to open it up to pain, and Elizabeth was born with a poet's soul. Love came naturally to her, but the experiences of her earlier life taught her to hang onto those close, guard her heart to further pain, devote herself to her father, and expect that life at best could give her only a measure of contentment.

"For years together," she wrote, "after what broke my heart at Torquay, I lived on the outside of my own life, blindly and darkly from day to day, as completely dead to hope. . . . Nobody quite understood this of me. . . . But God knows what is within."[3] Deep and abiding happiness was to be feared, for it could so easily turn to suffering. With her own health poor, the tenuous nature of living was a constant reminder. She huddled over her desk in a private room on Wimpole Street content with composing her poetry, coddling her pet dog, Flush, somewhat safe in her father's love and protective—though domineering and watchful—guardianship, feeling life had offered her all it could. She once wrote, "There is no kind of enjoyment which one can have on this side of the grave without paying its price in pain."[4]

A young woman feeling such pessimism is touched with an element of pathos and tragedy. Yet this she had come to believe. But providence had prepared for Elizabeth Barrett its deepest satisfaction and the fulfillment of her highest reaches of passionate yearning. To obtain it, however, would require sacrifices and courage born only in the wellsprings of a loving heart prepared to offer all in order to receive all. "Once I wished *not* to live," she wrote to a friend, "but the faculty of life seems to have sprung up in me again, from under the crushing foot of heavy grief."[5] The resiliency of the human soul and its innate desires for happiness, love, and fulfillment—the promise that they will always be possible—was still alive in Elizabeth and waiting, not only to spring up in her, but to blossom and fill her life with joy's fragrances. In time her very name would be associated with love's highest fulfillments.

CHILDHOOD

Elizabeth Barrett was born in 1806, the eldest child of Mary and Edward Moulton Barrett. Her life as a little girl was filled with the fullest joys of childhood. The large family lived near Ledbury, Herefordshire, the same area where Wilford Woodruff would convert large numbers of the United Brethren centering at Benbow's Farm near the Malvern Hills. Edward had a rather exotic new estate built for his wife and children far from the distractions of neighbors or society. It was a self-contained world, more than "off the beaten track," and this suited Elizabeth just fine. The outside world seemed not to exist in the isolation of the rolling countryside that surrounded the home. She had no longing for parties or gatherings such as those described in a Jane Austen novel. The estate was optimistically named "Hope End," the family supported by the profits from their Jamaica plantations. Edward was often in London, but his return was always a cause for joyful celebration.

Elizabeth spent days reading, playing with her many brothers and sisters, and, from a very early age, writing poetry. Her intellectual gifts were apparent from the beginning as she learned Latin, Greek, and even Hebrew. A trip to Paris with her mother resulted in assignments to write in French, yet Elizabeth was the center of fun for the other children, mothering them and creating new things to occupy their time, including plays, picnics, and camps outside. They were taught by their mother to help the poor and be aware of their responsibility to others. Novels were enjoyed and seriously commented on, especially those which described loving daughters in close relationships with their father.

When Bro left for school, Elizabeth began to feel the indignation of a girl who was encouraged to learn at home but denied an opportunity for more formal education. Her mind cried out for knowledge, but in her island of isolation near Ledbury the opportunity to communicate with others of active and alert mental seeking was limited. In this manner she passed the first fourteen years of her life. They were happy, active years, but this would all change with ill health from which she could seemingly never free herself.

The Upstairs Room on Wimpole Street

The happy, confident, somewhat tomboyish girl's troubles began with an illness her two sisters and she caught when she was fourteen. Henrietta and Arabella both recovered, but Elizabeth continued to suffer with pain, weakness, and an accompanying depression no doctor could confidently diagnose or treat. Her lungs, heart, spine, and overall constitution all seemed affected. Retreats to other parts of the country, the seaside, changes of doctors, and months suspended in a spine crib brought no long-lasting improvement. In time she increasingly saw herself as an invalid, confined to the house and her own private room, rarely going out and eventually needing opium in the form of laudanum to sleep, prescribed for her when she was fifteen. It would haunt her life until the day she died.

Her illness became somewhat self-fulfilling, prompted by her own hesitations, closeted lifestyle, and the solicitous and increasingly protective dominations of her father. She suffered from almost constant "congestion," which could cause her lungs to hemorrhage. The deaths in her family and her own frailty made her cautious, guarded, and somewhat distrustful of life, since a disappointment could be just around the corner. Better to avoid the corners altogether if possible.

Social interaction both repelled and frightened her. In this she was like her father. They shared their own type of societal shyness. Her family was her refuge, along with a few close friends with whom she communicated mostly through letters, though they would occasionally visit the inner sanctum of her private room. Inactivity had weakened her muscles, and lack of fresh air in her room had further stressed her lungs. Strong black coffee got her going in the morning and opium doses in the night brought her rest.

But her poetry! Here all the passionate nature and creative genius of her heart and mind could pour out. It was "the very soul of my being."[6] Though she did not crave fame or celebrity status, she had a growing satisfaction in the knowledge that her writing was becoming widespread and admired. It was during these years that the Barretts moved to a house on Wimpole Street in London. Elizabeth was now thirty-two and her life patterns set. Thus she lived and was content to do so, though she nourished a silent longing to travel, especially to Italy. Yet spread through it all was a sense that she was missing life's core experiences and that time would not allow her long to discover them.

Edward Barrett came to believe in an Old Testament view of fatherhood. His word was law and to be obeyed. In the beginning he was not so tyrannical, and loved his children, but the idea that they might have lives of their own to live outside of his tight family bonds was more and more unacceptable. All they needed they should find in each other. Besides, the world was a corrupt place and it was his duty to shield his children from it. He prayed daily with Elizabeth. He was a benevolent master, but a master nonetheless, and one that bordered on tyranny. The subject of marriage in particular was avoided. No man or woman could be right for his children, much to the heartbreak of some. Henrietta fell in love with a young man, but Edward would hear nothing of it. A scene erupted that Elizabeth never forgot, her sister's knees hitting the floor, desolated and pleading.

Edward felt calm, however, with Elizabeth's condition and love. She was too pure and faithful in her love for him to ever consider forming another attachment. For years, this was the accepted understanding between them. Besides, she was an invalid, just a little whisper of a woman, a flame one seemingly could extinguish with a breath. In the language of the time she was a spinster, approaching her fortieth birthday, the possibilities for a loving relationship with a man seemingly out of the equation life had granted her. She had consciously decided she would never marry. She waited instead for death to take her with the next painful coughing in her lungs. "It was a lonely life. . . . Books and dreams were what I lived in. . . . And so time passed, and passed."[7] But that was all before a letter arrived and Robert Browning entered her world.

"I Love Your Verses with All My Heart"

It all began with a poem written by Elizabeth called "Lady Geraldine's Courtship," in which she praised three of the poets of her age—Wordsworth, Tennyson, and the newcomer on the stage of Victorian authors, Robert Browning. Though she did not expect a response from any of them, Robert picked up his pen and wrote to her an amazing letter. Was it a love letter? How could that be possible? Yet she read Robert's opening, "I love your verses with all my heart, dear Miss Barrett." But there was more to come, as Robert's words aimed more directly and his feelings surfaced. "I do, as I say, love these verses with all my heart—and I love you too."[8] This was surely the surface playful posturing of a romantic man who shared her own love of the poetic muse, nothing more. Or was it? The letter was dated January 10, 1845.

They exchanged letters over the next weeks, each realizing they had found another who was sympathetic and understanding of all their deepest feelings, thoughts, and hopes. They would write 574 letters in a little less than two years. A relaxed, intimate, friendly attitude permeates the letters from the earliest correspondence and increases into deep trust. They began to share what had remained locked inside for years. Elizabeth believed the exchanges were sufficient in themselves; however, Robert desired to meet Elizabeth. This threw her into distress, for few ever invaded the privacy of her single-room existence. Her contact with men had been confined primarily to her eight younger brothers, her father, and the older gentlemen with whom she corresponded. Here was a man six years her junior who shared her passion for the rhyming line and beauty of expression, a man confident in the outside world of society that she had shunned throughout her life.

And, though she did not yet know it, here was a man whose heart and soul rang with the same intense passion of loving and living she did not yet know was capable of expression in her own allotted existence. The letters were so consoling, so important to her. If they met would he be disappointed? She was better on paper; would face-to-face contact end it all? He sensed her fears and tried to calm her. Nothing could change his feelings. She could trust him. Finally she wrote that he could come if he so desired, but warned him, "There is nothing to see in me; nor to hear in me."[9] She was only five feet one inch tall, wasted by sickness, slight of frame, with a thin, dark complexion, long black curled hair, and dark, brownish-green eyes. What would Robert think of her? The date was set for a Tuesday. "Well!" Elizabeth wrote, "We are friends till Tuesday—and after, perhaps."[10] It was May, a month of promise and renewing of nature, a green month of future harvests to come. She would look back on that day and call it, "my great Compensation Day."[11]

Robert was equally attached to his family, but his father was not so suffocatingly all-encompassing in his love. Robert Browning also had never loved a woman and believed he would never find one to whom he could completely give himself. His poetry was his bride, as Elizabeth's poetry was her husband. He was more direct, more sure of what he desired. Elizabeth's uncertainty, fear of what her love's affect on her father would be, and vacillations put up barriers all along the way. She doubted that Robert's love could be of long duration considering the circumstances of her life. Happiness was courting Elizabeth, had come unbidden into her presence. She didn't know how to grasp it without Robert's help, but help he would, patiently and selflessly. He would pull her out of her undeclared loneliness and allow all that was beautiful within her to emerge.

Footsteps on the Stairs

Robert did not know what to expect as he walked down Wimpole Street, flowers from his mother's garden in hand. His image of Elizabeth was of a slight woman, invalided, wasted from the cruelty of perpetual illness, permanently disabled with an injured spine. But he was confident. She awaited him with apprehension on the sofa, still dressed in black since the drowning of Bro. How could he possibly find her pretty? She heard his step on the stair: what would the opening door bring? An hour later she knew an elation never expected. Happiness was inviting her forward, urging her to lean into life, and she would not turn away.

Robert was more sure than ever and wrote asking for another visit on the following Tuesday. This was granted and Robert, with his always quick penchant for action, allowed his passion to move to the front. He seized the initiative and wrote her an unbelievable letter. Would she marry him and would she do so now? It shocked Elizabeth and was the only letter of the 574 she burned—much to our loss. He could call again, but marriage was not to be discussed. Who was she to be so desirable to this well-dressed younger man? They could talk of literature, London, anything but what pressed urgently on Robert's mind. And there was her father. The very thought of him terrified her. No! It would not do. Edward Barrett would never allow it. If Robert spoke "so wildly" again, *I must not . . . I WILL not see you again.*"[12]

Robert understood he had made a mess of things, but continued visits restored the easy relationship between the two. Letters became more intimate in nature. Elizabeth in time knew that marriage was at the end of the pathway they were walking, but it frightened her. How could she ever confront her father? Once when he was there at the same time as Robert, she said, "I was looking at Papa's face as I saw it through the floor."[13] How could she leave him? It would be "dreadful, dreadful."

Robert soothed her, instilled confidence in her. Her health improved under the lifting power of his love and the happiness she felt in his presence. She walked of her own power down the stairs instead of being carried by her brothers, to their shocked and speechless stares. She must get well—so much depended on her now. When she ventured outside just short of the one year mark in their love, she picked a flower and sent it to Robert, with the triumphant message, "Look what is inside of this letter—look! I gathered it for you to-day when I was walking. . . . Are you surprised?"[14] She wrote to a close friend that she was "growing and growing just like the trees—it is miraculous, the feeling of sprouting life in me and out of me—and now I begin to sleep and to look altogether like another person."[15]

All of nature was a wonder to her. "And to stand under a tree & feel the green shadow of the tree! . . . I seemed to feel the green shadow through & through me, till it went out at the soles of my feet and mixed with the other green below."[16] She was in love; perhaps more important, she knew she was loved, and that changes one. It is one of the deepest discoveries one can make in life—the knowledge that the woman or man you love loves you! It is helpful for us to remember as we visualize these two people that they were not flighty teenagers, rushing like Romeo and Juliet into tragedy. They were not young impassioned romantics in their twenties. They were mature adults, denied in younger days what they were now discovering with such release.

But then, they were also both poets sharing the poetic soul. Julia Markus, who wrote an excellent biography of the Brownings, described them well when she said, "A love relationship exists on balances, as well as shared sympathies."[17] They would demonstrate the power of that combination admirably throughout their life together—one that, unfortunately, would be all too short.

"My Election Is Made"

Robert visited once—and often twice—a week when Mr. Barrett was not at home for almost two years until it was unbearable for him. He pushed her to find a way to merge their lives more deeply than ink and one hour visits could offer. He made her restless, thirsting for change, open to escape into the fresher air of life to break the confines she herself had helped to erect. He awoke in her a renewed desire and tentative belief that happiness, happiness beyond what she believed she could know or was even worthy of, perhaps, just perhaps, was within her grasp. He eased her fears that he would in time tire of her, "My own Ba!—My election is made, or God made it for me,—and is irrevocable. I am wholly yours. I see you have yet to understand what that implies."[18]

Happiness and love are effective cures and Elizabeth thrived in their care, ready at last for the sacrifice and break she knew she would have to make. Unknown to Robert she had written a series of sonnets to him over the course of their letters. One of them simply asked, "If I leave all for thee, wilt thou exchange / And be all to me?"[19]

Leaving all would include her father. The thought frightened her to the point of paralysis. She had vivid memories of the scene the family had witnessed when her sister Henrietta wished to go out with a young man. Elizabeth assured him that her father would rather see her dead than married. Their solution was a secret marriage and escape to Italy. This troubled Robert because he dearly wished his own parents and sister to be present at their wedding, but he gave in to Elizabeth's distress and desire for secrecy. If her father knew what they were planning it would be terrible. Faced with the choice of Robert or Father she would choose Robert, of course, but her courage would come more easily if Robert was her husband and her father was told of the marriage when she was already on her way to Italy. A face-to-face confrontation was simply beyond her courage. Secrecy and a private marriage (not an elopement), was the only way for them. "Remember that I shall be *killed*—it will be so infinitely worse than you can have an idea," she wrote, expressing her worst nightmare: the discovery of their love and plans by her father.[20] Yet veined within those fears was guilt and real concern for what her departure would do to her father.

"I will go for a licence today," Robert wrote, "and we can be married on Saturday. . . . Your words first and last . . . have been that you could not fail me—you will not . . ." Elizabeth responded, "I shall not fail you—I do not. I will not."[21] The die was cast. There would be no bright wedding dresses, bridesmaids, flowers, or celebrations. There would be no announcements, no congratulatory wishes for their happiness, no gifts. There would be only Robert, only Elizabeth—that was more than enough.

ROBERT'S "BA"

After two years their happiness could not have been higher, Elizabeth confided in her maid Elizabeth Wilson. On the morning of the twelfth of September, 1846, Elizabeth and Wilson walked down Wimpole Street towards the church of St. Marylebone Parish. Waiting for her were Robert and James Silverthorne, a friend to act as witness. In a quiet ceremony viewed by only two people and the priest performing the marriage, Elizabeth Barrett and Robert Browning formed the eternal unit still celebrated as one of the most loving couples in history. She could call him husband, and he could now embrace her as his wife. She was *his* "Ba" now, and that is what he always called her. There was no music, no feasting, no procession among friends and family, but no woman was happier. "The many, many women who have stood where I stood and to the same end, not one of them all perhaps, not one perhaps, since that building was a church, has had reasons strong as mine for an absolute trust and de-votion towards the man she married—not one!"[22]

But their plan would not allow them to walk off together. Departure, honeymoon, and being completely alone for the first time in their lives would have to wait. They exited the church, climbed into two different cabs, and went their own ways, each to their home. A tense week of planning surrounded them as Robert arranged trans-portation to the Channel and then on to Paris, and in time Italy. The most difficult part still remained. It was suffocating living in the Barrett house. "It is dreadful . . . to have to give pain here by a voluntary act—for the first time in my life."[23] Elizabeth sat for the last time in her room, the room that had determined the boundaries of her world for so many years, and composed the most critical letters of her life—those to her friends, brothers and sisters, and, of course, her father. "With the exception of this act," she wrote to him, "I have submitted to the least of your wishes all my life long—Set the life against the act, & forgive me, for the sake of the daughter you once loved."[24] Would it be enough? She had not felt she could tell anyone, so that they could remain innocent of helping her marry Robert and thus not open to her father's fury. She posted the letters to arrive after she and Robert had left and would be too far a distance for anyone to stop their flight. She packed light so that no one would suspect what she was contemplating. But she had to have his letters, those words of openness, the fresh breezes of his emotions she had pored over so many times.

Robert had always known exactly what he wanted. He wanted Elizabeth. He wanted her with the first letter and first visit. Frail, delicate, dressed in black, vulnerable, awaiting (as her own words affirmed) only death's approach, closeted in the dark shadows of her room, he wanted her. He wanted her at the conclusion of almost two years of waiting and dreaming. He wanted her as he saw her clutching Wilson's steadying arm before the church where he waited for her. He never entertained second thoughts. Dark haired, dark eyed, diminutive, thin, self-assured only in her letters, her poems, and his love—he would always want her. She had to bring those letters—the letters that provide for us today the memorial and inspiration of their togetherness. "Your letters to me I take with me, let the 'ounces' cry aloud, ever so. I *tried* to leave them, & I could not. That is, they would not be left: it was not my fault—I will not be scolded."[25] Then she slipped into the package with her precious letters the sonnets she had written, so beautifully portraying all he meant to her, all he had saved her from, the poems whose existence were yet unknown to Robert, the ink-and-paper testimony of her love for him—her *Sonnets from the Portuguese.*

"Riding an Enchanted Horse"

Their flight, crossing of the Channel, and arrival in Paris taxed Elizabeth, but even exhaustion and fears of relapsing into sickness could not lessen her wonder. "Living as in a dream," she wrote, "loving & being loved better everyday—seeing near in him, all *that* I seemed to see afar. Thinking with one thought, pulsing with one heart. . . . It is like riding an enchanted horse."[26] These early days of elevated joy were only tempered by the knowledge that when they arrived in Orléans, letters would be awaiting her from her family. Of these she was afraid. They were her "death warrant."[27] When she received them she asked to be alone. The letter from her father was as she expected. She was disinherited, for she had "sold [her] soul," and would remain out of his affections and thoughts forever. "They were very hard letters from dearest Papa and dearest George . . . I do not seem to myself to have deserved that full cup."[28] There was simply no more Elizabeth *Barrett*. Her brothers were also outraged at her behavior. That hurt deeply, for she had hoped they would understand and had asked George to soften the blow for her father. Only her sisters and a few friends' letters were kind. She felt the balm of their joy for her in the soothing words.

Well, that was that. She was Elizabeth *Browning* now. The old life was truly dead. She was born anew and into a world of uncompromising love. A bright life awaited her; Italian sunlight awaited her. Her life would now be a world of places as well as writing, of doing as well as thinking, of being loved as well as loving. Robert spoke to her for hours, calming and comforting the blow, promising he would win back her family's affections. "It is strange," Elizabeth reflected later, "that anyone so brilliant should love *me*,—but true and strange it is . . . and it is impossible for me to doubt it any more."[29]

She wrote one poem during these early days of bliss. They were in Pisa. The abolitionist movement in America asked for a poem against slavery. Elizabeth's family fortune came from Jamaica plantations whose profits were drawn from the labors and abuses of slaves. She believed she had slave blood from the Moulton side of the family as she explained once to Robert: "Cursed we are from generation to generation!"[30] She was hostile to the system that abused black women in particular, which resulted in her own distant African blood. She was deeply anti-slavery, even after the laws terminating British slavery caused serious financial problems for her father, resulting in the loss of Hope End. She picked up her pen and wrote a ballad with passion. Robert's own father, also a product of Jamaican slave owners, was so revolted by the system after having visited Jamaica, he renounced his claim on his family, the possibility of a more easy living, and went to work for a bank as a clerk. Thus Robert and Elizabeth were also bound together by a similar aversion to one of the chief iniquities of the age. Throughout her life, Elizabeth would champion the cause of those who faced tyranny, certainly women, but also the establishment of a freer and more united Italy. She became their poetic voice, as passionate an Italian as any born in Florence or Rome.

Robert hoped the warm air, sunshine, and moderate climate of Italy would ease Elizabeth's persistent coughing and weakened lungs. Her health dramatically improved as they settled in Florence. Everything thrilled her—the places, the people, the scenery. "So now ask me again," she wrote to a friend, "if I enjoy my liberty as you expect. My head goes round sometimes, that is all. I never was happy before in my life."[31] Elizabeth endured four miscarriages, one almost killing her, but between them, a new element of love entered into her life as she gave birth to a robust boy who ended up, in true Barrett fashion, with the nickname "Pen."

Through the years she wrote numerous letters to her father, hoping always for reconciliation, for forgiveness. "He is my father. I would kiss his hands & feet at any moment."[32] He never responded, and Elizabeth wondered if he had even read them. In the warmer summer months the Brownings took trips into the countryside. She wrote poetry, read novels, doted on Pen, fussed over Robert, and consulted with him about finances and their son's education. She laughed in delight watching her husband desperately trying to master the spinning of a top for Pen's amusement. She composed reams of letters, made new friends, engaged in political as well as literary discussions, exercised, ate heartily, diminished her dosage of opium (which Robert wanted her to quit eventually), and in general lived a life she had never dreamed possible in her former days on Wimpole Street. They enjoyed weeks in Paris, the Alps, Venice, Rome, and finally back to London. Would her father see her and her son? Family was as strong in her as ever. They took rooms just a few hundred yards from the old residence on Wimpole Street. Robert wrote to Mr. Barrett an engaging letter asking for acceptance. He received a curt reply. For Elizabeth there was nothing—only the return of a bundle of never-opened letters, the letters she had written to her father over the years of her marriage. She was devastated, but pulled closer to Robert, "the tenderest and noblest of human hearts," and survived.[33]

The damp climate of England exacerbated her coughing, so Robert took her south again. Edward Barrett never forgave Elizabeth—and cut off in like manner her sister Henrietta and her brother Alfred when they married. He wrote her a hard, unnatural, condemning letter only once. That was all. He never spoke to her again, never wrote again, saw his grandson Pen only once and turned away. He died, still estranged, in 1857.

Sonnets from the Portuguese

Robert had his own crucible to face in the death of his mother. This pain Elizabeth knew, but commented she did not feel she had experienced grief at the depth Robert did. When nothing she could do would pull him out of his depression, she presented him with the forty-four sonnets she had written during their secret courtship. Perhaps they would help? They were deeply personal; Robert had once remarked in passing that he was not in favor of personal poetry or "putting one's love into verse."[34] She guarded them for the first years of her marriage without once letting Robert know of the depth of feeling she had poured out to him as he was freeing her from her former life's limitations.

"Do you know," she began, "I once wrote some sonnets about

you?" She then gave him the small bundle of poems. "There they are, if you care to see them."[35] She was tentative, hesitant, waiting for her husband's response, trying not to betray how much they meant to her. There is sweet poignancy in this moment that touches us in a wondrous way. He read them and fathomed the "depth and breadth and height / My soul can reach" of his wife's love—a love that reached "for the ends of being and ideal Grace." That love rested comfortably in "the level of everyday's / Most quiet need, by sun and candlelight." It soothed her "old griefs," and fulfilled her "childhood's faith."[36] Everyone should be loved to such a degree. Everyone should love in kind. He had healed her from hiding in the room at the top of the stairs, anticipating her own death; now she pulled him out of the sorrows and pain of his own loss.

Fifteen years they shared life. She had learned how to live it. "The secret of life is in full occupation, isn't it? This world is not tenable on other terms."[37] They rejoiced in each other's published works, disagreed about spiritualism (Robert thinking it was all bunk and Elizabeth enthusiastic to believe), delighted in Pen, visited family, dreamed of going to Egypt, mourned the loss of friends, but the old weaknesses began to last longer and Elizabeth's ability to fight back diminished. She had once indicated to her sister Arabel that in spite of the healthier climate of Italy, "you know my cough is always *there*, waiting like a lion in his den & ready to work on provocation." No matter what they did, Elizabeth was always living under the dark shadow. Yet she had learned to look beyond dying. "I look OVER death—& upwards."[38] Within the scope of that upward view she always saw Robert. Theirs was an eternal love. Both were convinced they would be together after death. When she did die, Robert wrote Dante's words from *Convito* in her Bible and incorporated them into one of his poems years later: "Thus I believe, thus I affirm, thus I am certain it is, that from this life I shall pass to another, there, where that lady lives of whom my soul was enamoured."[39]

"Beautiful"

In the summer of 1861, she complained of a sore throat that quickly grew into the protracted coughing she had known for so many years. She grew somewhat listless, a bit confused, "dozed constantly,"[40] needing to be carried by Robert from bed to sofa, but was uncomplaining. "She was cheerful as ever, with voice all but extinct."[41] Pen asked her repeatedly if she was feeling better. She replied, "Perhaps a little better."[42] Robert sat up with her through the night watching. She had so often rallied that everyone including Elizabeth believed she would this time also. Robert had strong chicken jelly made and encouraged her to eat some when she awoke in the middle of the night. She drifted in and out of sleep, but each time she awoke and heard her husband's voice she smiled at him and said she was better. The doctor had increased her morphine for the night and she stirred a little past three talking incoherently of a "steamer" which was very "comfortable" and Robert had done "right not to wait."[43] He felt her feet. They were cold though the night was sultry and the room warm. With the help of their Italian nurse, Robert brought hot water and bathed them, then sent for the doctor. "Well you do make an exaggerated case of it!" she told him gently, then feeling the effects of the warm water said, "My hands too."[44] She seemed to slip into semi-consciousness or half-sleep, which troubled him. Drawing close, he asked her, "You know me?" She took him in her arms, smiled, her face peaceful and joyful, and answered, "My Robert—my heavens, my beloved." She kissed him, holding on to him, then kissed him again, and again. "Our lives are held by God," she whispered. He tried to make her more comfortable, but she held him still. "God bless you," she repeated over and over again. "God bless you," kissing him continually "with such vehemence." He laid her softly onto the pillow, but she reached her hands to him and kissed the air. Still

Robert did not understand she was dying. "Are you comfortable?" he asked. "Beautiful," she answered.[45]

It was her last word. He took her into his arms again supporting her head. She tried to cough, but the struggle was faint. Her face contracted a tiny bit, then all was silent. It was the nurse Annunziata who finally said in Italian, "*Quest' anima benedetta è passata!*"[46] (This blessed spirit has passed!) Robert looked at her. She appeared so young now. The pain was gone and her face looked rounded and full—"how perfectly beautiful!"[47] Perhaps she also did not know she was dying. There was comfort for him in that. She passed happy, smiling, in the arms of the man to whom she had given her soul so many brief years ago when she read the words contained in his first letter, "I love your verses with all my heart, dear Miss Barrett. . . . And I love you too."

After her death, Robert wrote to his sister Sarianna while Elizabeth was still lying in the other room of their Florence home. "She is with God, who takes from me the life of my life in one sense,—not so, in the truest. . . . I shall live out the remainder [of my life] in her direct influence, endeavouring to complete mine . . . imperfect now, but so as to take the good she was meant to give me. . . . I shall live in the presence of her, in every sense, I hope and believe— so that so far my loss is not *irreparable*—but the future is nothing to me now, except inasmuch as it confirms and realizes the past."[48] The writing became painful and he closed, "I shall now go and sit with herself—my Ba, for ever."

Their love was *beautiful*, and it was rare. They shared what God desires we all share—the giving and receiving of love at its most refined levels. "Robert had a gift for me," she wrote her sister after years of marriage, "after the precious love undim through all these years."[49] Theirs was a love sanctified in gratitude, certainly for Elizabeth, but equally for Robert, in that neither one of them expected to know it, and therefore found it more welcome when it came. But experience it they did and in a manner that is so beautiful, so exceptional, as Elizabeth knew when she drew her last breath—as Robert knew when he wept with a close friend and simply cried, "I want her, I want her!"[50]

Robert wrote one letter to her brother, then stopped, pleading that he could not write the others as it was impossible for him to go over the details again. "I must write no more letters like this."[51] Elizabeth was buried in the English cemetery in Florence, where her grave can be seen to this day. It is a moving experience to stand beside it and reflect on her life and her love. Robert Browning returned to England with Pen. He never remarried, but went on to write some of his most powerful poetry—as Elizabeth believed he could and willed that he would. When someone suggested, proposed really, that he marry again, he strongly affirmed that his heart and soul was buried in Florence. Elizabeth knew it would be thus. Yet the gift they gave to the world was not contained in rhymed meters or beautiful imagery; it is in the love that ran pure as sunlight between them. It is in the hope of fulfillment and joyful giving their lives seem to promise us all if we can learn the sharing of the heart as they did.

Listen for the Footsteps

We never know what life will bring to us with the next ticking of the clock—the death of a most beloved brother in a squall at sea or the sound of a loving man's eager footsteps echoing on the stairs, climbing to reach us. The letters life sends us may contain undreamed-of love, past-hope fulfillments, or feared tragedy. What Elizabeth has taught me is never to doubt the possibility of the footsteps on the stairs, even those leading to heaven. Life is, at heart, simply "beautiful." As she testified: "Dancing is better for the soul than fasting, I believe," and "cheerfulness was a christian duty . . . the proof of a higher spiritual life."[52] I have a lovely friend who coined the expression "the unexpected life," a life she is living as am I since the death of my wife, Laurie. Neither one of us received what we anticipated. I think the first time I heard that expression, I assumed immediately that a life that is "unexpected" was by definition the undesired one—the dreams unfulfilled, the anticipated joys fading with the passing years. But Robert's and Elizabeth's love cry out against that perception. The unexpected life can be filled with promise, of answers beyond our dreams; we must never stop believing this. With Shackleton-like optimism we can await it. Around the corner may be an upset boat and a missing brother, but it may also be the beginning of 574 letters filled with emotion, elation, hopes, and fulfillment long since abandoned in the often invaliding nature of our personal fate.

"I always imagine that I was sent on the earth for some purpose!" Elizabeth wrote. "I know, I understand not how this is but I feel it to my heart core & so strong is this feeling that it amounts almost to presentiment!"[53] Perhaps, she thought, her purpose would be to change society or to "save by my death my country. . . . to suffer in the cause of freedom." But she joined with Robert in presenting to us love at its highest level and that oh-so-important hope we must never let die within us, so that happiness, however far or impossible it seems to be, may yet come into our lives. Her son, Pen, remembered Elizabeth as a woman full of happiness, which she spread into the world around her. This is how we must also remember her and try to live in grateful love and joy.

"EDUCATING INTO GLADNESS"

Elizabeth also wrote that people need "educating into gladness."[54] What a wonderful phrase! It is an idea she has bequeathed to us that we must try to fulfill. Joy, happiness, laughter, and optimism are not always inherent in our personalities or the circumstances of mortality. We are born to these things as part of our inheritance from God, but they also need to be educated into us. It is especially tragic when they are educated out of us, as they were Elizabeth early in her life. "Nothing is more true to me than that *gloom* is an immoral thing," she told her sister just before she died, "and as for solitude, I *know* it to be full of temptation."[55]

It is not sufficient that we simply wait for gladness in beyond-the-veil compensations as she once did, fearful of feeling happiness lest it be taken. Here and now the possibilities reach out to us. Some we must search for, stretch out towards—as Robert wrote: "Ah, but a man's reach should exceed his grasp, / Or what's a heaven for?"[56] Yet some come to us through the gracious gift of living. The unexpected life may be the best life we can imagine—not the shattered one. Goodness can be so mildly and gently given that we fear to awaken from the lovely dream we have entered. The last may be the best and eclipse all the pain and frustrations of the first. Just before her quiet marriage in the St. Marylebone Parish church, Elizabeth hinted to a friend what it all meant to her. "God intended me compensation even in the world and that the latter time would be better for me than the beginning."[57] Elizabeth certainly created some of the problems she struggled with, but then don't we all? In a number of areas of her life she was far from exemplary. In the final account, however, none of it mattered. Much of what we may presently believe to be impossible may still happen.

The human ear must ever be tuned for happiness climbing the stairs toward us. Robert Browning received from life exactly what he most desired from it, and Elizabeth Barrett accepted as a wondrous gift love she never anticipated, could not have conceived she was worthy of or that was even possible. Both knew they were blessed in each other and could appreciate and feel gratitude and happiness at the deepest levels. "I, who by a long sorrowfulness & solitude, had sunk into the very ashes of selfhumiliation—Think how I must have felt to have listened to [words of love] from such a man. A man of genius

& miraculous attainments . . . but of a heart & spirit beyond them all!"[58]

"TILL THE RE-UNION FOREVER"

My wife, Laurie, introduced me to Elizabeth Barrett Browning. As an English major, I had read and loved Robert's poems especially for their Christian affirmations, but Elizabeth, though very popular in her own time, has been less well-known than her husband, and I had largely ignored her. For her high school graduation, Laurie's grandparents gave her Elizabeth's *Sonnets from the Portuguese*. Since the day she showed them to me after our marriage, the Brownings—both of them—became a part of our own relationship. When she was dying, I whispered their words into her ear, and the last thing I did before veiling her face was to repeat to her one of Elizabeth's sonnets. I anticipate she heard it reaching to her through the curtained partition that now separates us. I too know what it means to cry out, "I want her!" Yet Elizabeth would undoubtedly respond, "All our grief is foolish, if we could see aright." Personally, I must not "disturb her where she is, by unreasonable sadness,—but rather by faith & assurance draw her 'nearer & nearer.' And still nearer, till the re-union forever."[59] It is difficult at such moments to know what to say, the feelings run so deep, but Elizabeth rescued me and placed hope in my soul and words in my mouth: the words of love I believe Laurie heard and accepted and understood and sent back again. Eve testified that it is necessary for us to pass through sorrow that we may know what true joy is.

Perhaps the greatest knowledge we gain as we "pass through" is the assurance of how precious it is to have someone to love as Robert loved Elizabeth and Elizabeth loved Robert. To gain that understanding is worth the grieving and the deep poignancy of those last moments in Florence as I'm sure the Brownings would affirm. And there is always the hope Elizabeth so wondrously expressed in one of the last of her beautiful *Sonnets from the Portuguese,* the verses I whispered to my Laurie:

> *I love thee with the breath,*
> *Smiles, tears, of all my life!—and, if God choose,*
> *I shall but love thee better after death.*[60]

THE HAPPINESS OF THE GREAT OCEAN

China
Fourth Century B.C.E.

The whole world tends to see one aspect
And think they have grasped the whole of it. . . .
The hundred schools . . . have their points
And each has its time of usefulness.
Though this is true,
Nevertheless not one of them
Covers the whole truth[1]
—CHUANG TZU

THE FROG AND THE TURTLE

THERE IS A PARABLE TOLD BY a Chinese Taoist sage named Chuang Tzu about a frog and a turtle. The frog lives in a well and is perfectly content with his life. The turtle has come from the great Eastern Ocean and is invited by the frog to share the well. "I have a great time!" the frog says, "I leap on the well wall, or I go down in the well, stepping along the broken bricks. When I enter the water, I float with it supporting my chin, feet up; on the mud, I dig my foot deep in. I look about me at the larvae, crabs and tadpoles and there is none that is as good as I. To have complete control . . . and not to wish to move but to enjoy the old well, this is great! Dear Sir, why don't you come down and see me sometime?" Being gracious, kindly, and patient, the turtle made an attempt to accommodate the frog's enthusiasm. He was not disdainful, aloof, nor judgmental, but he had a wider knowledge. "The turtle of the Eastern Ocean tried, but before he had put his left foot into the well, his right knee was stuck. At this he paused, shuffled backwards and then began to speak about the ocean. 'A distance such as a thousand miles doesn't come close to describing its length, nor a depth of a thousand leagues describe its deepness. In the time of Yu, nine years in every ten there were floods, but this did not raise the ocean an inch. In the time of Tang, seven years in every eight there were droughts, but this did not lower the ocean shore an inch. Nothing changes these waters, neither in the short term nor in the long term; they neither recede nor advance, grow larger nor smaller. This is the great happiness of the Eastern Ocean.'" Upon hearing this, the frog was amazed and filled with wonder.[2]

We are not told what the frog did as a result of his conversation with the turtle, but hopefully his curiosity was stirred with the desire to experience some of what his friend shared. Truth, beauty, and goodness are like the ocean—vast and deep. And, of course, there is also an ocean of lives waiting to be discovered. We can be content as was the frog with his well, but I think the Lord would have us test the larger waters. There is so much to wonder about, so much to learn in the lives of our Father in Heaven's children. The opportunity to be edified is limitless. As Chuang Tzu concludes, we don't want to "examine Heaven through a narrow tube or use an awl to explore the whole earth. Such tools are too small, aren't they?"[3] We don't want to spend so much energy on the fixed foot to the exclusion of the searching one, splashing in the well when the ocean awaits us. We must find balance. We must reach outward and draw a larger circle. Occasionally we must swim in the great Eastern Ocean.

I have wanted to write this book for many years, but have always hesitated. I don't consider myself proficient and knowledgeable enough to write on the level each life deserves. How do you put ten lives that have profoundly touched your own into a single book of a few hundred pages? These are character sketches at best, which try to draw lessons for living I believe can be beneficial to us all. If I have generated an interest in any one of these men and women I would feel gratified. I don't wish to be misunderstood in my own personal choices, nor represent the profound experiences of others in a superficial or inadequate manner. I have made the attempt because my late wife so wanted me to write it; the stories and truths call out to be told and retold.

I do so sincerely hope that it might touch a chord within and prompt us to reach out farther with our searching foot and discover in the lives and deeds and thoughts of great men and women the moving hand of God. I also hope to increase our gratitude and open up our thinking to include a little more of the goodness, beauty, and truth to be found in the world in other faiths and cultures. Perhaps the next time we reach for something to read we will choose a biography instead of the latest action, mystery, fantasy, romance, or spy novel. I have nothing against these really; I feel only a certain regret over all that is sometimes missed by the too-frequent reading of them. In the final analysis, none of them can compete with real life.

I would recommend as highly as I am able that each reader would pause and think, as did Marcus Aurelius, and find those people living or already passed on who have touched his or her life as these ten have touched mine. What have yours brought you? How have they enriched your life? When I think in these terms, it always motivates me to find new examples, new lives I have not yet discovered, anticipating my own will be substantially better because I have met them in the pages of the past.

At a minimal level I hope I've been able to reveal anew a little of what lies beyond our wells. Maybe one day in sacrament meeting or Relief Society we will hear a story about Patrick or Joan or a quote from the Dhammapada or a hadith from Aisha's memory, or deepen our own love because of Elizabeth and Robert, or be lifted by Darwin's fascination with creation or inspired by his noncombative humility. These lives and hundreds more await us. I do not wish to throw hammers in windows, as George MacDonald once intimated, unless it is to open us up to more light because the windows are clouded over.

The Lord shared with Joseph Smith one of the great eternal laws of existence. I call it the "law of attraction," and it has many ramifications in many different areas of life. "For intelligence cleaveth unto intelligence; wisdom receiveth wisdom; truth embraceth truth; virtue loveth virtue; light cleaveth unto light; mercy hath compassion on mercy and claimeth her own" (D&C 88:40). The verbs in this verse are simply wonderful! Let us cleave, and receive, and embrace, and love, and claim all the intelligence, wisdom, truth, virtue, light, and mercy we can discover. We will do so because there is a wholeness within the circle our searching foot can reach. We claim all truth, all goodness, all beauty because it is our own, as it is the inheritance of all God's children—and it is our commission to find it and share it. If Doctrine and Covenants 88:40 is true—and it is—our unique and central Latter-day Saint light will naturally draw these things from every other source on earth.

There are so many lives we can explore whose experience, worldview, religious devotion, or innate curiosity make them stand out even though they may come from a tradition much different from our own. We can ignore them, dismiss them, focus on their failings, or debunk them, as is so often the attitude of the modern, anti-hero world, but their achievements will stand as long as men seek inspiration and understanding of the highest that is within us. If we seek with an open heart and charity for all, we will ultimately conclude: "Is not humanity magnificent!"

> *He doeth that which is good among the children of men; . . .*
> *And he inviteth them all to come unto him*
> *And partake of his goodness;*
> *And he denieth none that come unto him . . . ;*
> *And he remembereth the heathen;*
> *And all are alike unto God.*
>
> —2 NEPHI 26:33

Notes

Preface: "The Beauty of the World"

1. William Shakespeare, *Hamlet,* in *William Shakespeare: The Complete Works, Second Edition,* ed. Stanley Wells and Gary Taylor (Oxford: Clarendon Press, 2005), 2.2.305–8. References are to act, scene, and line.

2. In *Journal of Discourses,* 26 vols. (London: Latter-day Saints' Book Depot, 1854–86), 14:231.

3. See Desiderius Erasmus, *Collected Works of Erasmus: Vol. 33, Adages: II i 1 to II vi 100,* translated and annotated by R. A. B. Mynors (Toronto: University of Toronto Press, 1991), 125 (adage II ii 93).

4. *Mencius,* rev. ed., D.C. Lau, trans. (Hong Kong: Chinese University Press, 2003), V. B. 8. References are to book, chapter, and section.

Chapter One: "The Voice of the Irish": Saint Patrick

1. *The Confession of Saint Patrick,* Thomas Olden, trans. (Dublin: James McGlashan, 1853), 49.

2. Jonathan Rogers, *Saint Patrick* (Nashville, TN: Thomas Nelson, 2010), 103.

3. Ibid., 106.

4. Ibid., 103.

5. Ibid., 104.

6. From St. Patrick's *Confession,* as cited in James O'Leary, *The Most Ancient Lives of Saint Patrick, Seventh Edition* (New York: Excelsior Catholic Publishing House, 1897), 5.

7. Ibid.

8. Ibid.

9. Ibid.

10. Ibid.

11. Ibid.

12. Ibid., 6.

13. Ibid.

14. Ibid.

15. Ibid.

16. Ibid.

17. Ibid.

18. Ibid., 7.

19. Ibid.

20. Ibid.

21. Ibid.

22. Ibid., 3.

23. Joseph Smith, *History of the Church,* 7 vols. edited by B. H. Roberts (Salt Lake City: The Church of Jesus Christ of Latter-day Saints, 1932–51), 1:299.

24. O'Leary, *Most Ancient Lives of Saint Patrick,* 14.

25. Ibid., 8.

26. Ibid.

27. Ibid., 9.

28. Ibid., 8.
29. Ibid., 9–10.
30. Ibid., 14.
31. Ibid., 9.
32. Ibid.
33. Ibid., 11.
34. Ibid.
35. Ibid., 16.
36. Ibid.
37. Ibid., 17.
38. Ibid., 14.
39. Ibid., 11.
40. Ibid., 13.
41. Ibid., 17.
42. Ibid., 11–12.
43. Ibid., 13.
44. Ibid., 19–20.

45. Ibid., 22.
46. Ibid., 20.
47. Saint Patrick, "Letter to Coroticus"; available at http://www.logoslibrary .org/patrick/coroticus.html; accessed 29 May 2012; emphasis added.
48. Ibid.
49. Ibid.
50. O'Leary, *Most Ancient Lives of Saint Patrick,* 14.
51. "Pangur Bán," in *The Poet's Cat: An Anthology,* compiled by Mona Gooden (London: G. G. Harrap, 1946), 23–24.
52. Saint Patrick, "Letter to Coroticus."
53. O'Leary, *Most Ancient Lives of Saint Patrick,* 18.

Chapter Two: "All Creatures of Our God and King": Saint Francis of Assisi

1. Donald Spoto, *Reluctant Saint: The Life of Francis of Assisi* (New York: Penguin Compass, 2002), 113.
2. Translation by author.
3. "All Creatures of Our God and King," in *Hymns of The Church of Jesus Christ of Latter-day Saints* (Salt Lake City: The Church of Jesus Christ of Latter-day Saints, 1985), no. 62.
4. Rosalind B. Brooke, *The Image of St. Francis: Responses to Sainthood in the Thirteenth Century* (Cambridge, UK: Cambridge University Press, 2006), 150.
5. "Onward, Christian Soldiers," in *Hymns,* no. 246.
6. See Brooke, *Image of St. Francis,* 14.
7. Brooke, *Image of St. Francis,* 16.
8. Ibid., 17.
9. "Franciscan Rule," A.D. 1220–1221, in Spoto, *Reluctant Saint,* 185.
10. Wendy Murray, *A Mended and Broken Heart: The Life and Love of Francis of Assisi* (New York: Basic Books, 2008), xvi.

11. See Father Cuthbert, O.S.F.C., *The Life of St. Francis of Assisi* (London: Longmans, Green, and Co., 1912), 299–300.
12. See Johannes Jörgensen, *Saint Francis of Assisi: A Biography,* Thomas O'Conor Sloane, trans. (New York: Longmans, Green, and Co., 1912), 318.
13. Ibid., 410.
14. Translation by author.
15. Jenny Oaks Baker, *Then Sings My Soul,* Shadow Mountain Records, compact disc, 2010.
16. Spoto, *Reluctant Saint,* 202.
17. In Julien Green, *God's Fool: The Life and Times of Francis of Assisi,* Peter Heinegg, trans. (San Francisco: Harper, 1983), 205.
18. Ibid., 261.
19. Translation by author.
20. Spoto, *Reluctant Saint,* 113.
21. Ibid., 215.
22. Ibid., 198.

Chapter Three: "We Have Burned a Saint": Joan of Arc

1. T. Douglas Murray, *Jeanne d'Arc: Maid of Orléans, Deliverer of France* (New York: McClure Co. 1907), 265

2. Lucy Foster Madison, *Joan of Arc: The Warrior Maid* (Philadelphia: Penn Publishing, 1919), 378.

3. Régine Pernoud and Marie-Véronique Clin, *Joan of Arc: Her Story,* trans. Jeremy duQuesnay Adams (New York: St. Martin's Press, 1998), 135.

4. Pernoud and Clin, *Joan of Arc,* 136.

5. Donald Spoto, *Joan: The Mysterious Life of the Heretic Who Became a Saint* (New York: HarperCollins, 2007), 193.

6. Ibid.

7. Ibid., 138.

8. Pernoud and Clin, *Joan of Arc,* 119.

9. Ibid., 19.

10. Ibid.

11. Ibid.

12. Ibid., 23.

13. Ibid., 24.

14. Ibid., 25.

15. Ibid., 28.

16. Ibid., 29.

17. Ibid.

18. Ronald Gower, *Joan of Arc* (London: John C. Nimmo, 1893), 46.

19. Pernoud and Clin, *Joan of Arc,* 57.

20. Murray, *Jeanne d'Arc,* 265.

21. Pernoud and Clin, *Joan of Arc,* 63.

22. Ibid., 79.

23. Ibid., 66.

24. Ibid., 67–68.

25. Denis Lynch, *St. Joan of Arc: The Life-Story of the Maid of Orleans* (New York: Benziger Brothers, 1919), 175.

26. Pernoud and Clin, *Joan of Arc,* 89.

27. Daniel Hobbins, *The Trial of Joan of Arc* (Cambridge, MA: Harvard University Press, 2005), 105.

28. Pernoud and Clin, *Joan of Arc,* 109.

29. Ibid., 111.

30. Ibid., 111–12.

31. Ibid., 112.

32. Ibid., 113.

33. Hobbins, *Trial of Joan of Arc,* 98.

34. Pernoud and Clin, *Joan of Arc,* 120.

35. Ibid.

36. Ibid., 121.

37. Ibid., 125.

38. Ibid., 127.

39. Ibid.

40. Gower, *Joan of Arc,* 168.

41. Ibid., 170.

42. Pernoud and Clin, *Joan of Arc,* 128.

43. Ibid., 129.

44. Ibid., 114.

45. Ibid., 130.

46. Ibid., 132.

47. Ibid., 133.

48. Vita Sackville-West, *Saint Joan of Arc* (Garden City, NY: Doubleday, Doran & Co., 1936), 339.

49. Spoto, *Joan,* 198.

50. Ibid., 136.

Chapter Four: The Childlike Heart: Mencius

1. *Mencius,* rev. ed., D.C. Lau, trans. (Hong Kong: Chinese University Press, 2003), IV. B. 28. References are to book, chapter, and section.

2. Ibid., IV. B. 19.

3. Ibid., VI. A. 8.

4. Ibid., IV. A. 1.

5. Ibid., IV. A. 12.

6. Ibid., I. A. 4.

7. Ibid., I. B. 6.

8. Ibid., II. B. 2.

9. Ibid., VII. B. 7.

10. Ibid., VI. A. 10.

11. Ibid., VI. A. 8.

12. Ibid., IV. B. 12.
13. *The Works of Mencius,* James Legge, trans. (New York: Dover, 1970 [reprint]), 322.
14. *Mencius,* II. A. 6.
15. Ibid., IV. A. 10.
16. Ibid., VI. A. 6.
17. Ibid., VI. A. 7.
18. Ibid., VII. A. 1.
19. Ibid., VII. A. 4.
20. Ibid., VII. A. 37.
21. Ibid., IV. B. 8.
22. Ibid., VII. A. 6.
23. Ibid., VI. A. 11.
24. Ibid., VI. A. 12.
25. Ibid., VI. A. 14.
26. Ibid., VI. A. 15.
27. Ibid., VI. A. 18.
28. Ibid., VI. B. 15.
29. Ibid., IV. B. 28.
30. Ibid., VII. B. 32.
31. Ibid., IV. A. 4.
32. Ibid., II. A. 2.
33. Ibid., VI. B. 2.
34. Ibid., VII. B. 15.

CHAPTER FIVE: THE KNOT IN THE CORD: KHADIJA AND AISHA, WIVES OF THE PROPHET MOHAMMAD

1. T.J. Winter and John A. Williams, *Understanding Islam and the Muslims* (Louisville, KY: Fons Vitae, 2002), 24.
2. Ibn Ishāq, Sira 145, in A. Guillaume (trans. and ed.*), The Life of Muhammad: A Translation of Ishāq's "Sīrat rasūl Allāh"* (New York: Oxford University Press, 2001), 100.
3. Winter and Williams, *Understanding Islam and the Muslims,* 42.
4. Ibid., 42, 44.
5. Ibid., 45.
6. Ibid., 26.
7. Ibid., 37.
8. Ibid., 63.
9. Ibid., 55.
10. As quoted in Karen Armstrong, *Muhammad: A Biography of the Prophet* (New York: HarperCollins 1992), 82.
11. Quran, Sura 96:1
12. In Armstrong, *Muhammad*, 83.
13. Ibid., 85.
14. Ibid., 89.
15. Ibid., 119.
16. Sigismund Wilhelm Koelle, *Mohammad and Mohammadanism* (London: Rivingtons, 1889), 493.
17. Quran, Sura 17:81.
18. Koelle, *Mohammed and Mohammadanism,* 489.
19. Ibid.
20. See ibid., 487–90.
21. Koelle, *Mohammed and Mohammadanism,* 489.
22. Ibid.
23. See ibid., 491.
24. Ibid.
25. See ibid., 492.
26. Koelle, *Mohammed and Mohammadanism,* 492–93.

CHAPTER SIX: THE WHEEL-TURNER: SIDDHARTHA, THE BUDDHA

1. *The Dhammapada,* second edition, Eknath Easwaran, trans. (Petaluma, CA: Nilgiri Press, 2007), 123.
2. "Abide with Me!" in *Hymns of The Church of Jesus Christ of Latter-day Saints* (Salt Lake City: The Church of Jesus Christ of Latter-day Saints, 1985), no. 166.
3. *Dhammapada,* 42–43.
4. Ibid., 79.
5. Ibid., 40.
6. Ibid., 45.

7. Ibid., 105.
8. Ibid., 116.
9. Ibid., 135.
10. Ibid., 117.
11. Ibid., 143.
12. Ibid., 157.
13. Ibid., 184.

14. Ibid., 251.
15. Ibid., 253.
16. Ibid., 61.
17. See, for instance, C. S. Lewis, *The Great Divorce* (New York: Macmillan, 1946), 72.
18. *Dhammapada*, 213.

CHAPTER SEVEN: THE BOY ON THE *BEAGLE*: CHARLES DARWIN

1. In *The Life and Letters of Charles Darwin,* ed. Francis Darwin, 2 vols. (New York: D. Appleton and Co., 1887), 1:195.
2. Ibid., 43.
3. John Bowlby, *Charles Darwin, A New Life* (New York: W.W. Norton, 1990), 402–3.
4. *Life and Letters of Charles Darwin,* 30.
5. Ibid., 26.
6. Ibid., 30.
7. Ibid., 28.
8. Ibid., 32.
9. Bowlby, *Charles Darwin,* 89.
10. *Charles Darwin's Letters: A Selection, 1825–1859,* Frederick Burkhardt, ed. (Cambridge, UK: Cambridge University Press, 1996), 102.
11. R. D. Keynes, *Fossils, Finches, and Fuegians: Darwin's Adventures and Discoveries on the "Beagle"* (Oxford: Oxford University Press, 2003), 16.
12. *Life and Letters of Charles Darwin,* 50.
13. Bowlby, *Charles Darwin,* 157.
14. *Correspondence of Charles Darwin, Volume 1,* 494.
15. Bowlby, *Charles Darwin,* 404.
16. Ibid.
17. Ibid., 76.
18. See *Life and Letters of Charles Darwin,* 51.
19. Charles Darwin, *The Voyage of the Beagle* (New York: D. Appleton and Co., 1902), 24.
20. *Charles Darwin's Beagle Diary,* ed. R.D. Keynes (Cambridge: Cambridge University Press, 1988), 23.

21. *Life and Letters of Charles Darwin,* 210.
22. *Beagle Diary,* 42.
23. *Voyage of the Beagle,* 496.
24. Ibid., 39.
25. *Life and Letters of Charles Darwin,* 213–14.
26. *Voyage of the Beagle,* 499.
27. Ibid., 41.
28. Ibid., 44.
29. *Correspondence of Charles Darwin, Volume 1,* 434.
30. *Voyage of the Beagle,* 100.
31. James D. Loy and Kent M. Loy, *Emma Darwin: A Victorian Life* (Gainesville, FL: University Press of Florida, 2010), 71.
32. Bowlby, *Charles Darwin,* 225.
33. Ibid., 229.
34. Ibid., 411.
35. Loy and Loy, *Emma Darwin,* 74.
36. Bowlby, *Charles Darwin,* 238.
37. Loy and Loy, *Emma Darwin,* 112.
38. Bowlby, *Charles Darwin,* 304.
39. *Life and Letters of Charles Darwin,* 95.
40. Ibid., 107.
41. Loy and Loy, *Emma Darwin,* 79–80.
42. Ibid., 85–86.
43. Ibid., 307–9.
44. *Voyage of the Beagle,* 324.
45. *Life and Letters of Charles Darwin,* 102.
46. Bowlby, *Charles Darwin,* 254.
47. *Correspondence of Charles Darwin, Volume 1,* 503.

48. Bowlby, *Charles Darwin,* 455.
49. Ibid., 336.
50. Ibid., 380.
51. Ibid., 306.
52. *Life and Letters of Charles Darwin,* 60.
53. Bowlby, *Charles Darwin,* 392.
54. Ibid., 11.
55. *Life and Letters of Charles Darwin,* 81.
56. Ibid., 81–82.
57. Loy and Loy, *Emma Darwin,* 283.
58. *Life and Letters of Charles Darwin,* 109.
59. Ibid., 275.
60. Ibid., 73.

Chapter Eight: "By Endurance We Conquer": Sir Ernest Shackleton

1. Ernest Shackleton, *South: The Endurance Expedition* (New York: Signet, 1999), 226.
2. Alfred, Lord Tennyson, *Ulysses,* in Harold Bloom, sel., *The Best Poems of the English Language: From Chaucer to Robert Frost* (New York: HarperCollins, 2004), 599.
3. Roland Huntford, *Shackleton* (New York: Carrol & Graf Publishers, 1985), 113.
4. Ibid., 18.
5. Ibid., 24.
6. As quoted in Beau Riffenburgh, *Shackleton's Forgotten Expedition: The Voyage of the Nimrod* (New York: Bloomsbury Publishing, 2005), 107.
7. Huntford, *Shackleton,* 261.
8. Ibid., 290.
9. Ibid., 231.
10. Ibid., 196.
11. Alfred Lansing, *Endurance: Shackleton's Incredible Voyage* (New York: Basic Books, 1959), 14.
12. Shackleton, *South,* iii.
13. Ibid., 85; emphasis added.
14. Huntford, *Shackleton,* 463.
15. Robert Browning, "Prospice," in *Pomegranates from an English Garden: A Selection of the Poems of Robert Browning,* introduction and notes by John Monro Gibson (New York: Chautauqua Press: 1885), 48.
16. Shackleton, *South,* 227.
17. Huntford, *Shackleton,* 625.
18. Shackleton, *South,* 246.
19. Huntford, *Shackleton,* 690.
20. Ibid., 693.

Chapter Nine: Love Right Through: George MacDonald

1. George MacDonald, *Unspoken Sermons,* First Series (Charleston, SC: Bibliobazaar, 2006), 118.
2. C. S. Lewis, *Surprised by Joy: The Shape of My Early Life* (New York: Harcourt Brace, 1955), 180–81.
3. Robert Bolt, *A Man for All Seasons* (Oxford: Heinemann Educational Publishers, 1960), 71.
4. C. S. Lewis, ed., *George MacDonald: An Anthology* (New York: Macmillan, 1978), xxxii.
5. Michael R. Phillips, *George MacDonald: Scotland's Beloved Storyteller* (Minneapolis: Bethany House Publishers, 1987), 165.
6. Greville MacDonald, *George MacDonald and His Wife* (London: George Allen and Unwin Ltd., 1924), introduction.
7. From *Ranald Bannerman's Boyhood,* as quoted in Phillips, *George MacDonald,* 70.
8. MacDonald, *George MacDonald and His Wife,* 117.
9. In Phillips, *George MacDonald,* 182.

10. MacDonald, *Unspoken Sermons,* 118.
11. Phillips, *George MacDonald,* 88.
12. From *Weighed & Wanting,* as quoted in Phillips, *George MacDonald,* 124.
13. MacDonald, *George MacDonald and His Wife,* 180.
14. Ibid., 536.
15. As quoted in Phillips, *George MacDonald,* 248.
16. C. S. Lewis, ed., *George MacDonald: An Anthology* (New York: Simon & Schuster, 1996), xxxiv.
17. Ibid., xxxv.
18. MacDonald, *George MacDonald and His Wife,* 373–74.
19. MacDonald, *Unspoken Sermons,* 34–36.
20. From *Paul Faber, Surgeon,* as quoted in Phillips, *George MacDonald,* 190.
21. MacDonald, *Unspoken Sermons,* 22.
22. Ibid., 168–69; emphasis added.
23. MacDonald, *Unspoken Sermons,* 176.
24. Ibid., 38.
25. Ibid., 366.
26. Ibid., 321.
27. From *Thomas Wingfold, Curate,* as quoted in Phillips, *George MacDonald,* 351.
28. MacDonald, *Unspoken Sermons,* 270; emphasis added.
29. MacDonald, *Unspoken Sermons,* 52–53.
30. Ibid., 93–94.
31. MacDonald, *George MacDonald and His Wife,* 525.
32. Phillips, *George MacDonald,* 333.
33. MacDonald, *George MacDonald and His Wife,* 528.
34. MacDonald, *Unspoken Sermons,* 358–59.

CHAPTER TEN: "IF I LEAVE ALL FOR THEE . . .": ELIZABETH BARRETT BROWNING

1. Julia Markus, *Dared and Done: The Marriage of Elizabeth Barrett and Robert Browning* (London: Bloomsbury, 1995), 88.
2. Markus, *Dared and Done,* 23.
3. Ibid., 83.
4. In Margaret Forster, *Elizabeth Barrett Browning: A Biography* (New York: Doubleday, 1988), 51.
5. Forster, *Elizabeth Barrett Browning,* 103.
6. Ibid., 27.
7. Markus, *Dared and Done,* 28.
8. Ibid., 3.
9. Forster, *Elizabeth Barrett Browning,* 147.
10. Ibid., 148.
11. Markus, *Dared and Done,* 38.
12. Ibid., 30.
13. Ibid., 60.
14. Ibid., 49.
15. Forster, *Elizabeth Barrett Browning,* 155.
16. Markus, *Dared and Done,* 50.
17. Ibid., 160.
18. Ibid., 44.
19. Elizabeth Barrett Browning, *Sonnets from the Portuguese* (Portland, ME: Thomas B. Mosher, 1910), Sonnet 35, 37.
20. Markus, *Dared and Done,* 72.
21. Forster, *Elizabeth Barrett Browning,* 178.
22. Ibid., 180.
23. Markus, *Dared and Done,* 74.
24. Ibid., 72.
25. Ibid., 74.
26. Ibid., 81.
27. Ibid.
28. Ibid., 84.
29. Ibid.
30. Ibid., 106.
31. Ibid., 88.

32. Ibid., 92.

33. Forster, *Elizabeth Barrett Browning,* 253.

34. Markus, *Dared and Done,* 164.

35. Forster, *Elizabeth Barrett Browning,* 237.

36. *Sonnets from the Portugese,* Sonnet 43, 45.

37. Markus, *Dared and Done,* 248.

38. Ibid., 211, 190.

39. In *Major British Writers, Enlarged 2nd Ed.,* G. B. Harrison, gen. ed. (New York: Harcourt, Brace, World, 1954–59.), 532; see also Robert Browning, *The Agamemnon of Aeschylus: La Saisiaz [et al.]* (New York: Houghton Mifflin, 1894), "La Saisiaz," 61.

40. Robert Browning's letter to his sister Sarianna, 30 June 1861, reproduced in *Robert and Elizabeth Barrett Browning: Everyman's Library Pocket Poets* (New York: Alfred A. Knopf, 2003), 247.

41. Ibid., 245.

42. Ibid., 247.

43. Ibid.

44. Ibid., 248.

45. Ibid.

46. Ibid.

47. Ibid., 250.

48. Ibid., 248–49.

49. Markus, *Dared and Done,* 211.

50. Mrs. Sutherland Orr, *The Life and Letters of Robert Browning, Volume 2* (Boston: Houghton Mifflin, 1895), 358.

51. Forster, *Elizabeth Barrett Browning,* 368.

52. Markus, *Dared and Done,* 314, 308.

53. Ibid., 133.

54. Forster, *Elizabeth Barrett Browning,* 213.

55. Markus, *Dared and Done,* 314.

56. "Andrea Del Sarto," in *Selections from the Poems and Plays of Robert Browning,* 216.

57. Forster, *Elizabeth Barrett Browning,* 173.

58. Markus, *Dared and Done,* 83.

59. Ibid., 310, 308.

60. *Sonnets from the Portugese,* Sonnet 43, 45.

EPILOGUE: THE HAPPINESS OF THE GREAT OCEAN

1. *The Book of Chuang Tzu,* trans. Martin Palmer with Elizabeth Breuilly, Chang Wai Ming, and Jay Ramsay (New York: Penguin Classics, 1996), 297.

2. Ibid., 145.

3. Ibid., 146.

INDEX